BY VICKI CONSTANTINE CROKE

*Elephant Company: The Inspiring Story of an Unlikely Hero
and the Animals Who Helped Him Save Lives in World War II*

*The Lady and the Panda: The True Adventures of the First
American Explorer to Bring Back China's Most Exotic Animal*

*Animal ER: Extraordinary Stories of Hope and Healing from
One of the World's Leading Veterinary Hospitals*

The Modern Ark: The Story of Zoos: Past, Present, and Future

ELEPHANT COMPANY

ELEPHANT
COMPANY

THE INSPIRING STORY OF AN
UNLIKELY HERO AND THE ANIMALS
WHO HELPED HIM SAVE LIVES
IN WORLD WAR II

VICKI CONSTANTINE CROKE

RANDOM HOUSE / NEW YORK

Published in the United States by Random House,
an imprint and division of Random House LLC,
a Penguin Random House Company, New York.

RANDOM HOUSE and the HOUSE colophon are
registered trademarks of Random House LLC.

Images on pages 37, 56, 60, 88, 197, 198, 199, 247, and 289
courtesy of Di Clarke. All others courtesy of Treve Williams.

LIBRARY OF CONGRESS CATALOGING-IN-PUBLICATION DATA
Croke, Vicki.
Elephant Company: the inspiring story of an
unlikely hero and the animals who helped him save lives in
World War II / Vicki Croke.
pages   cm
Includes index.
ISBN 978-1-4000-6933-0
eBook ISBN 978-0-679-60399-3
1. Williams, J. H. (James Howard) 2. World War,
1939–1945—Campaigns—Burma. 3. Elephant Company
(Great Britain) 4. Bandoola (Elephant) 5. Animals in logging—
Burma—History—20th century. 6. Asiatic elephant—
Burma—History—20th century. 7. Working elephants—
Burma—History—20th century. 8. Animals—War use—
History—20th century. 9. Burma—History—Japanese
occupation, 1942–1945. I. Title. II. Title: Inspiring story of
an unlikely hero and the animals who helped him
save lives in World War II.
D767.6.C76 2014 940.54'259591092—dc23   2013032280

Printed in the United States of America on acid-free paper

www.atrandom.com

11 13 15 17 19 18 16 14 12
Book design by Barbara M. Bachman

For Christen Goguen

CONTENTS

———

PART TWO

LOVE AND ELEPHANTS

———

PART THREE

WAR ELEPHANTS

———

JAMES HOWARD WILLIAMS WAS A WORLD WAR II LEGEND. Newspapers and magazines around the world, including *The Times* of London, the Melbourne *Herald, The New York Times, The New Yorker,* and *Life* magazine, loved telling the story of the quietly charismatic war hero with a dash of mysticism, who could talk to elephants. He had gone to work in the teak industry in Burma in 1920, and over the years displayed a remarkable gift for understanding the hearts and minds of the great beasts who pushed, pulled, and dragged the logs to the riverways. Without any veterinary training, Williams had evolved into a skilled and intuitive animal doctor. He knew more about elephants, one paper said, "than any other white man."

When World War II broke out, Williams formed a unique and indispensible unit for the Allies. His Elephant Company not only helped defeat the Japanese in Burma, it also saved the lives of countless refugees. For much of the war, he operated far out in front of the Allied forces, facing the enemy in wild mountainous terrain.

The work of elephants, it turned out, was vital to troop movement. They made bridge building possible, and they hauled supplies to units bogged down in places even mules couldn't negotiate. Their services were so crucial that they were coveted by both the Allied forces and the Japanese.

Williams's fearless snatching of elephants from Japanese hands made headlines and earned him a popular nickname, Elephant Bill. As part of the elite Force 136, fighting behind enemy lines, he waged what the *Daily Mirror* called "a holy war against the Japanese." His extraordinary exploits became nearly mythic when he saved a group of evacuees, and like the famous military hero from 218 B.C., conducted his own "Hannibal trek," crossing not the Alps, but several mountain ranges between Burma and India with his train of elephants.

The *Daily Mail*'s headline "Elephant Bill Won His War: Beat Burma Japs" might have been reductive, but Williams was awarded the Order of the British Empire and mentioned in dispatches twice for gallantry in facing the enemy. His efforts led famed field marshal Sir William Slim to write movingly about how much he owed Williams and the elephants.

All the correspondents of the time touted what Williams did to help elephants. But Williams thought they'd gotten it backward. It was the elephants who had helped him. Not only did they give him joy and a reason to live in the lonely jungles, but they became his teachers. "Look," he told one reporter, "I've learned more about life from elephants than I ever did from human beings." And there, hidden in the inverse of all those newspaper articles, was the even more astonishing, if overlooked, story: how the elephants had transformed a carefree young man into a war hero.

Living day by day with elephants, he had absorbed their deeper, more philosophical cues. In fact, he discovered in them the virtues he would work to develop in himself: courage, loyalty, the ability to trust (and the good sense to know when to be distrustful), fairness, patience, diligence, kindness, and humor. "Not a bad way to learn," he said, because "the elephant takes a more kindly view of life than we do."

Some of the most pivotal moments of Williams's life were guided by the elephants' creed. He won the faith of a monstrous boss by refusing to back down, just as he had seen serious bull elephants do when tested by bigger, older ones. Two elephants who scrapped one day, he learned, would forage together the next, because they had won each other's respect. Williams would also forgive an employee who tried to kill him when he realized that the attack never would have happened if he had treated the man with the dignity he accorded his elephants. He would not make that mistake again. Even his courtship of Susan, the woman who would become his wife, mimicked the graceful tuskers who gently followed a female, reading her mood and approaching when invited. Finally, when Williams came to command men in war, he fully understood the difference between a leader and a bully. The elephants had taught him this distinction, too, when they organized themselves at treacherous river crossings. Time and again, he found that the universal truths he had observed in the jungle applied not just to elephants but to people, too.

Williams had witnessed a life among the elephants that would be hard for those outside to fathom—in fact, he reported behaviors that many would not believe until they were validated decades later by biologists in the field. He had seen these creatures thoughtfully solve problems, use tools, protect one another, express joy and humor, stand up for something more important than their own safety, and even, perhaps, comprehend the concept of death. There was a largeness to them that was about more than their physical size, a quality triggered especially when their sense of decency or outrage was provoked.

Could one really call it decency? Williams thought so. Courage defined them. He had witnessed their bravery—mothers defending babies, tuskers squaring off against each other, closely bonded females running toward danger, not away, to protect one another.

There were simple lessons from the animals, like how to be content with what he had. And there were more complex ones, too: the realization, for instance, that trust requires much more than affection; it depends on mutual confidence—strength, not niceness. Or that sometimes it's not necessary to know what elephants or people are thinking, as long as one honors what they are feeling.

He called his elephants "the most lovable and sagacious of all beasts," "the most magnificent of animals," and "God's own." His time in the logging camps of Burma was spent studying them, healing them, learning from them, and, he was never ashamed to admit, *loving* them. "The relationship between man and elephant," he would say later, "is nine-tenths love." Several elephants would be like family to him, and one in particular, a noble tusker named Bandoola, would be his kindred spirit. Through accidents, illness, and the loneliness of the forest, elephants not only made his plight bearable; they helped give it meaning. He told intimates, "I am convinced that life in such conditions would be impossible if it were not for the elephants."

Later in life, Williams would have an epiphany. What the elephants meant to him had gone beyond notions of friendship or even family. The great animals, he decided, had become his religion. Through them he had been saved, reborn, and even christened— renamed as Elephant Bill. With them, he had gained a world of wisdom and compassion. In a way, he proudly told one writer, he had even become one.

MAP OF

BURMA

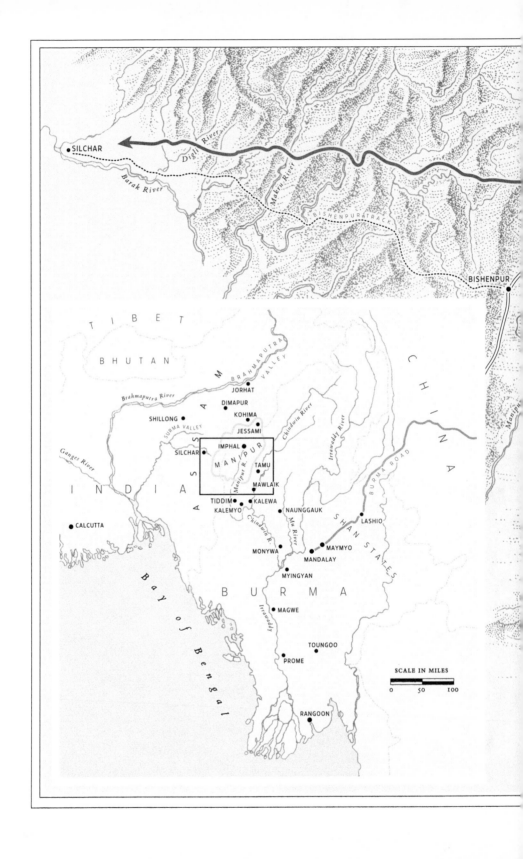

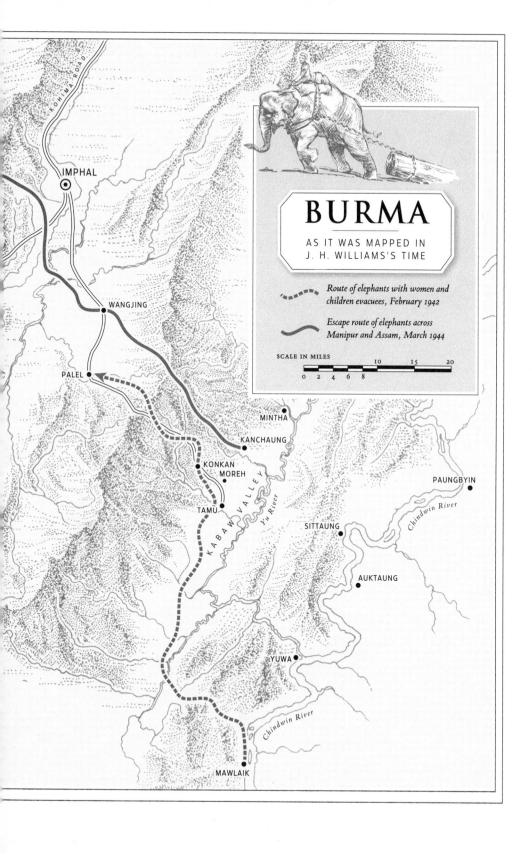

KOHIMA ROAD

IMPHAL

BURMA

AS IT WAS MAPPED IN
J. H. WILLIAMS'S TIME

- - - - Route of elephants with women and
children evacuees, February 1942

——— Escape route of elephants across
Manipur and Assam, March 1944

SCALE IN MILES

0 2 4 6 8   10   15   20

WANGJING

PALEL

MINTHA

KANCHAUNG

KONKAN
MOREH

PAUNGBYIN

TAMU

Yu River

SITTAUNG

Chindwin River

AUKTAUNG

YUWA

Chindwin River

MAWLAIK

K A B A W   V A L L E Y

PART ONE

THE MAKING OF AN ELEPHANT WALLAH

CHAPTER 1

THE SHOULDERS OF A GIANT

———

Deep in the jungle-clad hills of northwest Burma, close to the border of the Indian state of Manipur, Billy Williams, delirious with fever, began to regain consciousness. Half dreaming, he scrambled to piece together what was happening. His lanky body felt cockeyed and unresponsive. Even opening his eyes seemed impossible. As hallucination gave way to reality, he remembered his predicament: He was stranded in an inaccessible forest, on the wrong side of the raging Yu River, during the dangerous, unrelenting monsoon rains of 1927, and he had never been sicker.

His spiking fever was accompanied by chills. The lymph nodes at his groin were swollen to the size of fists, and some of the small pustules lining his feet and legs had broken open. For days he had been unable to eat and could barely drink. That morning he could not even stand.

As the lashing rains tore at his clothes, he suddenly felt something that he couldn't make sense of: His cot was lurching, as if it was trying to buck him off. Forcing his eyes open, Williams realized he was not on the wrong side of the river, but smack in the middle of it, riding an elephant through the churning avalanche of water. Around him, deadly two-ton tree trunks shot down the rapids like missiles, crashing into one another with a sound like thunder.

Blinking against the pouring rain, he seized the rail of the large bamboo cargo basket, or "kah," he lay in as it rocked him back and forth, perilously close to the frothing current. The elephant was pitched at a steep angle, leaning his flank into the wall of water, shouldering all his weight against the chocolate-colored torrent in an effort to keep his footing. Yet Williams felt oddly lucky. That was because of the elephant he rode. There was no way Williams could mistake the animal's identity—even in his feverish state, slumped high up in a basket. The broad expanse of the gray back, the delicate pink freckling bordering the ears, and the rakish slant of the gleaming white tusks, their tips just visible from this viewpoint—this was the only elephant who could brave the crossing: the strongest and most stouthearted creature in the forest, the best friend Williams ever had. Bandoola.

Williams, who managed several teak logging camps, would eventually know a thousand elephants by name during his years with the Bombay Burmah Trading Corporation. Of all of them, Bandoola was dearest to him, owing to his intelligence, virtue, and strength. Williams had confidence that even without a rider's guidance, "the great elephant knew what he was doing," using his own instincts and judgment for this passage.

Not that a human voice could be heard over the pounding water, but Williams probably mustered the breath to at least whisper encouragement. He had made a habit of speaking to the working elephants in the language they were trained in—Burmese. More than any other animal, he believed, they craved conversation. Their vocabularies, the number of words they understood, were astonishing, but to Williams, impressive as that was, there was something that counted more. These creatures could read underlying emotion, understand intent, perceive what was really being expressed. Now, verbalized or not, Williams would make plain to Bandoola that he was grateful and believed in him.

The bull already knew how ill Williams was. Earlier that day, the mahouts, or "uzis" as they were called here, who worked for Williams had cinched a cargo basket to Bandoola's back. It was an unusual event for the tusker, who was a logging elephant, not one of the small pack elephants called "travelers." Nonetheless, he had stood patiently, head held high, ears flat against his neck, as the rain pelted his back and ran off his wrinkled hide in runnels. Soaking wet, his skin had inked into a deep purple. Elephants in Burma knew how to cope with monsoon. If he tilted his head forward, his large, bony brow ridge would shield his eyes from rain, and he could keep water from spilling into his nostrils by hanging his trunk down straight, curling it under at the very end. When a limp Williams was carried out of his tent, Bandoola's dark eyes, beneath their heavy, wrinkled lids and long lashes, tracked the movement, lending him the meditative look particular to elephants. Bandoola not only recognized Williams, he knew something was wrong. This person was different from the energetic, confident man who when visiting camp invariably produced a sugary tamarind ball treat for Bandoola, spoke to him, scrubbed his sandpaper skin exactly where it needed scratching, ran his hands along his hide, swabbed ointment on abrasions, and then slapped his flank good-bye. He had nursed Bandoola back to health for a whole year after a fight with another tusker, spending every day cleaning the wounds and applying antiseptic and fly repellent. Now Williams, the elephant saw, was as broken as Bandoola had been then.

The order *"Hmit!"* was given, and Bandoola sank down, back legs buckling first into the sludge, then the front. Several Burmese men, their colorful sarong-like longyis sodden with rain, struggled with slipping hands and feet to hoist the senseless Williams up to the basket atop Bandoola's shoulders. Two of them, Williams's closest servant, Aung Net, and another camp worker, would ride with him.

As the body was passed upward, Bandoola swiveled his trunk, pressing his nostrils to Williams, and breathing in deeply. Even through Williams's clothing Bandoola was picking up organic clues, especially from the armpits and between the legs. Like all elephants, he was a master chemist, analyzing much of the world through his sensitive nose. Bandoola could ascertain innumerable facts about any animal: last meal eaten, fitness, anxiety level, or hormonal state. Elephants read one another—and people—this way. Bandoola's prodigious brain, highly evolved to negotiate a complex social world, kept a dossier of the men around him, especially Williams, whom he had known for seven years. Scent was a critical part of that inventory. Williams's transformation into a seasoned forest man was telegraphed to Bandoola in large part by his body odor. Billy Williams smelled different as a veteran than he had as a recruit. Over time, his diet and smoking habits changed, the ratio of fat to muscle shifted, and his confidence around elephants grew, meaning certain hormones that often signaled fear were reduced. The city washed out of the man, and the jungle seeped in. When Williams had an opportunity for sex, Bandoola could smell that, too.

BANDOOLA

Williams did not possess a single photograph of Bandoola,
but commissioned this rendering of the great tusker.

What Bandoola inhaled this day was misery. With just a few whiffs of Williams's body, the tusker processed the rank breath, the change in hygiene, and the yeasty scent of an infection. Elephants routinely help other ailing elephants, lifting them when they cannot stand, feeding them when they are unable to forage. Are they capable of doing the same for people? Williams couldn't prove Bandoola was aware of his dire condition, but it damn sure felt that way to him during his flashes of consciousness.

Like all the European teak men, Williams was a nomad of the forest. He knew illness and accident went with the job, that bouts of malaria were as frequent as colds were back home. Hundreds of miles—roadless, muddy, rain-drenched, wooded, and mountainous—from any medical help, he and his colleagues toughed out such episodes. Even the most robust among them could wither and die within days of something seemingly innocuous: a headache, a cut, a chill. "No one who works in the jungle," Williams once wrote, "calculates on a ripe old age as a near-certainty." The tropical forest was capricious in its blessings and curses. Indigenous people made sense of it with a pantheon of jungle sprites that they called "nats": some cruel, sneaky, and slick, others kind and generous. The nats personified the soul of the forest.

Staying alive—especially for outsiders like Williams—took every trick a man could muster. The company's numbers told the story: Williams had been one of forty-one young recruits hired for the Bombay Burmah Trading Corporation in 1920. Now, seven years later, only sixteen of them were still on the job. The others were either dead, dismissed, or disillusioned. Though he knew the attrition would continue, he hoped he wouldn't be the next to go. With Bandoola, at least he had a chance.

First, they had laboriously waded through nearly fifty miles of thick sludge. "Each stage of that agonising trek was about ten miles," Williams wrote. "At every step Bandoola sank two or three feet deep into the mud. Each foot he lifted made a loud sucking noise and even his gigantic powers were sorely taxed."

Then came the river. Progress was slow. The churning water was level with Bandoola's chest, and the animal had to pause before each stride, feeling the boulder-strewn riverbed with his feet for his next purchase. Often, he would freeze in place for what seemed like "an eternity of time in the middle of the angry waters," as the current sloshed over his back, soaking Williams and the two men. Then Bandoola would find a foothold and lunge forward again. "His massive head and tusks ploughed a passage through the water like the nose of a submarine," Williams wrote years later in one of the several memoirs he would produce. "Riding on his powerful back brought home my own fragility."

Precarious as his situation was, Williams could not keep his eyes open. The fever pulled him back into oblivion, as, step-by-step, Bandoola made his way. By the time they reached the far shore, Williams was unconscious. Aung Net and his helper pulled him from the basket and dragged him to a hut. There were still maybe a hundred miles to go between them and a station with a doctor. Once he was awake, Williams would have to make a tough decision: whether to travel overland through impenetrable virgin forest, or by water, shooting down the dangerous rapids. Either way, he needed to reach the more populated banks of the mighty Chindwin, the river where, it seemed an eternity before, Williams had first met Bandoola and his life among elephants had begun.

CHAPTER 2

INTO THE JUNGLE

———

O N A CRISP NOVEMBER DAY IN 1920, JAMES HOWARD WILLIAMS, called "Billy" by friends and "Jim" by his family, saw the Chindwin River for the first time. The waterway originated far to the north near the Himalayas, in the wild Hukawng Valley, and stretched for 750 miles, eventually spilling out into the even greater Irrawaddy River near Mandalay, Burma. The Chindwin, the history books and magazines promised, ran through savage country where villagers still practiced head-hunting, performed human sacrifices to appease the spirits of rice production, and could transform themselves into ghost cats. Famous explorers wrote of remote and little-known corners of the area that harbored barbaric tribes. It was enough to scare any of the new British recruits routinely hired by the logging companies. But Billy was different. Striking a match to one of his Players cigarettes and looking out over the water and the limitless jungle beyond, he was amused by such flights of imagination. A forest teeming with monsters? He knew better and had seen worse.

Tall, clean-shaven, and built like a loping hound, Williams may have looked young in his freshly pressed khakis, but he had been through the kind of hell that quickly burns away a man's innocence. Months earlier, on January 26, 1920, the British Army had demobilized him with the rank of captain. During four years of brutal, bitter fighting in the Great War as part of Devonshire Regiment, or the "Bloody Eleventh," Billy had led other men into battle and served in several battlefronts in a wide sweep across North Africa, the Middle East, India, and Afghanistan. In the deserts of Egypt, he was part of the Camel Corps, facing the jihad raised by the Senussi, a group of Muslim guerilla fighters. Along the Tigris, he had been a bombing officer engaged in ghastly battles with the Ottoman Army as part of the Mesopotamia (Iraq) Campaign, in which close to one hundred thousand soldiers from the British and British Indian Armies died. Finally, in 1919, he endured his last two assignments. The first brought him into the turmoil of Lahore, India, where martial law was declared to quell rioting against the British. And later that year he fought hand to hand against fierce, well-armed tribesmen in Waziristan, a remote mountainous outpost on the border with Afghanistan.

A gallant soldier and sensitive soul, J. H. "Billy" Williams was certain that the forests of Burma would offer tranquillity, adventure, and, most of all, elephants—an antidote to all he had experienced on the battlefields of the Great War.

He knew he was lucky to be alive. Nearly a million British soldiers had died in the Great War, and those who survived were forever changed. Some obviously so—faces half blown off, hands trembling from shell shock, trouser legs folded neatly and tacked up where a leg should be. Others carried the trauma inside.

During World War I, James Howard Williams (center) served in several battlefronts in a long, wide sweep across North Africa, the Middle East, India, and Afghanistan.

Billy Williams would never write or speak about his experiences in the war, for he had a lifelong tendency to lock away his deepest emotions, especially the painful ones. The less he talked about something, the closer it was to his heart. It wasn't in his nature to dwell on the darkness of combat. He wouldn't mention what ailed him, only what might cure him. When he came home, he said that the vision of Burma's lonely jungles, filled with wild animals, called to him. It was no surprise to his family. As social as he so often appeared, they knew that solitude was his true bent. He could do without the parties and pranks he was known for in school; in fact, he truly thrived in the kind of isolated wilderness that would turn other men mad.

His opportunity to do just that came from a chance meeting

shortly before being discharged. An army buddy he was drinking with had a connection to a teak logging company and suggested an adventure in Burma. Williams fell in love with the idea even before locating the country on a map. Clinching it was the mention of elephants. "My way has been from a very early age the companionship of animals," he once wrote.

His fondness extended to most creatures, but it was individual animals who affected him most deeply. He recognized their distinct personalities even when few others did. First, there was Prince, his childhood donkey, with whom he would wander the moors, hitching him up to a jingle, or carriage. "I developed a longing for big open spaces," Williams wrote, "and used to talk it over with old Prince who seemed to understand." The donkey, he said, "was the first animal with which I enjoyed a joke." When he left Prince to go off to boarding school, he was bereft, feeling that the separation created a "blank in life."

In wartime, he "really fell in love" with his camel named Frying Pan. And of more than one dog, he would simply say, "We loved each other dearly." When circumstances such as school or war uprooted him, the worst part was saying good-bye to a pet. It created an emotional tear he believed could be mended only by time and the company of another animal. But an elephant? Was he really up to that kind of challenge?

Instinctively, he felt the answer was yes. A jungle full of elephants sounded like the ideal corrective for what he had witnessed on the battlefield. He dashed off a letter to the logging company.

It was perfect timing: The war had thinned the ranks of forest men who roamed the jungles overseeing logging work at far-flung camps for the Bombay Burmah Trading Corporation. At the moment, "Bombine," as the company was nicknamed, was in a recruiting frenzy. And Williams was just its kind of man. The big Burma-based British companies liked to fish from different pools. Rival Steel Brothers, trading in rice, teak, and oil, sought candidates from the wealthy, elite schools. Bombay Burmah, founded by six Scottish brothers in 1863, specialized in teak, tea, cotton, and oil. And it recruited from universities, with a bias toward athletic over academic skill. "The life is a roughish outdoor one," the company had written of the position Williams was being considered for. "A robust constitution, trustworthiness, sobriety, and ability to learn languages are the chief qualifications wanted."

Williams was subjected to a rigorous vetting process. These firms required applicants to undergo a withering interview, a written examination, and a physical at their London offices. Candidates also had to provide stellar personal references. Williams had it all. Just under six feet tall, he was fit, smart, indefatigable, unflappable, good with languages (having easily picked up Hindustani in the service), and, by all accounts, of "good moral character."

His official offer came via a letter dated June 30, 1920, which began, "We have the pleasure of engaging you on behalf of the Bombay Burmah Trading Corporation Ltd." Passage out would be paid, starting salary was four hundred rupees per month, and he would be provided with housing. The one-year contract could be extended pending review.

At home, his joy over the offer was not shared. Every day during the war, British newspapers had printed long lists of the dead, and like all parents of soldiers, Jimmy's had anxiously scanned them, praying they would not find his name. He had returned not only alive, but, just as miraculously, whole. Yet he was set on leaving again. His father, who had settled down as a country squire after his own wandering days in Australia, Brazil, South Africa, and Spain, wanted at least one of his three sons to succeed him. The elder, Nick, was a lawyer with a firm in Calcutta, while Tom, the younger, was headed for a career as a mining engineer in India. Jim was the only hope. So his father tried bribing him: He offered to buy three adjacent holdings, at formidable expense, to set Jim up as a farmer of means. When he made his pitch, he told his son not to answer right away. "Go down to Penamel cove, have a swim, and let me know when you get back," he said. Jim sprinted along the familiar fields that led to the shore, and plunged into the icy waves. He returned, dripping wet and gritty with sea salt, carrying the answer his father had feared. On July 7, 1920, he signed the Bombay Burmah contract accepting the terms offered.

———

WEEKS LATER, ON SEPTEMBER 23, 1920, he boarded the cargo-passenger liner *Bhamo* in Liverpool with a one-way ticket to Rangoon. It was a mild, hazy Thursday without enough wind to blow away the curtain of fog that clung to the horizon. The ship was fairly empty—just eighty-three passengers—as it was still monsoon season in Burma, and travel between the two countries tended to flow westward.

As Williams found his cabin and stowed his grip, he was pining already for Cornwall. He knew that because of the company's home leave schedule, he wouldn't see his family for at least three years, possibly five or more. But he was also thrilling at the prospect of the coming adventure. The war had revealed to him his fearlessness, independence, and recognition that his happiness was of his own making. His old roles—Cornish loner, well-liked high school student, tough soldier, obedient son—no longer applied. He would forge a new identity: elephant wallah. It sounded electrifying, even if he didn't know exactly what it entailed.

Williams, a fearless adventurer with boundless energy, was eager to explore the mysterious jungles of Burma.

Once on board, Williams, realizing he would spend most of the next year tucked away in a remote forest, made the most of his time meeting young women at dances and playing games such as skittles, a top-deck version of bowling. By the time the *Bhamo* approached the south coast of Burma and the mouth of the Rangoon River a few weeks later, the young suitor had a stack of addresses, which would serve as a romantic lifeline for his lonely journey up-country.

The five-hour-long approach to the capital on the silty waters of the Rangoon River sliced a wide brown ribbon through the lush green land, and, standing on deck, Williams saw miles of tall kaing grass, patches of mangrove swamp, and occasional huts surrounded by crops. On the horizon, ten miles upriver, he could just make out the golden dome of the famous Shwe Dagon Pagoda rising high above the city. The paddy fields began to diminish and in their place mills, sheds, refineries, factory chimneys, storage tanks, and industrial buildings lined the shore. Williams could even see elephants working the big logs at the mills. Once the ship pulled up to the wharves, and with the gangway in place, throngs of visitors and "shore boys" looking for work hauling luggage stormed aboard.

The offices of the Bombay Burmah Trading Corporation, Williams discovered, were just steps away from the dock. During the short trip to the office on Strand Road, the main thoroughfare that ran along the river, he had a whole world to take in: The wide street was impossibly congested, filled with bicycles, cars, rickshaws, and bullock carts. Colorful buses, crammed with people and poultry, were decorated with images of animals—snakes or tigers or elephants—to identify their individual routes, the way numbers or addresses did back home. Pedestrians—and not just Burmans, but many Chinese and Indians and Westerners, too—were everywhere. Dressed in bright colors, local men and women both wore long traditional skirts, the women topping them with spotless white jackets and flowers in their hair.

In no time, Williams was standing outside the imposing colonnaded white Bombay Burmah building and soon escorted into the cool of a teak-paneled office, a matting fan swinging rhythmically overhead. The manager of the firm described what would be expected of Williams in the jungles of that portion of the country referred to as "Upper Burma." He did not sugarcoat any part of the message—just the opposite, in fact. This was the company's last chance to scare off any unsound hires before investing any more in them. It was noted that only 4 percent of Europeans who chose the life of a teak man completed their full service. And that didn't even take into consideration the recruits who never started the journey—those who lost their nerve the day they were due to sail from home.

The company knew that most of the arrivals would be gone within months. Loneliness may have been one of the most common complaints, but it certainly wasn't the worst. Some of the working elephants were notorious killers. And the men frequently died from accidents or tropical disease. Recruits could become unhinged by the remoteness of the forest, their fear of the elephants, or the jungle sounds at night. There was no way of knowing in advance which men would have the peculiar, undefined traits that brought success in such outposts.

The Bombay Burmah manager in Rangoon generally spent about a half hour with each new man, providing a comprehensive overview of the work ahead. There was a lot to say: Williams was joining the biggest company in one of the country's biggest industries. At the time, Burma, under British rule, produced 75 percent of the planet's teak. And Bombay Burmah was the top "teak-cutting" operation. The hard, elegant wood, resistant to the elements and impervious to destructive insects such as termites, was highly sought after. The timber even contains a type of oil that prevents metal corrosion. Particularly treasured by the Royal Navy, it was used in boat-building and as decking for ships around the world.

Tectona grandis did not grow in large plots like orange groves, but was scattered among many kinds of trees. As a *National Geographic* from the era noted, "a teak forest 10,000 square miles in extent may be capable of producing only seven or eight thousand trees a year."

The government's forest department was charged with deciding which trees should be extracted. Those eligible for harvesting were killed by girdling them: A two-inch ring of sapwood (the outer, younger wood) was removed from the circumference. Then the tree would be ignored for two or three years while it died and dried out. This was a vital step, since fresh "green" teak sinks, and logs needed to be transported by floating down rivers. As one British educational pamphlet explained, "The rivers of Burma with their vast network of feeder streams make possible the economical extraction, sometimes over distances of 1,200 miles and more, of teak and other waterborne forest produce to the sawmilling and shipping centres of Rangoon and Moulmein."

Because the country had few roads and railways, an army of elephants would drag the harvested logs to waterways. Rudyard Kipling described the process in his famous poem "Mandalay" as "Elephints a-pilin' teak / In the sludgy, squdgy creek."

Elephants. Finally. Billy Williams listened attentively when the subject turned to these animals. In non-monsoon seasons, the manager explained, timber was hauled by elephants to dormant, dry creeks. Then, when the rains arrived in the summer, stirring the tributaries to life, the lumber would rise with the flowing water and begin its journey to larger rivers such as the Irrawaddy. Hurtling at high speed, the logs threatened the lives of anyone foolish enough to enter the water. On the big rivers, trunks would be bundled into rafts of about 125 and guided by five-man crews. Then, from the Irrawaddy, the barges would be steered to the Rangoon River to float down to the mills of the capital city, where "their contact with primitive things would be ended." Given all the variables of the monsoons, the mountains, and even the men who worked the forests, it could take anywhere from five to twenty years for a log to become a milled plank.

Sitting behind an ornate carved desk and glaring through his old-fashioned pince-nez, the manager asked, "What made you think you were cut out for this sort of life, Williams?"

Billy Williams could see that this was a well-worn tactic meant to intimidate new hires.

"Well, sir. . . . I imagine it's difficult to know if one is until one's been out there some time, but there were all sorts of things that appealed to me. I'm fond of animals for one thing . . . then the open air life . . . sense of adventure."

The manager cut him off abruptly, "In fact the usual romantic illusions that bring all you youngsters out East, eh?"

Williams said, "I suppose so, sir. . . ."

"Hmm. Well, there's nothing wrong in that, but because they are illusions, you're on trial only, for one year. Is that clear?"

"Perfectly," Williams said, understanding that the manager wasn't really interested in his thoughts. "It seems very fair to both sides."

"I'm glad you think so," the manager noted sarcastically.

Williams learned that he would be under the thumb of a boss living in the forests northwest of the capital, along the Chindwin River. His own territory would be near his superior's in the Myittha River valley.

"You better spend the rest of the week fitting yourself out from the Company stores," the manager said. "They'll tell you all you'll need. And catch Monday's boat. All right, Williams, I hope the jungle life will suit you."

"Thank you, sir, so do I."

The manager rang a buzzer, and one of the company's Chinese office workers silently appeared in the doorway. The clerks had the packing down to a science. Steamer trunks were stuffed with everything a recruit would eat, read, wear, sleep in, get drunk on, and shoot with for the next six months in the jungle: portable typewriter, canteen, mosquito netting, canned goods, tea, chocolate, and even hops to bake bread. Every calorie Williams was expected to consume (including the village chickens it was assumed he would purchase for the pot) had been accounted for. There was a shotgun, a rifle, and whiskey. Packed in a teak box were magazines and reference books crucial to his education.

Williams's days were spent preparing for departure, but at night he squeezed in some socializing. Rangoon was full of British architecture, French wine, English beef, and exclusive clubs, such as the Rangoon Sailing Club, "one of the stickiest Europeans Only clubs in Burma," as Williams recalled.

As much fun as was available to Williams, Burma did not hold the social cachet of other colonies. In fact, government workers who lived there were given an extra allowance, since by some accounts young British officers in country had a tendency to suffer nervous collapse.

That wouldn't be Williams's problem—especially not with other recruits to knock around with in the exotic city. Over beers with two pals, he discovered they had a few things in common: They had given up traditional opportunities to go to Burma, and family and friends did not understand their impulse. Maybe they didn't, either. None of the three could articulate why he had made the choice, but together they could laugh about it. "Just crackers, the whole lot of us," one of them said. Though he took the responsibility seriously, Billy Williams acted the cool adventurer, saying, "What the hell! A year's probation, passage home guaranteed. We're on a marvelous wicket. And *if* we make the grade—which I should say is most un-likely—we might as well forget all the dames we've ever known, because I must remind you gentlemen that working for this outfit marriage is out for ten years."

On nighttime escapades in Rangoon, Williams was a shy flirt. Genuinely interested in women, he would often ask them about themselves rather than dominate the conversation with stories of his own exploits. And he would rarely sit out a dance. Good-natured and good-humored, he quickly met more single women than he'd expected. Many were members of what was referred to as "the Fishing Fleet." These were eligible Englishwomen who set sail for the far corners of the British Empire, where they could improve their odds of catching a husband. The toll of war had changed the gender balance back home in England, with women outnumbering men by 1.9 million. Some found their way to Burma, where there was a concentration of young single men, desperate for the company of home-grown girls. During his few days in Rangoon, Billy Williams gathered more names and addresses, but did not fall in love.

It wasn't the high life but the forests that called to him. Once packed and briefed, he traveled the first leg of his journey—four hundred miles north from Rangoon—by rail. Paddy fields became thick woods, and the urban din gave way to primitive jungle sounds.

He could hear the deep *coo, click-hroooo* of Green Imperial pigeons, and from somewhere deeper in the forest, the cries of macaque monkeys.

When he arrived at the wide, milky-brown Chindwin River, framed by lush tropical forest, he found the Burma he had dreamed of. There he was met by the company's stern-wheel paddle steamer, a miniature version of a Mississippi riverboat. Painted a spotless white with a trim black stack and outfitted with four comfortable cabins, two saloons, a small library, and ample decks, it was a conspicuous colonial apparition.

Williams spent several days aboard the sturdy little vessel as it made its way up the Chindwin. Weaving and dodging among sandbanks and shallows, guided by painted bamboo channel buoys, the Indian crew took soundings with bamboo poles, singing out the depth to one another. The water was full of timber rafts making their way south, as well as native boats piloted by old Burmese men, shaded by umbrellas. Each evening at dusk, the stern-wheeler would tie up for the night, and at dawn winches would once again take in the mooring chains.

The skipper was a drunk "who had reached the terminus of thirst, Crème de Menthe frappe," and the engineer played the same gramophone record over and over. Both were emblematic of the eccentric characters the jungle seemed to attract. And, in his own way, Williams figured he was a member of the misfits club, too—a nonconformist, even from boyhood.

He had been born on November 15, 1897, and grew up on the coast of Cornwall in the little town of St. Just in Penwith. From his bedroom window at night, in the little cottage set high on a hill, he'd watch the slowly turning beams of seven lighthouses. He was the middle of three brothers who rambled the moors, "as wild as March hares." And though they sometimes banded together as the Three Musketeers, more often, young Jim spent whole days in solo expeditions into caves, over cliffs, and across fields.

He was a daredevil, exploring abandoned shipwrecks or the nearby copper and tin mines. He secreted art supplies in a remote grotto, where he would go to paint for hours. But mostly, he followed animals. He loved every creature he came across, and, with very rare exception, they seemed to like him, too. It meant, he wrote, that he was never lonely.

He spent so much time observing animals that he felt he could anticipate their impulses and movements. He developed a knack for framing the world as they did. "I never looked for a wren's nest, I merely walked to some spot where I thought one would build, stopped, then with sure hands parted the ferns, and in some mossy overhanging bank inserted two fingers into one of a dozen holes and felt ten warm eggs—mother wren might have shown it to me," he wrote.

His formal education was at Queen's College, a boarding school in Taunton, for senior school, or high school, where he was a good student and popular friend. From there, in 1915, he was off to war. He was brave and able wherever he was assigned, but found the best of himself in the Camel Corps.

On the river trip, Williams's thoughts were dominated by the hope that he had the talent to become a true elephant man. In the teak box filled with books and articles, he discovered treasures: instructions on elephant management. The standard texts of the time included "Notes on Elephants and Their Care," written by William Hepburn, a young veterinary surgeon who had died in Burma of some tropical malady just a few years before, and "Elephants and Their Diseases," by Griffith H. Evans, published in Rangoon in 1910.

The state of elephant medicine at the time might have been primitive, but Williams savored every detail. He chain-smoked cigarettes, enjoyed cold beers from the saloon, and read hungrily. Evans's book was exhaustive in its tables of illnesses and treatments. Copious soap and warm-water enemas were considered a good purgative. Allspice could cure elephantine flatulence. For "inflamed and indolent boils," there was nothing like a poultice of roasted onions. And eight to twelve ounces of diluted brandy was recommended for large cases of stomach upset.

The text, a humane treatise by a veterinarian who had spent decades with elephants, made clear to Williams that he would be interacting with one of the most enchanting species known to man.

Elephants "have few vices, are gentle, obedient, and patient," Evans wrote. But despite their formidable size, he cautioned, their health could be rather fragile. In fact, "if neglected they rapidly go to pieces."

The elephants in Burma were Asian elephants. They usually weighed well under eleven thousand pounds and stood about seven to nine feet tall at the shoulder, as opposed to African elephants, who could weigh as much as fifteen thousand pounds and reach thirteen feet in height. Both male and female African elephants have tusks, while only some Asian males have tusks, and none of the females do. Their body shapes differ, too: Asians are more compact; Africans lankier, with a more concave back. The Africans' ears are enormous and wide (like maps of Africa, it's said)—the biggest mammal ears in the world—while those of the Asian elephant are smaller and closer to square.

In fact, the African and Asian elephants are not only separate species but separate genera—a whole other level of taxonomic rank, as distinct in genetic heritage as a cheetah is from a lion. And some say it shows in their temperaments—the Africans active and more high-strung; the Asians more serene.

Physically, all elephants are astonishing. They are the largest animals walking on land. And their appetites are commensurate. Hard-working logging elephants in Burma can eat six hundred pounds of fodder a day, gathering their food with those incredible trunks. Longer and heavier than a man, and much, much stronger, the trunks provide elephants with a sense of smell that may be five times more acute than that of a bloodhound. And by narrowing or widening their nostrils like musical instruments, they can modulate the sound of their voices.

They have extraordinary brains built for memory and insight, and they use them to negotiate one of the most advanced and complex societies of all mammals. To those who have spent time with them, elephants often seem philosophical and perceptive, and appear to have deep feelings. They can cooperate with one another and have been known to break tusks trying to hoist injured relatives back on their feet. Further, their behavior suggests they have an understanding of death, something believed to be rare among nonhuman animals.

And then there's their secret language. Using infrasound, which is too low-frequency for human hearing, elephants communicate with one another not just in close range, but also over long distances—as great as five miles. They can reach others far away, and decide to meet. Identifying this sound in the 1980s explained a lot of the mysteriously coordinated movements of widely separated elephants, which to some researchers, witnessing it from the air, resembled some kind of elephant ESP.

So much about elephants—their seeming awareness of death, their ability to cooperate, their empathy, and the extent of their intelligence—were yet to be revealed to science. But Williams, who saw more in animals than most anyway, had an inkling.

AT THE FOOT OF THE CHIN HILLS, in the far western shoulder of Burma, the exact territory where Billy Williams was headed, a magnificent tusker fitted with a braided harness and thick dragging chains began his day's work towing teak logs toward a jungle creek.

Huge and healthy, the animal carried himself differently from the other elephants around him. There was a majesty, if not yet complete maturity, to him and an ease in the company of both elephants and men. Twenty-three years old, he already stood over eight feet at the shoulder, taller than many of his elders. And because he would continue to grow throughout his life, adding perhaps half an inch a year for the next twenty years, it meant that he would likely join the tallest bulls, who measured over nine feet. He wasn't just big; he was beautiful. He had the kind of tusks, angled up and outward, that the men, likening them to the arms of a Burmese dancing girl, called *Swai Gah*. Those tusks gave him a wicked, roguish appearance that was accentuated when he cocked his ears. In the company's ledger book for him, it was noted that his feet were "perfect," with five nails each in the front, and four on each back foot. His back was shaped like a banana bough—the most suitable for logging. His skin appeared loose and heavily corrugated; his ears were fine, "heavy-haired in orifice." He certainly possessed a physical refinement that elephant connoisseurs admired. Burmese tradition held that "an elephant of good quality has a skin that is wrinkled like the rind of a custard apple, and darkish grey in colour." The elephant named Bandoola unmistakably had that. The drapes of his baggy skin arranged themselves in the shape and form considered auspicious. Right under his tail, thick folds resembling a frog's head would provide some protection from the tusks of another bull during a fight. Bandoola also had a dewlap under his chin, and a bag of pendulous skin—what the elephant men called *Pyia Swai,* or honeycomb—that ran all along his underbelly.

The lavender shade of his skin was exquisite, and splashed across his trunk and high cheekbones were pale pink freckles, as delicate as a field of flowers. Yet, he was as tough as any wild elephant. So superb a specimen was he that every forest assistant—no matter where in Burma he was based—would claim to have managed him at one point in his career.

It was said that he did things that no other elephant could. He had a vast understanding of human language, and while most elephants could distinguish among a few of the camp tools, Bandoola knew them all. When asked to choose a hammer from items laid out before him, the big tusker would reach with his trunk and pull it out. Though he appeared to enjoy the work, no one would call him obedient; Bandoola had a mind of his own. But from birth it proved to be a wise and generous one.

He even seemed to have a sense of humor. Occasionally, after he hefted a large log to the very edge of a cliff or the bank of a river, he would pretend he could push it no farther. He would pantomime the effort of a shove again and again, and behave as if the wood were suddenly unmovable. Only after his uzi would beg him to stop clowning would he suddenly flick the log over the precipice with no effort at all. Then, as all the people who knew him would attest, the elephant would rumble at his own joke.

CHAPTER 3

MEETING THE BOSS—AND THE ELEPHANTS

———

AFTER SEVERAL DAYS ON THE CHINDWIN, WILLIAMS, STAND-ing on deck dressed in new khaki shorts, shirt, and stockings, reached his destination: a clearing along the bank, where he saw a man in his fifties sitting in the portico of a large cottage tent. The man who would show him the ropes. The boss. Williams had no idea what to expect, but plenty of others like him had found strong, paternalistic forest managers who nurtured them. He hoped for the best. After all, this would likely be the sole Englishman he would see or speak to for the next six months.

Deposited on the shore by dugout canoe, Williams took several moments to survey his new world where "range upon range of mountainous country lay away to the east." By the time he looked back over the water, the big white boat was disappearing behind a bend. The sight triggered a pang of abandonment, which Williams described as "almost a yearning." He lifted his hat to wave good-bye but no one was looking in his direction. He pivoted and walked the short distance to the camp.

His new boss, a man he referred to in later writing by the pseu-donym Willie Harding, and occasionally as Freddie, was sitting in a camp chair, sun weathered, balding, and wearing a short-sleeved gray shirt and pressed gray flannel trousers. His light blue eyes were focused far away. From his war experience, Williams could tell the boss was "down with fever." On the table before him lay papers, a survey map, a bottle of good-quality black label whiskey, and a soda siphon. Drinking, most forest men found, helped mitigate loneliness. British companies allowed the habit for their employees working in distant outposts, and some, such as the East India Company, encouraged and underwrote it. It was just noon, but Harding was already knocking back hard liquor. He held in his hand a Burmese cigarette, or cheroot, which gave off a slight scent of incense. Though it was a simple, homespun smoke, he held it with care, as if it were an expensive cigar.

Po Pyan, the head servant, or *lukalay,* waited on the boss with formality, calling him "*Thakin,*" or "Master," the customary address for all Englishmen. After working for the Bombay Burmah Trading Corporation his whole adult life, Harding was the picture of the colonial British "jungle salt": reserved, taciturn, and, above all, capable. His only acknowledgment of Williams's arrival was the deepening of his sour expression.

Striding up to the table, his right hand outstretched, Williams offered a cheery greeting. "Good afternoon, sir."

"There's no 'sir' business in the jungle," Harding replied without looking up.

Williams dropped his hand and after a few awkward moments, went about raising his own brand-new tent next to Harding's. One thing he knew: This was "quite certainly one of the most obvious ways of how not to receive a young recruit."

Billy Williams was stung but not rattled by the reception. He was good at winning people over, and by four, he was ready to emerge for another try.

He sat down at the table, and when a camp attendant asked to take his order, Williams requested a cup of tea. Harding snorted. To him, anything short of a whiskey and soda was unmanly. Humiliated, Williams silently vowed to drink Harding under the table later. Since conversation did not seem welcome, he sat mute. Talking to Harding, it became clear, was a hazard that everyone in camp avoided. At about five, a worker came by and wordlessly placed seven hidebound

notebooks on the table. Simultaneously, seven elephants materialized at the edge of the clearing.

They were paraded into camp, a driver sitting on each animal's
neck. Huge as they were, they made a hushed advance on broad,
cushioned feet. It was just as Kipling had described—elephants walking "as silently as a cloud rolls out of the mouth of a valley." The
only noise Williams heard was the warm symphony of the teak bells
under the elephants' chins, and the crackling of bamboo as they
pushed their way into the clearing. Two tuskers carried in their
trunks the ends of the tying chains fastened to their back legs; this,
Williams would learn later, was to ensure that the next elephant in
line would not step on them.

Without a word, Harding rose from his camp chair and headed
for the assembly. This was the moment Williams had been waiting
for. The reason he had traveled halfway around the world. Elephants.

They were a magnificent sight, lining themselves up and then
standing in perfect, swaying formation—a hypnotic movement that,
Williams would come to learn, actually aids the circulation from
their legs to their hearts. If he looked down, he would see that, as
they shifted pressure from one foot to another, the circumference of
each foot would increase or decrease nearly 10 percent.

The elephants commanded attention. And their immensity was
only part of it. Their "fragrant" scent, a clean barnyard smell that
Williams could almost taste, filled the clearing. They flapped their
ears, some silently, some producing a sound like hands clapping. Even
the air itself throbbed with their presence. It wasn't a fanciful notion,
but a physical fact, as their low vocal tones were felt as a vibration in
his chest. Their chatter—everything from incongruous little shrieks
to low rumbles, like a lion's growl—seemed full of meaning.

The seven huge gray animals remained in motion even when
parked. They rocked, shuffled their feet, and cocked their heads so
they could stare down, focusing the nearest eye on him for a better
look. Their trunks danced—touching their own bodies and those
nearby. When they made contact, Williams heard a faint sound, a
dry rustling or rasp, as skin scraped skin. Those long, fleshy noses
became megaphones, amplifying sound.

Williams focused on individuals. There were a few males, not all of them tuskers. Because tusks are actually the elephant's elongated incisors, even the tuskless males and females had short, mostly hidden versions of them—tushes, or nubs of ivory. One of the females, a gaunt, dignified old dame, "looked as if she were the mother of the other 6," Williams noticed. She was called Ma Oh, or Old Lady, though her real name, given to her a lifetime ago, was Pin Wa, meaning Mrs. Fat Bottom. She was hardly that now. Her head seemed like little more than gray skin stretched over a great craggy skull. Her movements were slow and deliberate.

She might have been suffering from any number of old-age complaints, just like a human—including heart disease, cataracts, and arthritis. By this stage, she shouldn't have still been in service. Over their lifetimes, elephants successively wear away big sets of molars that are replaced by new ones, not from underneath, but as if moved forward along on a slow conveyor belt. They have six sets in total; when there are no new ones to move in as replacements, the animals starve to death, no longer able to chew the tough vegetation that makes up the elephant diet. Ma Oh likely had reached this point.

Harding called out a name—Bo Shwe—and a tusker from the middle of the line stepped forward, stopping five paces away from him. Harding walked up to him. Holding the lobe of the animal's ear, he told the uzi, *"Hmit."* And the uzi called out to the elephant, *"Hmit!"*

Williams was astonished by the graceful descent of the big bull: He sank his hindquarters into a kneeling position—curiously, looking more like a churchgoer in prayer than a horse or a dog whose legs bend backward when reclining. Then came the slow folding drop of his front legs, also into a tucked position. The whole motion had a certain precise formality.

Williams observed, or thought he observed, an expression he recognized. Though Bo Shwe obeyed every instruction, the tusker's eyes seem to convey that he found the strict rules a little ridiculous. Williams felt an immediate connection with him.

If Harding caught such a nuanced emotion, he showed no sign.

He approached Bo Shwe, spreading his hands and placing his palms along the animal's flank. He rubbed and kneaded the skin along the barrel of his back, inspecting by touch. Then came a close examination of eyes and feet. What he was looking for was still a mystery to Williams, though his reading of the dry text on elephant care might have come back to him. Griffith H. Evans, the veterinarian, had written that working elephants "are constantly disabled from sore backs and feet, the majority of such cases being due to want of a little care and supervision." The portions of their skin likely to be irritated must be "regularly examined before and after work." The color of their gums, their temperatures, and the clarity of their eyes gave clues about their general health, too.

The *Hmit,* or down position, for working elephants.

When Harding had finished, he stood back and said, *"Htah."*

The elephant rose with slow dignity, returning to his place in line. The boss repeated the examination down the line, scribbling comments into separate logbooks, one for each animal.

Though smaller than African elephants, the tuskers in Burma
could stand nine feet at the shoulder. To Williams they were
every bit as magnificent as he had hoped.

Williams could observe the features of the elephants from front
to back. And every inch held a fascination. Their trunks. The single
organ that most identifies an elephant as an elephant. It acts, among
other things, as a hand, an arm, a nose, a snorkel, a sledgehammer, a
trumpet, and a hose. It possesses more than sixty thousand muscles.
Without containing a single bone, it is strong enough to lift heavy
logs, and sufficiently nimble to pick up a coin. It is both nose and
upper lip. In Asian elephants there is a single "finger" at the tip while
African elephants have two. The tissue of the tip, the nerve endings,

and the short hairs all help elephants sense vibration, lift chemical signals, and dexterously manipulate objects.

Relaxed, their lower lips hang down like fleshy pendants behind the trunk. The skulls of Asian elephants are double-domed on top and full of ridges and hollow places below. There is a very large brain inside.

When the elephants opened their mouths for Harding's scrutiny, Williams could see their blocky, muscular, bright pink tongues. Wet and mobile, a tongue can shift shape dramatically, so that it becomes a ball, a wave, or a trough. On either side were their huge, strange yellow molars, washboard ridged and ancient looking, like giant tri-lobites. Williams counted four of them, two up, two down, each about nine inches long and weighing four pounds apiece. Some of the elephants invited Harding to rub their tongues, an approximate version of their trunk-to-mouth greetings with one another.

The elephants' ears seemed tissue thin in places, and everywhere tracked by veins. Williams would learn to look at the tops of them to help determine age. The farther they were folded down, the older the animal.

The females displayed two mammary glands, quite similar in size to a woman's breasts, and placed as humans' are—on their chests, rather than in rows of four or six as is typical for mammals. On the elephants' rumps, each had the letter "C," marking them as company animals—not seared there with a hot iron, but painted with a caustic substance that burned into the flesh permanently. It was supposed to be more humane. Just past the brands, at the very end of their bodies, were their four-foot-long tails—small in contrast to their bulk, but Harding was careful around these appendages, and Williams would soon find out why. The tails were strong enough to pack the jolt of a baseball bat. Below those tails, in the bulls, something seemed to be missing: testicles. They had them, all right, but they were nestled high up inside the abdomen.

The whole inspection process took about a half hour, during which Harding shared nothing with Williams—not even a glance. Williams, filled with curiosity, suppressed his impulse to ask questions, knowing "I should only be called a damn fool if I did so."

As Harding handed off the book for the last elephant, he looked at Williams. "Those four on the right are yours, and God help you if you can't look after them." He turned and walked back toward the camp table.

Williams returned to his own tent astonished on two counts—by his first moment face-to-face with elephants, and by Harding's order. How exactly, he wondered, does one take care of an elephant?

CHAPTER 4

INITIATION RITES

———

AT SIX O'CLOCK THAT EVENING, THE LIGHT DRAINING FROM THE sky, Williams rejoined Harding at the table where two full bottles of black label whiskey—one at each place setting—had materialized. Exhausted from his journey, Williams would have to wait to challenge Harding in a drinking competition. Both men had changed into clean, pressed clothes and sat glumly across from each other with a campfire burning nearby. No matter where the outpost in Burma, forest managers had their dinners served properly—white tablecloths, bone china plates, and perfectly cooked English meals, starting with a soup course.

Williams removed the lead foil from the top of his whiskey bottle and pulled out the cork. They drank. When Harding emptied his glass, Williams lifted his own bottle. "May I fill yours, sir?" With a withering look, Harding informed him, "It's the custom to stick to our own bottles." The silence persisted through dinner with only the hum of the jungle insects amplifying the sullen formality of it all.

After about half an hour, Harding finally spoke up to ask Williams about his skill with firearms: Was he "safe with a shotgun"?

"Yes, I think so."

More silence. While Williams seethed over this treatment, Harding refilled his glass several times then spoke again.

"I drink a bottle a night, and it does me no harm. If I never teach you anything else, I can tell you this: There are two vices in this country. Woman is one, and the other 'the bottle'—take which one you please, but you cannot mix them. Anything to do with jungles, elephants, and your work you have to learn by experience. No one can teach you but the Burman, and you'll draw your pay for ten years before you will ever be earning your salary."

As a forest assistant, Williams would labor all year round, in hot weather and monsoon, touring in succession the logging camps in his district. He would witness plenty of trees being felled, but chopping wood was not his job. Instead, he would oversee the men, the elephants, and the camps where the work was done. Forest assistants brought cash to pay the men, they doctored the elephants, and they made sure that the task of dragging logs was proceeding at the proper pace. They were constantly on the move following a circular route, often made up of nothing more than a narrow game trail that connected all the camps in their domain.

Harding told him that the next day he'd be given maps to study, in preparation for being sent off for three months on his own. Williams's mood brightened at this news. Harding said, "You can do anything you like, including suicide if you feel lonely, but don't come back to me until you speak some Burmese."

Despite the bottle of liquor in him, the old man managed to stand and stagger off to his tent without saying good night. Williams swiveled his chair toward the fire and stared into the flames.

Harding was right about speaking Burmese, and Williams knew it. One fellow recruit said that he began to have an insight into the work only when he had mastered some of the language. "A knowledge of Burmese is a necessity for every jungle man and it entails many months of hard and serious work," A. W. Smith wrote in *National Geographic* magazine. "It is a difficult language in itself, a language that depends on an infinite variety of vowel sounds that, written in English character all have the same appearance." Williams also felt strongly that in order to connect with the men, he needed to be able to joke with them, and Burmese would be "the gate to local humour."

Harding had not said much, yet he had left his recruit with a lot to think about. When Williams turned in, he found his tent glowing with the warm, dancing light of an oil lamp. His cot was dressed with soldierly precision, his trunks were neatly stacked next to it, and there was a lovely six-by-four dhurrie rug set out. There was only a thin canvas wall between him and Harding's own tent, but he was happy for the refuge. He slipped out of his clothes and sat down. Surrounded by the dark jungle, Williams was alert to every sound and sensation, the repetitive *chounk-chounk-chounk* of a large-tailed nightjar or the mournful *kwo-oo* of a collared scops owl. A few elephants scrounging near camp snapped branches as they passed. The teak box with his traveling library was within easy reach. His reading materials underscored his heated and hallucinatory nighttime impression of the place. "This is Burma," Rudyard Kipling had written, "and it will be quite unlike any land you know about."

Company maps showed Williams that the country was about the size of Texas, shaped like a kite—including the long tail—and was carpeted in diverse forests, with everything from mangrove swamps to thickets of pine, evergreen, and deciduous trees across tropical, subtropical, and temperate forest types. Much of it was still unknown to travelers, and whole swaths of it remained largely unmapped. Over its thousand-mile length, it changed from steamy tropics in the south to snow-capped mountains in the north, and all of it was teeming with wild animals—three hundred kinds of mammals and a thousand bird species. An old volume on game listed many of them: elephants, tigers, leopards, bears, and an astonishing three species of rhino (Indian, Javan, and Sumatran).

It was easy to see on these maps how Burma had retained its secrets. It was cut off from the rest of the world by natural barriers: to the north, west, and east, a horseshoe of mountains; to the south, the sea. The British framed the country as Upper and Lower Burma. Lower Burma included the capital city, Rangoon, and the plains, valleys, and deltas of the southern portion of the Irrawaddy River, shot through with hundreds of streams that found their way past mangrove forest out to the Bay of Bengal. Upper Burma, where Williams sat this night, was different country. Here was the heartland, marked by mountains and forest. This region stretched to the borders of Assam, Tibet, China, French Indochina, and Thailand. It was home to many tribes including Shans, Kachins, Chins, and the notorious head-hunting Nagas. Burma was an ethnically diverse country: Two-thirds of the population was Burmese, with several other groups and subtribes making up the rest.

At the very crown of the country, past the northern city of Myitkyina, where the rail line ended, was some of the roughest and most remote wilderness—what was often referred to as the back-of-beyond country.

The maps only hinted at the ruggedness of the terrain. Burma was not only tough to enter, with mountains and sea at its borders, its interior was, significantly to Williams, extremely difficult to negotiate, too. The land was corrugated: Its many mountains and rivers ran north to south, making horizontal movement—east to west—nearly impossible. No highways or railroad tracks penetrated these obstacles: the Arakan Mountains to the far west, the Pegu Range in central Burma, and the Shan Plateau to the east. In between these mountain ranges lay fertile valleys and rivers. Burma's great rivers, including the Chindwin and the Irrawaddy, originated in the north, the "hills," the area that according to *Time* magazine, was "where God lives." These waterways all ran southward into the Gulf of Martaban and the Bay of Bengal.

To Westerners, Burma was an icon of the exotic East and all its mysteries. During his boat trip up, Williams had caught glimpses of village life along the banks of the river. The country was almost entirely Buddhist. Williams constantly noticed the golden spires of pagodas rising above the green forest. Monasteries were ubiquitous, and at sunrise, the saffron-robed priests would emerge to tend to nearby villages.

It was late. The new recruit extinguished the light, and, as he did every night, said a silent prayer and got into bed. He hoped for a fresh start with Harding in the morning.

SUNUP THIS TIME OF year was chilly. Williams rose from wool blankets shivering and discovered that attendants had warmed his clothes

Even in the most remote outposts,
Williams would find lovely pagodas.

by the fire. Logging camps throughout the country were coming to life in just the same way—clearings were quiet, shrouded in a thick mist. Sunlight would begin to filter in hazy shafts through the surrounding trees, and birds would be singing. A hearty English breakfast, including bacon, awaited him.

After the morning meal, Williams continued to tiptoe at the fringes of camp life until he was suddenly in the heated center. Without telling Williams, Harding had ordered the camp workers to speak only Burmese to him. When Harding overheard Williams speaking some broken Urdu, which he had picked up in India, to the cook, the poor man was fired, no appeals allowed. Williams was stunned by the swiftness and cruelty of Harding's command, eaten up by the fact that he had caused the man's unemployment and that he was helpless to intercede. Harding's decisions were final.

That evening, the elephants were once again paraded into camp. This time, Harding told the novice to inspect his own four elephants. Williams decided the wise course was to mime what he had seen his boss do the night before. This would be his first intimate moment with an elephant. He walked up as Harding had done and ordered an elephant down. This was Chit Sa Yar, or Lovable, a calm male who could stand stoically even when his rider fired a rifle from his back. Williams would later choose him as his personal elephant to carry only his belongings. When the animal lowered himself, Williams approached. Strangers always inspire curiosity in elephants. As Williams looked Lovable over, the animal's trunk naturally followed.

Up close, Williams was astonished by the size of the great head. It was longer, wider, and heavier than he was himself. Lovable swiveled his trunk around and oriented his wet nostrils toward the new man, likely targeting the richly aromatic regions on Williams's body—his mouth, armpits, and crotch. Lovable was taking in the lanky white youth before him. Williams was trying to do the same thing, but with his arsenal of human tools. He didn't have the analytical olfaction of an elephant, but he appreciated Lovable's wholesome smell. Reaching up, he made contact. That trunk was remarkable: the weight of it, the obvious strength, the tough tire-tread ridges on the underside that could leave a friction burn on his arm. The elephant's exhalation could blow his hair back with a great whoosh, or gently tickle his skin.

Williams ran his palms along the male's spine: rough, wrinkled skin punctuated all over by harsh, wiry hairs. Sand and dirt, which had lodged in the folds of the tusker's hide when he had dusted himself, loosened and rained down on Williams's head and arms. It was an elephant baptism.

As the elephant was commanded to stand, he rose, as solid as a tree, but still yielding, breathing, warm. Williams felt a strong connection, even as his hands throbbed from the rasping coarseness of the contact. He moved on to the next animal.

There were two healthy females, including Chit Ma, who was in the prime of her life. But then came Pin Wa, whose tough old hide hung gaunt from her bones. There were more hollows than heft to her. And the filminess of her eyes gave her a mystical aspect.

Each elephant seemed to enjoy engaging with him. Just as they had the day before, they rumbled audibly and also inaudibly, as Williams could feel but not hear. In fact, there were maybe three times as many of the silent kind, which caused a rippling of the skin on a small patch of the elephants' foreheads—the highest area of the trunk, where the nasal passage enters the skull.

As he pressed his hands along so much elephant hide, Williams had no idea what he was meant to be groping for, but it didn't matter. Inch by inch, he was learning elephant.

At dinner Harding was as stony as before. During the soup course, he produced a homemade condiment—a shaker-topped bottle of sherry in which lethally hot Asian chili peppers had been fermenting for more than a month. Since it looked like ordinary Tabasco sauce, Williams hammered out several mean doses into his bowl. Harding kept a poker face as Williams raised the spoon to his mouth. The first swallow scorched a path from his mouth all the way down his throat. Even his stomach seemed set afire.

But Williams refused to give his tormentor the satisfaction of seeing him surrender. He ladled the blistering soup, spoonful after spoonful, into his mouth. His eyes watered, beads of sweat formed on his brow, and, still, he kept eating. Deflated, Harding upped the ante, prodding Williams to speak by asking a simple question: Was he homesick? Williams patiently finished his bowl, wiped the water from his eyes, and finally answered "No."

It was his turn to surprise the old man. Far from being afraid to leave the nest, he told him he wanted to launch his first tour far sooner than Harding had decreed. In fact, he said, "I'd like to start off on my jungle trip tomorrow." Harding struggled but failed to conceal his surprise.

"That remark got inside his guard," Williams later noted with pleasure.

From the start, Harding had been deliberately trying to break Williams. But his effort, Williams would come to believe, was a kindness. If a recruit could be broken, Harding felt, it was better to uncover it in the safety of camp rather than out in the forest. It was said of Williams that his Cornish and Welsh heritage made him "self-reliant and tough in many ways, and yet gave him his sensitive and sometimes almost psychic qualities." This combination of traits found expression in the odd friendship that he was developing with Harding: Williams craved Harding's respect, but he was also brassy enough to want to fight, and even triumph over him in the process.

When Harding rose from his chair at the end of the night, he was "a bit staggery," Williams noticed. Harding took his empty bottle of whiskey, corked it, flipped it upside down, and steadied it on its head. "By dawn that bottle will have drained its last [jigger] into the neck, and will lace my morning tea," he said.

Williams said good night to Harding's back as the old man lurched toward his tent.

The next morning when Williams emerged, Harding, already scrubbed and dressed, glared at him from the breakfast table. "Good Lord!" he cried out. "You still here?"

The boss soon gave him his orders: Williams was to hike into the Myittha valley, a lush forested area between the Chindwin and a string of hills close to the Indian border. Here a village leader named U Tha Yauk ("U," or uncle, is a polite form of address for a mature male) would begin his training in forest life. Harding would give Williams those four elephants to serve as pack or baggage animals, known as travelers.

Before dawn on the day he was to depart, Williams silently rose and peeked out at the darkened camp. The flaps to Harding's tent were down. The old man was still asleep. Hallelujah. At least he could embark on his first expedition without ridicule. He conveyed to the uzis that he wanted to pack up quietly. They, too, were eager to leave without waking Harding, and had already silenced the knockers on the elephant bells by tying them tight. After Williams watched his last bit of gear handed up and placed in the kah, on the back of an elephant, they started off: four elephants, four uzis riding them, a cook, two bearers, and two messengers; a good-sized entourage for a twenty-three-year-old rookie.

Williams was heading into the forests of Upper Burma with enthusiasm, despite the fact that so many experienced outdoorsmen had lost their lives in the field there, including, just the year before, the forty-year-old famed botanist Reginald Farrer, who had died of diphtheria. For Williams, the jungle was already restoring some of the wonder of his boyhood.

He was outfitted for a good hike—wool socks, well-made boots, khaki shorts and shirt. Sunbeams burst through the branches of the tall trees. Exotic birds called out. Ahead of him was the unknown. The war, Billy had thought, had drained him of the kind of innocence required to appreciate all this. He had feared he was "past the age of adventures." But now he gratefully realized he was wrong.

Right away, there was a commotion among the elephants. Back at camp, a female named Me Tway was trumpeting, and Williams's elephants stopped the procession to respond, cocking their ears forward to listen. After some back-and-forth, the most vocal and strong-willed among them, Chit Ma, broke away, rampaging back to camp with her rider on board. Williams's men and those back at camp had to sort it out. The elephants won: When Chit Ma returned to the expedition, her friend Me Tway came with her, which meant one of the other travelers had to be returned to camp.

Already Williams was seeing how strong the bonds among the elephants were. When Harding had split the group in two, it had taken an emotional toll. Captive elephants did not form the mother-daughter-sister dynasties that wild ones built over generations. Circumstances didn't allow it. But they did cleave to one another just the same. Among the logging elephants, blood kinship wasn't necessary—they had figured out how to sustain ties just as enduring among themselves. Often the uzis would witness a kind of shared parenting, in which females bonded with one another so closely that they reared their calves together. The men used the term *twai sin* in reference to these inseparable female elephants: aunties. When a calf bellowed in distress, not only his mother, but his auntie would come running. Separating such bonded elephants was wrong, "indeed cruel," Williams thought as soon as he saw the consequences.

With peace restored, Williams was off on his first elephant journey. What would become the musical score to his life—the warm, resonant tolling of the elephant bells, soon began. Carved from teak by each uzi, with two clappers on the outside, every bell delivered a slightly different note, allowing one to distinguish his own elephant even when he couldn't see her. As the animals stepped in natural unison, the four bells layered into song.

Williams's boots became wet with the morning dew, and he breathed in the pungent scent of the vegetation, which in the deep shade still carried its nighttime perfume. He marched his group nine miles, stopping just short of the clearing where they would pitch camp. Following protocol, the elephants were halted outside the compound while they relieved themselves. Four big bladders noisily emptied about three gallons each (over the course of a day, the small group would expel enough urine to fill a rain barrel). Plus, there were the unmistakable thuds of defecation. Asian elephants produce about eight boluses twelve to twenty-four times a day, which for some individuals could total more than two hundred pounds. It was best to keep their output away from the camp perimeter. When they were finished, the animals came into the clearing to have the packs unloaded. Then, after all the saddlery, harnesses, and straps were removed from the elephants' backs, the animals headed into the forest, snatching and stuffing bushels of vegetation into their mouths as they walked. Williams's tent was then set up and a cooking fire started, and the uzis began constructing a rough bamboo platform about a foot up off the ground, with a baggage tarpaulin as a roof. It would serve as their communal bunk. An uzi, Williams noted, had "a pretty hard life." He worked to exhaustion, put up with meager accommodations, ate what was available, faced danger not only from the elephants, but from the game he might meet in the forest, and often lived a hundred miles or more from his native village.

In camp that night, Williams had some time and privacy to reflect and record his thoughts. He lit a cigarette, took a long drag, and stared into the roaring campfire. He wrote simply, "My jungle life, to be spent with elephants as my breadwinners had started."

The following four mornings, he moved camp quickly at dawn so as to be safely out of Harding's reach. Then, he could afford to

A page from Williams's photo album showing his typed caption. Each day, the elephants were eager for this moment, which marked the end of their work shift and the beginning of their night life in the forest.

Arrival in camp. Unloading kit.

slow down and take in his surroundings. November in the forests of Upper Burma, he discovered, is a time when "every day was like a perfect English summer's day." Clear air, mild sunshine, no humidity. Each evening he relaxed by a log fire. When he could, he indulged in his great passion: recording the life around him in small watercolor scenes. Most of his compositions would be mailed off in weekly dispatches to his mother. Perhaps a few would go to the girls he had met on the way to Burma. He certainly wrote letters to them.

Away from Harding, Williams could be himself. That meant getting to know elephants, and there was so much to learn. As he did with all animals, he opened himself to them. "I have never studied them as a naturalist," he said, "but I have tried to establish an understanding with them, to find some common ground, some way of seeing the world through their eyes rather than through my own."

Williams was a talented artist and loved sketching
and painting scenes from the jungle.

Dogs, camels, rabbits, horses. And now, the most magnificent creatures he had ever been near. During working hours, they were at the disposal of their handlers—marching, carrying kit, and obeying orders. But there was a change—in attitude, behavior, and movement—as soon as their packs were removed, and they were set free from the afternoon until the next morning to forage and socialize. These captive elephants, he realized, were creatures of two worlds. They lived by one code during the day and quite another at night, transforming themselves with ease from disciplined workers to free jungle animals. He saw that they could go back to free living when on occasion they eluded capture. Over the years, foresters found they lost dozens in this way. Williams thought they were closer to their wild state than any other working animal he had seen. In fact, he wrote, these elephants could be considered "domesticated for only eight [hours] out of the twenty-four."

Because elephants need little sleep, only two or three hours a day, their nightly immersion into the wild world was leisurely and lengthy. The bulk of their time was spent foraging for food. Elephants need a lot of it—they're big and their digestive efficiency is low. Asian elephants consume anywhere between two hundred and seven hundred pounds a day in forage. The working elephants in particular burn up calories, so they might spend as much as twelve hours feeding.

While their uzis slept, the animals would wander the forests and stands of fifteen-foot-tall kaing grass. They rarely went far, usually less than eight miles, because they didn't have to. Camp was almost always set up in an area with their needs in mind: plenty of fodder and a close water source. While they were roaming, they might interact with wild bulls who liked to mate captive females and challenge captive tuskers. Over time, young working males learned to stand their ground with a glare, a shove, or even a fight.

At sunup, the wild animals became working stiffs again. They weren't eager to return, and the forest was so thick that they couldn't be seen from a high perch, but the bells around their necks, called "kalouks," revealed their location to the searching uzis. The elephants appeared to know that the kalouks betrayed them: Almost all of them had a technique for evading their uzis in the morning. It was a trick they played when they didn't want to be interrupted from an especially pleasurable activity, such as feasting in a cultivated banana grove, where they could eat not just bunches of bananas, but sometimes a whole tree.

Williams was amazed to learn the elephants' tactic. "Many young animals develop the trick," he reported, of muffling the effect of the exterior clappers by stuffing the inside of "the wooden bell which they have suspended around their neck, with good stodgy mud." In darkness and complete silence, they could stealthily clean out even a guarded field. It was almost like a well-executed bank heist.

The more Williams saw of elephants, the more he wanted to know. So he investigated them as he had the wrens and rabbits on the moors back home, recording his observations with a fountain pen in his two-penny notebook.

The elephants of the night, the free elephants, especially drew Williams in. "It is impossible to understand much about tame elephants unless one knows a great deal about the habits of the wild ones," Williams wrote. Right away, he established a routine unlike that of any other recruit. Like the elephants, he became two different characters by day and night. During working hours, he was the boss of men, a kindly one, who wanted to learn from the uzis. But starting in the afternoon, when the elephants were discharged, he would follow quietly on foot, turning into a field biologist.

Me Tway and Chit Ma, of course, stuck together. They left camp in each other's company and returned together in the morning. Lovable, the male with short, blunted tusks, went off on his own, and poor Pin Wa ambled slowly and, it appeared, painfully into the forest.

But even following old Pin Wa wasn't easy for Williams. He occasionally had to climb or descend fifteen-hundred-foot hillsides, and his progress was slowed by thick undergrowth and all kinds of jungle tortures: reedy canes whose long tendrils were dotted with hidden barbs as sharp as "trout hooks." Prickly canes, "edged with teeth as sharp as the finest saw," that tore his clothes and cut his body. A bamboo that would shower anyone disturbing it with a fiery dust that would have its victim clawing his skin. A stinging nettle called *petya,* which caused painful welts. And one frightening and common plant that provoked intense skin irritation, and could, on contact with the cornea, cause permanent blindness. Harding would have been enraged if he knew of Williams's pursuits. Any forester would have said following dangerous, loose elephants in the dark was insane. But he kept at it.

By moonlight, he saw elephants sleep, lying down or going into a standing slumber. Sometimes, he even heard one or two of them snoring. But one aspect of their life eluded him in those early days and for long after. No matter how closely he tracked them, he was unable to observe them mating.

The uzis, as mahouts were called in Burma, were brilliant observers of elephant biology and behavior.

What Williams couldn't learn directly from the animals, he could pick up from the uzis. He was fascinated by their communication with the elephants: the way they spoke to them and how much was conveyed by their body language. Leaning back rigidly meant stop. Leaning forward and down commanded an elephant to kneel. Pressure on one side was to turn left, the other to turn right. When the uzi dragged his foot up one side of the elephant, the animal would raise the foot on that side.

Most of all, Williams was charmed by the intimate relationships he witnessed. The men seemed to have been born with an uncanny elephant proficiency, and in a way they had. They often grew up around the animals, helping their fathers who were uzis, and from the age of fourteen, they could start earning a wage as apprentices, helping with harnesses and chains. By the time they were uzis themselves, they were walking encyclopedias of the art and science of elephant life.

Williams couldn't yet speak their language, but he watched them closely. The astonishing skill of an uzi was displayed each morning when he set off to retrieve his elephant. First, he'd study the trampled ground at the edge of camp. "He knows the shape and size and oddities of his own elephant's foot print with such certainty that having determined it," Williams wrote, "off he sets following the trail." Williams found the uzis to be infallible, never confusing their own elephant's prints with another's. The trail showed the uzis not only which direction the elephant had gone, but where his elephant had rested and with whom. If there had been a disagreement between males, there might be trampled vegetation, broken branches, or even blood.

Usually, the morning report was peaceful, the trail marked by evidence of digestion, not duels. The uzi would examine droppings, kicking them open and checking the contents. A bolus revealed what the elephant had already eaten, and perhaps what she would crave next. After consuming bamboo, for instance, the elephants tended to seek out succulent kaing or elephant grass, which grew on the banks of the creeks. So the uzi who found bamboo in his elephant's excrement would head for the water to look for her.

Once there, he would listen for her kalouk. Upon hearing it, he would begin his approach, first with song. Elephants have fairly poor vision, seeing the world mostly in shades of gray. So as not to startle the animal, a rider would serenade her from a distance, his voice acting like his own kalouk, alerting her to his advance. If the uzi were in the kaing grass, which grows to nine feet, he might find a safe high rock to sit on and then call to her: *"Lah! Lah! Lah!"* "Come on! Come on! Come on!"

The elephants were not like dogs; they didn't run with wagging tails to the handlers. It was a ritual. When an elephant showed herself, the patient rider would speak softly to her: "Do you think I've nothing else to do but wait for you?" He might rub her trunk. "You've been eating since noon yesterday, and I haven't had a bite of breakfast." Williams couldn't translate all the words yet, but he grasped the forbearing attitude the men had toward the elephants. The uzi would then unfasten the cane or chain shackles on the elephant's legs and order her down so he could scramble aboard and head back to camp. Once returned to the clearing, the uzi would eat his first meal and then wash his elephant to start the day's work.

Williams's study of the animals became an addiction. "Everything of interest became elephants, elephants, elephants," he wrote. In particular, he was falling in love with his four travelers. He fed them the treats they liked—sweet tamarind balls or bananas—and learned where they liked to be rubbed or scratched. Pin Wa worried him most. Their hikes each day were not strenuous, and Pin Wa carried the lightest pack, but still the old girl looked creaky. Her skin was sagging and the tops of her ears had folded far down with age. Her movements were deliberate and dignified. She worked without complaint. Williams hoped to find a way to release Pin Wa from her toils, but nature would beat him to the punch.

One morning before sunup, he was woken by the uzis. It was sad news—"tragedy overtook me," Williams wrote. Pin Wa was dead. The men led him through the forest to her body. It looked as though she had died in her sleep. As peaceful as she was lying there in the silence of the forest, to see the huge animal down was still a terrible sight for Williams.

He didn't have the luxury of sustained mourning. First, he thought about Harding—"God help you if you can't look after them"—and the rebuke he would receive. Next he saw an opportunity to learn what his elephant textbooks couldn't teach him. He decided to hold an amateur postmortem. This was no easy task on an eight-thousand-pound animal. Without special equipment or training, he'd just have to make do. Here in the forest, men like Williams were called upon to act as mechanics, architects, veterinarians, doctors, engineers, undertakers, and even priests—whatever was needed.

He gathered the sharpest knives and machetes available and began. "Her body was scarcely cold before I was literally inside," he wrote, "the ribs of the flank being a canopy over my head from the sun, and I 'learnt' about elephants from her."

The first cuts released foul-smelling methane gas into the air. Sawing open her torso, he needed help pulling away the skin, which felt as heavy and unwieldy as a waterlogged carpet. Next there were three tough layers of muscle. And then the huge, protective omentum, an opaque apron of connective tissue laced with branching blood vessels. It supports the blood vessels for the intestines, making a kind of girdle or scaffolding for the great loops of the gut. He hacked at the tissue that kept the viscera in place. When the digestive organs slid out, they seemed to expand as they exited, and the escaping gas was noxious. Though she, like all elephants, looked portly, there was actually little fatty tissue. Her great barrel of a body was filled with the vast workings of digestion. Elephants can eat 8 percent of their own weight in vegetation every day, and they need a very big gut to process it all.

He began to excavate the organs, pulling them out and placing them with care into a straight line to study. Laid out, the intestines and stomach alone looked bigger than the elephant herself. It seemed impossible they had come from inside her. There was her heart, the size of a well-fed bulldog, with two apexes instead of the one a human heart had. This feature led another novice forest assistant to conclude that one of his elephants had died of a broken heart.

Williams had to work to slice Pin Wa's lungs free from her chest wall. This was another puzzle, for almost all other mammals have a space around the lungs—the pleural cavity. But the elephant's lungs are anchored right to the rib cage. No other mammal breathes this way. Elephants don't inflate and deflate their lungs as humans do, but instead depend on chest muscles to do the work. That's why they have trouble breathing if their chest is restricted—for instance, if they lie down too long.

He spent all day on what he called his "Jonah's journey," quitting at sundown covered in blood and gore. It was a sign of his determination that he had gotten so far alone, using only the knives on hand. A meticulous man who regularly pumiced tobacco stains from his fingers, he scrubbed himself clean before returning to his tent to transcribe his report. Sitting at a makeshift desk in front of the typewriter, he struggled. Though he had learned a great deal, he could not see any obvious reason for Pin Wa's demise. That night as he pecked out his observations, it dawned on him that Harding had saddled him with an old animal unfit for work. Under cause of death, he simply reported "Found dead."

Because Pin Wa's pack had been so light, it was easy to redistribute her load among the remaining three elephants to continue their march. But the quiet old elephant remained much on Williams's mind.

ALONG A DRY STREAMBED, almost always the most unobstructed travel lane available through the thick Burmese forest, Williams made his way forward, often leaping from rock to rock. He was well ahead of the animals when he spotted U Tha Yauk, the man he had come to meet, sitting high on a boulder. Striding toward him, he uttered the few Burmese words he had committed to memory. Unsure of his usage and pronunciation, Williams laughed at himself—and U Tha Yauk responded with a kindly laugh of his own. After the experience with Harding, Billy Williams reveled in the warmth of the moment.

U Tha Yauk led him to the village clearing, which consisted of about ten bamboo huts set high on stilts, topped with peaked thatched grass roofs. Williams, the European company man, was given the royal treatment. A beautiful young Burmese woman wearing her best *htamein,* or sarong, a traditional white muslin jacket, and a flower in her hair, rushed out with a cane stool for him to sit on. Others brought a little hand-forged copper cup and green coconuts to pour juice for him. Biting bugs were fanned away by a little boy as Williams gulped down the drink, his cup refilled each time he emptied it. Taking out one of his handkerchiefs from home, which was embroidered with a foxhunting scene, Williams made a hat for the boy as a gift. Everyone was so solicitous, he felt struck by the "wonderful gentleness in these jungle people."

That night, when Williams was treated to a colonialist's dream, he had anything but a colonialist's response. An immaculate hut had been prepared for him, lighted by little oil lamps and decorated by pretty woven dhurries covering the floor. His bed, encircled by mosquito netting, was dressed in spotless linens. Clean flannel trousers and a white shirt were laid out. His revolver was placed, for nighttime emergencies, by his pillow. His camp furniture, which traveled with him—table and chair—were unpacked and arranged, with framed photographs from home set out.

He took a steaming hot bath in the tin tub placed in the middle of the room. And then a parade of village men served his roast chicken dinner in several courses, handing them up to his designated "valet." After finishing the feast, as he drank his coffee, one villager quietly prepared the mosquito netting, tucking the bottom hem in securely for him, and then vanishing.

On his own in the quiet, Williams heard the faint tinkling of the many delicate village pagoda bells, like the music of fairies. He felt humbled by the care these strangers lavished on him. "Left alone, I was overcome by a great homesickness," Williams would recall years later. "The overpowering kindness of the Burmans was too much for me, and I asked myself what I had done to deserve it." The people in the village, he said, "wanted to show their sympathy with me in my loneliness and my ignorance of their language and all the difficulties that lay ahead." He would never take them for granted.

The next morning, Williams was pulled gently awake by dozens of distinctive kalouks, sounding like a babbling brook. He rose to see the clearing now alive with elephants. While he had been introduced to the traveling elephants, these were the real working elephants of Burma, the ones who wrestled the giant teak logs. The sight was thrilling. It was a sea of gray, and yet he saw anything but uniformity with variations in hue and markings and in the amount and placement of pink freckling. Some even had the spotted pigmentation inside their trunks. Here were big tuskers, tuskless males, and the much smaller females, a few with babies by their side. There were so many patterns of tusk sets and physiques that there were categories to sort them. Tusks that curved up and inward, looking like a monk carrying a begging bowl, were called, appropriately enough, *thabeik-pike,* or bowl-carrying type. Short, fat tusks that resembled small bananas were called just that—*hnet-pyaw-bu.* Tusk girth, not length, helped indicate age.

The shape of the back fell into five categories, including *wet-kone,* which most resembled a pig's back; *kyaw-dan,* which was straight and flat; and then the one considered best for logging work, a back that would slope gently down toward the tail, like the bough of a banana tree—*hnyet-pyaw-gaing.* For a new elephant lover such as Williams, this was an embarrassment of riches.

He quickly washed up and shaved so he could sit outside with his traditional English breakfast and watch the scene unfold. The uzis sat squatting in small groups, silently eating their own morning meal of steamed rice served on a "plate" of wild banana leaf. One by one, as each man finished, he would rinse his mouth with water from a coconut shell cup and then quietly mount his harnessed elephant to begin the day's work. They headed up to the work site where the elephants would spend the day moving felled teak trees into a dry streambed ready for the monsoon.

U Tha Yauk came to him, carrying a map. Spreading it out before Williams, he traced his finger over five parallel creeks, all flowing west into the Myittha River. Williams understood that over and around these watersheds and hills of three or four thousand feet, they would make their journey to the ten elephant camps of his division. It encompassed an area of about four hundred square miles. Without a better command of the language, he could ask no significant questions. But he deduced from the map that the distance between camps was about seven miles.

WAITING FOR WILLIAMS IN one of those ten camps was an elephant man named Po Toke. He was a leader among the workers, and an independent thinker. Po Toke was not Bandoola's uzi nor his owner. He was the master mahout who had trained him and oversaw his care. Handsome and slight, with his graying hair kept in a neat braid, and intricate tattoo patterns decorating his torso and legs, Po Toke looked "Siamese," meaning his family was ethnically Shan, the Burmese word for Thai. Married and childless, Po Toke was an authority to the men. But he wasn't entirely popular with his British bosses, who suspected him of harboring nationalist leanings.

Still, he had managed years ago to wrangle an agreement with Bombay Burmah that he would always work with the magnificent Bandoola. After all, he had helped raise the animal from infancy. Now nearly forty, Po Toke was only fifteen when he took on the elephant's care. His entire adult life had centered around Bandoola. Their relationship was like that of father and son.

The most strenuous logging work went to the biggest, most mature bulls. At twenty-three, Bandoola wasn't ready to compete at their level.

Po Toke had something to prove to the world, and Bandoola would be his masterstroke. But, at twenty-three, Bandoola was still a tender, immature bull. He wasn't ready for the most strenuous logging work. The tusker was in the midst of a growth spurt that would last a decade. In fact, it might not be until Bandoola's forties that they would see the full extent of his magnificence. So there was danger in the coming transition of management. This raw recruit, a man named Williams, who as yet knew nothing about elephants, was about to be Po Toke's boss. His word would be law. Out of inexperience or cruelty, the young Englishman could undo a lifetime of Po Toke's work in a matter of weeks. Sent into the heavy logging area, Bandoola could be permanently injured. The master mahout had a lot to protect. As he waited, he did what he could: He appealed to the spirits and plotted with the men.

WILLIAMS KNEW WHAT TO expect. Assistants like himself were generally given a territory "larger than an English county," where they would be in charge of about three hundred men and one hundred elephants. He would be required to monitor the health of the elephants at each camp, oversee the logging, and take care of all administrative duties: paying the men; settling disputes; hiring, firing, and communicating with headquarters. "By continual touring during all seasons of the year," the forest assistant "saw each camp about once every 6 weeks, so that it was a matter of time before he knew his charges, not only by name, but by temperament, and capabilities of work." By luck, Williams had fewer elephants in a smaller area than most, which meant he could see each elephant twice a month. It was perfect for a man who wanted to really know them, not just canvass them.

This would be his life: a nomad in the forests, making the rounds of the widely distributed teak camps in his district. The people he would be interacting with included, as he wrote, "the elephant oozies and their camp followers; . . . jungle villagers such as fire-watchers, fellers, rice traders and bazaar vendors; . . . elephant contractors, who might equally well be Indian, Karen, or Siamese as

Burman; and dacoits—men who, for one reason or another, had put themselves beyond the law and who existed by robbery, and, on occasion, murder." And then there would also be occasional visits with other forest men, Europeans like himself.

Each camp had its own personality, but physically they tended to look alike. Generally there were two or more bamboo-floored long huts in a clearing, raised about six feet off the ground. Some camps housed the families of the riders. These villages were often set in clearings and surrounded by rough fences. There were usually about a dozen tidy houses, all with thatched roofs and walls made of woven bamboo, set up on stilts, with ladders to climb up to the front doors.

The logging camps were well-organized villages that always contained a clean hut for visiting forest assistants such as Williams.

There would be a pagoda, and one bungalow would be retained for the visiting forest assistant. Palm trees provided shade. Chickens, pigs, and skinny little pariah dogs wandered around under the houses. Always, the villagers were welcoming with smiles and little gifts of food. The women, he noticed, seemed to care for each other's children—even to the point of breast-feeding one another's babies. It wasn't just the human children who benefited from this nurturing attitude. More than once Williams found a village mother suckling an orphaned forest animal, such as a baby bear, kept for a time as a pet.

Most good-sized villages also held a monastery. The monks, in their orange-gold robes, were responsible for the country's high literacy rate, for they taught young boys to read and write.

For now, Williams would be the student of U Tha Yauk. The men packed up once again, to begin his education.

CHAPTER 5

HOW TO READ AN ELEPHANT

———

WHEN THE GROUP REACHED THEIR FIRST CAMP, U THA YAUK conveyed to Williams by hand signal that they would spend just one night there for the time being. During the monsoon, from about mid-May to October, it would become their home base. Chosen for its earthly and divine features, the little clearing was level, open, and said to hold no malignant spirits.

About twenty men were erecting a set of jungle buildings, including a shrine to the good nats. Williams's hut was raised up on stilts, topped with a thatched roof. There was a veranda in front, whose height had been calculated for loading elephants. A bamboo ladder would serve as a staircase. Inside, one large room contained an office, dining room, and bedroom. In the back was a small bathroom and a set of stairs for the servants to deliver meals.

The sea of forest around the site was Williams's classroom. U Tha Yauk demonstrated for him some simple forest tricks. The teacher went over to a large Shaw tree and cut a notch. He then grabbed the bark, pulling upward and out, so that an eighty-foot line of it separated from the tree all the way to the top, like a narrow strip of wallpaper. Plaited together like jute, the material made harnesses for the elephants. Cutting a stalk of bamboo at the knuckle and tipping the short length to his mouth, the Burman showed Williams the hidden drinkable water that was all around them.

As much as he loved the elephants he knew, Williams still used his jungle stalking skills to shoot a wild elephant in the name of science. Big game hunting and "collecting" were British passions in Burma. Williams didn't kill the animal for the tusks, though, but rather to conduct another necropsy, or animal autopsy, and to become versed in the biology of a healthy elephant. "To hunt is to learn," he explained. Within a year he would be speaking of killing elephants in a very different way.

Each day began at dawn to avoid the highest temperatures. Forest assistants might have as many as twenty traveling elephants and a greater number of camp men, so marching along they sounded like a gypsy caravan. The kalouks around the animals' necks rang out, empty kerosene cans clanked, and the men chatted. Williams, craving the quiet, made it his habit to leave early on his own.

Hiking ahead of the men, Williams knew that even as a keen observer of nature he didn't see half the animals who saw him. Tigers were plentiful but not known as man-eaters in the area. So he walked with confidence. It would take several days to travel from logging camp to logging camp. His group would always start early and, before lunch, choose a clearing where they would spend the night. Williams would fill out paperwork, and when they eventually arrived at a site, he would meet with ten to thirty men, examine the working elephants, and settle any matters that needed attention.

Logging in Burma, Williams discovered, was strictly monitored by the British in the government's forest department. In the name of progress, they had adopted a German concept of scientific forestry in the mid-1800s. In essence, the philosophy was to balance regeneration with extraction in order to prevent the kind of deforestation that had taken place in India.

A new generation of foresters was particularly proud to be part of a novel kind of conservation and stewardship of the forests. The problem was that the actual extent of tangible conservation was questionable. Teak forests could be cash cows for the empire, and forest managers were under pressure from senior government officials to chop down ever more trees. With increasing demand came increased production, from sixty-three thousand tons of teak a year in the late 1800s to more than five hundred thousand tons annually in Williams's early years. The industry may have been hacking at an unprecedented pace, but all the while, they promoted the perception that this was more responsible than indigenous practices would be.

There were Burmese-owned timber companies, too, but very few. Their harvest was dwarfed by that of the European firms. At the beginning of Billy Williams's career, the five big European outfits owned three-quarters of the teak extracted, while the Burmese share was less than 5 percent.

Williams did not oversee the felling of trees as part of his regular duties, but he occasionally joined the men to observe the awesome sight of trees over a hundred feet tall crashing to earth and then being prepared for transport.

Williams sometimes headed up into the forest with the logging crews. The men, using only axes and simple saws, with blades two inches across, would dispatch teak trees that were often well over a hundred feet tall and nine feet in girth. It was remarkable to witness the huge trunks falling toward earth, pulling down neighboring saplings and vines and landing with a ground-shaking bang that could be heard for miles. Unlike other kinds of harvested wood, teak trunks would not be crosscut into eighteen-foot lengths. Instead, the branches would be trimmed, and the trunk, about twenty-nine feet long, would be left intact. Drag holes, to accommodate heavy chains, would be bored into each end.

Teak stump and logs ready for hauling.

Another captioned photo from Williams's own album. This shows a pair of well-trained, mature elephants working in tandem.

The big, experienced elephants would then transport the massive two-ton logs from stump to stream. The drag chains were attached to the elephants' nine-inch-wide plaited breast bands, and then run up and over a wooden saddle on their backs. The saddle was padded underneath with thick layers of woven bark. Logs twenty to thirty feet in length and about seven feet in girth could be hauled by a single elephant, with the bigger logs requiring teams of two or even three. The elephants would use their heads and trunks to position the wood. The uzis and their helpers would attach the elephants' harness chains to the logs, and the animals would tow them to the closest feeder stream, where they would be placed in orderly lines. The trip could be harrowing, though the elephants knew how to manipulate the load when descending steep hillsides so that the log didn't end up dragging them. The men were fearless, too, darting in between the legs of the tuskers to free snagged chains.

The elephants drag teak logs down to creeks to await the monsoon.
The heavy rains would then move the logs along to larger waterways.

These elephant crews had other jobs, too. They showed Williams how to use logs four to six feet in girth to construct a staple of the forest, "an elephant bridge," a simple but sturdy span over a creek. And they taught him the importance of pulling debris out of dry streambeds. When the rains hit, one jammed log could cause a pileup of hundreds behind it. By observing everything and becoming familiar with the men, Williams began to form his own forest family. The first, and most beloved, member was a funny-looking little village urchin named Aung Net.

The fourteen-year-old in ragged clothes had noticed during one of Williams's visits that a spaniel had kept hunting with Williams, even as she dropped newborn puppies in a section of dense reeds. When the shooting was over, Aung Net appeared, "grinning from ear to ear," and carrying a bundle of five puppies to Williams. Struck by the boy's "humor and kindliness," Williams instantly offered him a coveted job as jungle follower traveling with him from camp to camp. Immediately, Aung Net became indispensable. He first learned how Williams liked his tea, then worked his way up to attending to Williams's clothing and setting his table. The boy wasn't sophisticated—indeed, the others teased him for his earnestness— but he was exceedingly capable in all his tasks. And he proved able to read people and animals alike. When all the men went tearing off in pursuit of a green three-foot-long reptile called a "water dragon" (whose eggs were a delicacy), it was always Aung Net, Williams noted, who would emerge from the brook holding the prized lizard in his hand.

Despite the thrill of new friends and adventures for Williams, when the December holidays arrived, there was inevitably melancholy and homesickness for the family and the life he had left behind in England. His mother sent a traditional Christmas hamper, or gift basket, from the famed British provisioner Fortnum and Mason. Filled with astonishing delicacies such as tins of quail in foie gras, pots of Stilton cheese, ham, biscuits, cakes, chocolates, Christmas pudding, cognac, and Montebello 1915 champagne, they were especially joyfully received by men like Williams—colonialists in the far corners of the world. Alone in his tent, he binged on the contents. In no time, he was delirious with fat, sugar, and booze.

The next day he was back to work. As he sat eating a curry lunch in one of the logging camps, he looked out from the covered veranda of his hut. About a hundred yards below, where the fast-flowing brook opened into a large pool, he saw five elephants bearing uzis. They walked into the stream and lay down in about three feet of water. The uzis slipped off the elephants and knotted their long tubelike longyis into loincloths, exposing some of their traditional tattoos that resembled "skin-tight underwear" from knees to waist. The intricate patterns of dark blue tracery were hypnotic and chimerical: tigers, ghost tigers, cats, monkeys, spirits, and elephants, each bordered by scalloped lines and the circular letters of the Burmese alphabet.

The elephants loved their spa—it not only felt good but signaled the end of the working day—and their joy was infectious. The uzis were using special tree bark and loofah-like creepers from the acacia family, which lathered up thickly like soap, to wash the animals. Every inch from trunk to tail was scoured. Williams found the scene irresistible. He wiped his mouth with his linen napkin, stood, and abandoned his warm, spicy meal to stroll down to the bank for a closer look.

Bath time for the elephants was always a draw for Williams,
who was unfailingly moved by their joy.

It was the same, and was never the same. This time, fuzzy-headed babies rolled over and over in the water, chasing one another with their tails sticking straight up in excitement. They still had so much hair it often looked in need of brushing. They planted themselves in the mud, or slid down the banks into the water, bulldozing each other and running with abandon despite the presence of two big bulls. The males, who had worked out any dominance issues between them long ago, were lying placidly having their teeth brushed.

The uzis took handfuls of the gritty silver sand and used it like tooth-paste to scale their gleaming white tusks.

The baby elephants in particular reveled in the fun of a good soak.

Out of the pool, the animals headed for sand, using their trunks to either suck or scoop it up—depending on the texture—and then blanket themselves with it. The process helped keep them cool and served as a barrier to various swarms of bloodsucking parasites. They also might grab sticks with their trunks to use as back scratchers, and if they didn't quite reach, they'd drop them and pull longer ones off a tree: what scientists would later identify as tool use.

Once they had dried off and the uzis had changed into clean clothes, everyone lined up for inspection. By now, Williams under-stood the formality of the process. He wanted to respond with equal respect as U Tha Yauk bowed before him, handing him a stack of ragged books, each one with the name of an elephant printed on the cover.

Williams called each animal in turn. The first male marched for-ward, halting just in front of him. He was "a splendid beast, with his head up, his skin newly scrubbed but already dry in the sun, a black skin with a faint tinge of blue showing through it," Williams wrote.

The bull's "white tusks, freshly polished, gleamed in the evening sunlight." The tusker's uzi sat on his neck, one leg bent at the knee, the other hanging down behind the elephant's ear ready to signal movement and direction.

Williams opened the top book and read the Burmese entries about the mature male standing before him. His language skills had improved enough to recognize the frequently used designations: *F* for female; *CAH* for calf at heel, if the baby was under five and not yet weaned; *T* for tusker; *Tai,* a male with only one long tusk; *Tan,* for one short tusk; *Han,* a male with a pair of short tusks; *Haing,* a male with no tusks at all. Height, as well as a description of the eyes, tail, ears, and skin, and any identifying scars were noted, as were the mother and date of birth if known.

Though written in shorthand Burmese, the book painted a detailed portrait; a whole life could be conjured up from the scribbles that grew with nearly every inspection. Born in Siam (Thailand), this bull had been purchased by Bombay Burmah at the age of twenty and was once placed on medical leave for a whole year after having been badly gored by a wild tusker.

Williams felt along the elephant's body as he had watched Harding do, and he himself had done months ago upon arrival in the jungle. But now it wasn't just a pantomime. His hands were developing knowledge of their own. The men were even teaching him how to doctor the galls he had read about: slice them open and apply disinfectant. He added his notes into each book.

The histories were recorded not only in these books, but also on the elephants' skin. Their bodies were maps of their experience. Females who had fended off tigers in order to protect their young sported long scars from the claws that had raked them. Mischievous young animals might have notches in their ears from scrapes with other elephants, and bulls who had been belligerent toward people might have had their tusks "tipped" (shortened) for safety.

It was from a male with short, blunted tusks that the recruit learned about another practice that sickened him. As he bent down to look at the animal's feet, Williams recoiled at the sight of ropey, discolored, raised scars that encircled the ankles. He ran his hands along the tracks of thickened and toughened hide. The uzi told him they were training scars, where heavy-gauge holding chains had bitten through flesh during the brutal, weeks-long "kheddaring," after the elephant had been captured from a wild herd.

Kheddaring targeted animals between the ages of fifteen and twenty. A colleague of his would later amplify, describing the process in detail: "Elephants in the wild are generally taken in traps known as *keddahs,* which may be several acres in extent and capable of capturing a whole herd at a time. The *keddah* is formed of a strong stockade of tree trunks with a bottle-necked entrance, into which the victim is either driven or wanders of his own free will. Once in the *keddah,* there is no escape, and trained elephants are then used for securing with ropes the animals thus caught."

As Kipling characterized it, elephants would tumble into the enclosure "like boulders in a landslide." Panicked, and heaving themselves against the heavy posts, they would be taunted and jeered, with torches thrust at them. Empty cartridges would be fired off around them.

During the day, the frightened elephants might be left in the sun with no access to water. They would be chained and beaten, and the air would fill with the shouts of men and the groaning and trumpeting of elephants, until, in exhaustion, pain, and confusion, the animals submitted to the wranglers.

Williams would soon see these practices for himself. He found them barbaric. "When wild elephants are caught by Kheddaring," he would write, "there is undoubted cruelty in the training and particularly in the breaking of the spirit." The animals would often lunge at their handlers, who then would retaliate "with a spear stab to the cheek, leading to wounds which are almost impossible to treat, thus becoming fly blown and ulcerated. Finally the young animal becomes heart broken and thin," Williams wrote; "covered in wounds it eventually puts up with a man sitting on its head, realising finally that it is for ever in captivity which it accepts after a heart breaking struggle." It was, in short, he said, "the very essence of brutality."

But it was also steeped in tradition, relying on techniques dating from ancient times. The large-scale capture of elephants was left to private contractors. Williams knew this had to change, and that the big teak firms shouldn't buy from kheddaring operations. He surmised, however, that the old-timers would not want to hear about reforms from a man who had been on the job a few months. Kheddaring kept them supplied with elephants. If he wanted to put a stop to the custom, he'd have to figure out an alternative. But if they didn't pull elephants from the forest, where else would they come from?

CHAPTER 6

THE FAIREST TUSKER
OF THEM ALL

———

As Williams traveled to the next logging camp, the men told him he was in for a surprise. There was a famous elephant in residence whose name was known throughout the forest: a tusker so blessed, he was like a god. The recruit was intrigued.

On arrival, the workers unloaded the travelers, and Aung Net set about unpacking Williams's clothes and gear. It was soon afternoon and time for the timber elephants to quit for the day. They were bathed and then presented for inspection. In the lineup of about seven, sure enough, one tusker stood out. Strapping, substantial, and confident, he was named Bandoola. Williams approached him and, as was becoming habit, spoke a little Burmese to the bull. The elephant's deep-set dark eyes at first seemed vicious, Williams thought, "but on closer scrutiny kind, for their true colour was the equal of the pearl, with a pupil like a black bead." There was intelligence in the animal's gaze, too—a sense of knowing.

Williams reached out to pat Bandoola's trunk and felt a very odd sensation. A meeting of souls. He was certain that a current of mutual recognition had passed between him and this elephant. "It was not merely that chance or fortune brought me together with him," he would write years later. It was destiny. Rubbing the high-up portion of the tusker's trunk, he sensed an unbreakable bond being formed. In that instant, Williams had "a feeling of understanding him as a fellow-creature closer than many human beings."

That thought fit Billy Williams's ideology. A superstitious man, he jingled the coins in his pocket at the sight of the new moon for financial luck, and was adamant that peacock feathers with their circular "evil eye" patterns did not belong inside the house. He was spiritual, too, for he felt moved by forces that weren't necessarily visible or easily explainable. Coming to Burma had only amplified those leanings. "There are ways of knowing things quite certainly but not by reason," he would write, "and in the East both the wise and the simple accept this."

The moment with Bandoola seemed transcendent. And yet there were earthly reasons, too, for him to feel so drawn to the tusker. They were classmates in a way: born in the same month and year, November 1897. At the time of their meeting, they had both just turned twenty-three and were beginning their adult lives in the jungle.

From Bandoola's ledger Williams learned a great deal and wanted to know more. In halting Burmese, he spoke to Po Toke, the curious man who handled Bandoola. Williams's interest in Bandoola was the best thing Po Toke could have hoped for. He was eager to provide a complete picture of the great bull who was on the cusp of his most powerful decades.

Po Toke, it turned out, had blueprinted a new kind of training for logging elephants, and Bandoola was the living embodiment of it. Over the loud sawing of jungle insects, Williams learned about a method of schooling that resonated deeply with him. Po Toke's revolutionary strategy was built as much on love as it was on logic.

Bandoola had been born under a full moon on November 3, 1897, in the forested area that would later be called "Pyinmana." His mother was Ma Shwe (Miss Gold), a formidable female who was working in a logging camp. Given her temperament and bearing, there was no doubt that as a wild elephant, she would have been a matriarch, a wise leader. But she never had the chance. She had been kheddared by a Burmese contractor before she had fully matured.

Because Ma Shwe was always released at night like the others to feed herself, it was believed that she had mated with a wild bull, a common enough occurrence among the logging elephants. What was uncommon was the mate himself, an especially wily and notorious bull, whom the locals, out of fear and awe, dubbed the "beast of the local forest" or "Bwetgi Monster."

Thus, from both sides of his lineage, Bandoola received size and intelligence.

Although tigers and elephants generally avoid each other, a two-hundred-pound baby elephant can be very tempting for a five-hundred-pound predator. Soon after Bandoola was born, a big cat came for him in the night just outside the logging camp. Bandoola's mother and her *twai sin,* or bonded female friend, bellowed, trumpeted, and fought the killer off. Bandoola was just a shuffling, rubbery little tub of energy with a shaggy coat of baby hair who couldn't yet properly use his trunk. But during the chaos of the assault, he managed to stay with his mother.

Po Toke was among the men who raced to the scene of the attack that night. Just fifteen years old and working far from his home village, he had begun to believe that calves, raised and trained with kindness, would grow up to be better workers than grown elephants who had been beaten into submission. This calf seemed like an ideal candidate to prove his point. Then and there, years ahead of the normal naming time, Po Toke christened the fat calf Maha Bandoola (most often spelled as "Bandula" now), after a courageous Burmese military hero who had fought the British in the 1820s. It was an expression of Po Toke's respect for the elephant and his wish for independence for his country.

Right away, the uzi's confidence seemed deserved. The calf showed an unusual autonomy—leaving Ma Shwe's side to explore on his own for substantial intervals. And he did something else that seemed comical, but amazed the men even as they laughed: If his mother was given a command, Bandoola followed right along with her, so that when a rider told Ma Shwe, *"Hmit!"* big elephant and tiny elephant sat simultaneously. A shout of *"Htah!"* snapped them both to their feet. Simply by observing his mother, Bandoola had absorbed all the basic commands of working elephants without being taught. In the wild, this is precisely how these babies learn.

Though the captive life would seem inherently safer, Bandoola faced dangers that wild calves didn't. The elephant contractors and the British loggers thought that rearing elephant calves, who wouldn't be strong enough to work until they were twenty-one, was a waste of money. Why squander resources for a growing animal, they reasoned, if a full-grown wild one could be caught and trained in a short time? When a baby was born, the men put the mothers right back to work. The calves tried their best to tag along, but they simply could not nurse as often as they should, nor even touch their mothers as frequently as they were meant to. Inevitably, they grew up smaller and weaker than their wild cousins. Worse, because they didn't receive constant maternal protection, they often got lost, were attacked by tigers, and died. The system guaranteed high mortality rates; by some counts it was nearly 70 percent.

Tiny calves suffered high mortality rates at camps where
their working mothers were forced to neglect them.

It was a lucky calf who survived, and Bandoola was nothing if not lucky. The spirits of the forest, the nats, favored him, the uzis always said. That good fortune began at birth, when Po Toke had taken an interest in him. Po Toke not only cared for the baby; against policy he made sure Ma Shwe stayed healthy and unencumbered enough to dote on her calf. But he had to do it surreptitiously. He subtly steered her away from the dangerous work zones and placed her with teams who maintained lighter loads. It would not be easy to conceal for long, especially from his fellow uzis. So he needed everyone in camp to believe, as he did, that Bandoola was exceptional. With the help of the others, and by converting the pretty daughter of the man who owned the elephants to his cause, he had a chance. In a country devoted to Buddhism and mindful of the pantheon of nat spirits, his best bet was to seek a special spiritual status for the animal.

He traveled eighty miles to consult a *pone nar,* or astrologer, hoping to have Bandoola designated a white elephant, for these sacred animals were part of the very soul of Burma. After all, it was in the form of a white elephant that the Buddha chose to enter the world. White elephants came to symbolize all that is pure, strong, and celestial.

Once confirmed by special holy experts, a white elephant would be honored as the earthly embodiment of the universe's gods and godlike beings, and transported to the capital in a royal barge, accompanied by musicians and dancers. There he would live in his own palace, lavishly adorned by items blessed by monks: bangles, headdresses, necklaces, velvet robes, tusk rings of gold, and harnesses studded with precious gems.

The blessings spilled over, in the form of titles and rewards, onto the lucky jungle men who provided these animals. So Po Toke fantasized as he looked at Bandoola. In his favor were two important factors. It was said in Burma that a white elephant emerging from a bath would appear to have red skin, not black as on most other elephants. Bandoola did have a purplish-pink glow when doused with water. And, best of all, in the stiff dark tuft of Bandoola's tail, there were four white hairs.

The *pone nar* agreed that Bandoola might qualify. He told Po Toke to observe the elephant closely as he grew, and he provided auspicious dates to mark for Bandoola's training. He instructed him on specific rituals and offerings to appease the nats. Armed with this chance for sanctification, Po Toke returned to the village, conscripted the support of the other uzis, and followed the astrologer's calendar.

When Bandoola was five, Po Toke built a teak-log holding pen for the calf and tried out his gentling process, rather than "breaking" the animal as was done to wild adults. Bandoola would do anything to get a sweet treat, while threats and abuse seemed fairly ineffective. So Po Toke avoided punishments and focused on rewards. He expanded on the commands Bandoola had learned by observing Ma Shwe. The young elephant quickly began to learn more complicated directives about moving logs that only much older elephants knew.

The method was such an immediate success that Po Toke's status rose among the elephant men. Soon after, when all the elephants of his camp were sold to a teak firm, Po Toke married the boss's daughter and became a high-ranking elephant man with the buyers. He and his wife, Ma Pyoo, followed the elephants to their new assignment in the western part of the country where he continued his work with Bandoola. Though he was clearly a great bull in the making, Bandoola's conditioning was far from over. He still needed time to mature before he was assigned the heaviest log work.

Po Toke hoped that Williams, the new boss, would understand his methods. He did. More than that, Williams realized that Po Toke was a master mahout, the kind of elephant expert Williams hoped to become. For Williams, the proof of Po Toke's gifts was Bandoola, "a rare elephant in his generation, born in captivity and educated to man's service not through cruelty and the breaking of his spirit, but by the indomitable patience of Po Toke. He represented a new generation of elephants."

Bandoola's singularity was made plain by the entry in his ledger book next to "Identification scars": "nil." The tusker was the only unmarked working elephant Williams had come across. It was something he wanted to replicate—in fact, to establish as the standard.

Williams's vague thoughts about elephant care were beginning to crystallize. In Bandoola, he could see the direction of his life and career. He would make sure to visit Po Toke's camp as often as he could. To make the lives of elephants better he would need an ally in the company. Unfortunately, just as this spark hit, it was time to report back to Harding.

CHAPTER 7

THE BURNING BOSS

———

WILLIAMS LOATHED THE IDEA OF LEAVING THE FOREST, ESPE-
cially to return to Harding's camp. "Naturally," he wrote, "when I
arrived I got the greeting I expected: sarcastic remarks." The first
issue the old man confronted him about was one that seemed to have
taken place a lifetime ago: the death of Pin Wa. Harding taunted
him, saying Pin Wa must have been crushed under the weight of
Williams's kit, overstuffed with the novice's gadgets, clothes, and
books.

Williams had seen young male elephants in the logging camps
shove back if bumped by another male. After three months among
the bulls, he was primed for this conversation.

"I'm surprised she lasted as long as she did," Williams replied,
looking squarely at Harding, "considering that her liver was riddled
with flukes and her heart was so enlarged."

Harding wheeled on him. "How do *you* know how big an elephant's heart ought to be?"

"I shot a wild tusker that Tha Yauk told me was forty years old,
and I did a post-mortem on him in order to see how the organs of a
healthy elephant compared with hers," Williams said. The heart of a
healthy animal should be about fifty pounds.

Surprisingly, the old curmudgeon did not react with fury. In fact, Williams noticed that he actually looked *pleased*.

Though Harding did admire Williams's seriousness and inquiry about elephants, the shooting of an elephant on its own wasn't something that made him happy. "Don't make a practice of it," he said. Williams quickly discovered that Harding, as crusty and unsentimental as he seemed, had no patience with so-called big game hunters. In fact, "he felt far more sympathy with any creature which was part of his jungle than with any new arrival."

It would take Williams only a short time to agree. After the first elephant he shot, there would be at least two more: another in the interest of science, and one a rampaging elephant. By the time he shot the rogue, he was a changed man. The action had been necessary, but once it was done, he dropped his rifle, doubled over, and vomited with fear and remorse. Just a little over a year in Burma, he would be done with such behavior for good. Later in life, Williams said it was hard for him to believe there was ever a time when "I allowed the thrill of big game shooting to dim my eyes to the fact that [the elephants] were God's own." He said his only consolation was that it actually helped him develop "as deep a reverence for the jungles and all in them as anyone possibly could." Ultimately, he came to feel that big game hunting was a product of fear, not courage.

It was all part of making sense of his life in Burma. Things were coming together so quickly that on his return from his very first jungle tour, he had one-upped Harding. That night when darkness fell, the familiar two bottles of black label whiskey were set out with glasses. Something had shifted, though. There was peace. Williams looked across the table at his boss, who was settled in his camp chair, his very English face looking even ruddier in the glow of the flames. "That evening I became a companion with whom he could enjoy rational conversation," Williams wrote, "instead of an interloper who had to be bullied and kept in his place." In particular, "the way I had pleased him was by my interest in the elephants."

Moved by the new sense of camaraderie, Williams showed Harding the sketches in his diary and some of the feathers of the jungle fowl he had shot for food. The evening was so convivial that Harding insisted on gin before they graduated to double rations of whiskey.

Williams had not forgotten his vow to drink Harding under the table. So he matched the old man, glass for glass.

After several hours, Harding slumped unconscious in his chair. The moment the boss's chin touched his chest, Williams felt unexpectedly sorry for the crumpled figure. To avoid embarrassing the senior man, he slipped away to his tent, securing the canvas flap open so he could watch the snoring figure from his cot. Harding looked small, old, vulnerable. Finally, the dozing man shuddered and then stood. But rather than heading to his bed, he stumbled toward the campfire and toppled over into the flames. Williams sprang from his tent, reaching his boss just as he was reflexively rolling away. The skin of Harding's arm was already charred bloody and black. Williams pulled his boss to his feet.

Now nose-to-nose with Harding, Williams took in his sour, boozy breath. The old man spit out his words: "What the hell are you doing? Do you insinuate that I am drunk?"

Williams was shocked. "No. But you've burned your arm badly."

Told to mind his own business and get back in the tent, Williams stomped away, shouting: "Well, if you fall again, I shall let you sizzle."

For the next several days, camp was a sullen, silent place. It must have galled him, but eventually Harding was forced to request Williams's help in dressing his burned limb. As the two men sat close, with Williams ministering to the tender, blistered skin, the fragile friendship began to knit back together.

About this time, Williams found out by chance that he had passed his first probation. Harding never mentioned it, but the recruit saw his note to headquarters, which merely said that Williams "would do."

A few days later, as Williams prepared to leave again for his forest travels, Harding pulled him aside for a talk over drinks. Forest assistants became invaluable by focusing on specific aspects of the work, he said. And it had occurred to him some time before that no one had taken up a serious study of elephant management. That had always been a Burmese expertise, not a British one. Clearly, Williams had the interest and talent to fill the gap.

Here was his ally. Williams was gratified to discover that Harding wasn't as oblivious as he liked to appear. The creatures who fascinated Williams would be his life's work and the route to something else he yearned for: advancement in the company. His ambition and passion would be on the same trajectory. He could now establish a humane standard of care for elephants and outline what needed to change most urgently. Williams spoke at length about his ideas.

He wanted to overhaul the system from cradle to grave—starting with the way elephants were recruited into the logging life. He hoped to create a school to gradually induct the young ones, already born into captivity, and even to establish a hospital to ensure better doctoring.

When he finished, there was silence. Harding poured himself another drink, paused, and then spoke. As long as Williams rationally made his case, and documented proof of his success, Harding said, "I'll back you." That was vital because there was sure to be a battle ahead. "You're challenging accepted methods," Harding said. "Some people won't like that." In fact, the boss figured, the campaign might make or break the young recruit. He'd better be prepared. The example of Bandoola went only so far. Williams had to demonstrate the success was repeatable. If he could do that, Harding said, then "the days of kheddaring will be numbered."

Over the next months, Williams campaigned for his ideas, taking every opportunity to seek out opponents as well as supporters, and tell them, "If you saw Bandoola—he's the only domesticated elephant we've got—Bandoola works smoothly. He uses his brain. He knows exactly what to do and when to do it. The kheddared elephants rush the job. They're not skilled."

The gentler concepts that Williams believed in, he said, "appeared to the senior men in Bombine as sentimental, unpractical, uneconomic." He knew he wouldn't change their minds until he could prove that his plan was financially beneficial.

So he worked out some figures. While baby elephants were being thrown away to die, the company was spending a fortune obtaining grown elephants. In a single decade, it would purchase nearly two thousand mature workers for Burma logging alone. And each one cost anywhere between $500 and $3,000, as much as $180,000 today. Meanwhile, what would it cost the company to keep the babies alive? Very little. The elephants primarily fed themselves, so the only expenditures would be from making up for the loss of output from mothers who would temporarily be given lighter workloads, and the pay for extra uzis as the calves grew. The price tag would still be less than it would be for buying kheddared animals. And these elephants would be healthier and more trustworthy. It was, he said, "at the same time practical and humanitarian." As for creating an infirmary and improving veterinary care, making a case was easy—healthy animals produced more work than sick ones.

Williams had worked it all out on paper. Now it was time for Harding to go to bat for him.

CHAPTER 8

SEX, CRICKET, AND BLUE CHEESE

———

WHEN WILLIAMS NEXT RENDEZVOUSED WITH HARDING, THE boss was waiting with a reproach. This time it was about the mail. In his loneliness, Billy was corresponding with every young woman he knew from London to Rangoon. The bundle of responses was taking up too much space in the company's green canvas mailbag, which was shared by the two men. Harding wanted more room for the truly important items in life: whiskey, cigarettes, and the specialty cheeses, including blue Cheshire, he regularly requisitioned.

To be in camp with Harding, Williams knew, was to suffer days at the mercy of his sharp tongue. But now there was a new wrinkle: Harding asked him to play cricket. It was clear this wouldn't be just an amusement. First of all, while Harding waited, Williams and the elephant men in camp were directed to hack out a playing field in the jungle. That finished, the tense match between Englishmen began. Right away, Harding was furious that Williams jokingly claimed to be left-handed: "What the hell do you think you're going to do, mow corn? Stand up and bat right-handed like a gentleman." When Williams took a real whack at the ball they were using, sending it deep into the shaded forest, Harding's face went "purple with rage," and he fumed, "Do you think tennis balls grow on trees, you idiot?" Worst of all, it turned out that the old man was actually quite good, "a well-known bat in county cricket." Williams would later recall, "Cricket has never been my favourite game; but my fanatic loathing of it dates from that afternoon."

When the rains washed out their cricket playing, Williams was overjoyed. But Harding was undaunted. He had a new sport for them: Northern Quoits, a game like horseshoes played with a steel discus set. If the discus landed with the convex side down, Harding explained, "that's what we call a 'lady,' but you're too young to know why." After some play with the discuses, Williams said, "I don't mind admitting I've never seen so many ladies lying on their backs."

"Nor have I," Harding said, "and I'm over fifty."

"This I remember as a very important afternoon," Williams wrote years later, "because in it I had made Willie smile once and laugh once. It was the beginning of the thawing process, almost as gradual as the melting of the polar ice-cap, but at least a start. And as I got better at the game, so Willie in his unbending way unbent."

On this trip, Williams led his boss to his favorite place, Bandoola's camp. It was becoming nearly a second home to Williams. The men arrived early and watched the logging elephants as they neared camp for their afternoon baths. Williams spotted Bandoola immediately. They knew each other by sight now, and Williams often brought the elephant tamarind balls as treats. Bandoola would take them gently from Williams's hand, curling the end of his trunk around the offering and then popping it into his mouth. He'd then chew slowly, his mouth making loud smacking noises, his eyelids remaining half closed. Williams would pat the front of his trunk or scratch the ridged underside of it. The thickness and weight of Bandoola's trunk, bigger than both of Williams's thighs put together, always astounded. The bull himself seemed larger every time they met. While so many things could befall these working elephants, Bandoola was thriving. Harding wouldn't have any criticisms of him in the lineup.

But then Williams saw another big tusker from a different camp. He had a large abscess on his chest that had clearly gone untreated for some time. Williams figured that Harding would probably erupt over this, though when the old man saw the swelling, he was silent. Williams walked in front of the elephant and tapped his lower jaw so he would raise his head. He touched the abscess, which, he wrote, was "twice the size of my fist." Still, Harding said nothing. As Williams ordered a knife be brought to him, Harding walked away and sat down on a log to watch.

"I stabbed the abscess with the dagger," Williams wrote, "and the pus poured down the animal's chest and foreleg in a stream. I cleaned the abscess out with my fingers, then syringed it with a dilute disinfectant, which I also used for washing the animal's leg and my own hands and forearm." It was fast and good work. Williams proudly strolled over to Harding, figuring "that if I had not earned any praise, at least I had avoided a rocket." But Harding moved away, saying they would discuss the matter later. That evening, the two men sat down for their evening ritual. As Harding sipped his first whiskey, Po Toke appeared and fell to his knees before him in submission. Williams, who felt equally responsible for the abscess, wouldn't let him face the firing squad alone, and knelt beside him, an extraordinary act for a British man here.

Harding addressed Williams first: "Didn't this headman tell you the animal was dangerous?"

Williams said no. Harding said it was in the book, and if Williams's Burmese were better he'd know that. "It's a wonder the animal didn't knock your block off," he said.

Williams was perplexed. He may have been on his knees, but now he was full of fight. "Well, why didn't one of you stop me operating?"

Harding's answer was opaque. "For precisely the same reason that the animal *didn't* knock your block off," he said. The boss and the tusker were acknowledging that Williams could get away with liberties around elephants that no other man could.

Then Harding lit into Po Toke, and every one of his words "seemed to go home like a body blow." Po Toke was shaken when he was dismissed.

Harding turned back to Williams, saying that he didn't trust Po Toke. Any Burman suspected of nationalist leanings was a threat to the old guard colonialists. Aware of Williams's loyalty to Po Toke, Harding issued a pointed warning: "Watch him as you go."

Williams and his big-hearted village dog, Jabo, entertain a visitor.

Williams returned to his regular rounds. But the rainy season brought three serious attacks of malaria. As he had during the war, he would tough them out, but the cumulative effect was telling. He was helped through them by the companionship of a young red-and-white village dog he had picked up named Jabo, who showed him sympathy.

When Harding summoned Williams out of the forest for a trip to headquarters in Rangoon, they hadn't seen each other in three months. Williams looked so haggard that Harding went easy on him his first night in camp and for the several days of travel down to the capital.

The first thing Williams did when leaving the jungle was catch up on the news from the outside world. He was hungry for it. Aboard the company paddleboat, during the periods of wakefulness, Williams could stay curled up in his bunk reading the newspapers. Back in England, that summer of 1921, unemployment soared, the coal miners ended their strike, and in September, Ernest Shackleton was making his way to Antarctica on what no one knew would be his last voyage.

Harding provided more important news closer to home: He was about to go on leave, so Williams would be temporarily reporting to a different forest manager, a man named Millie. In addition, in a few months' time, Williams would be overseeing a large district as the replacement for a forest officer going on leave—another move up the ladder for the ambitious young recruit.

Williams and Harding were finally enjoying each other's company as they cruised down the Chindwin. It felt good to have the boss confiding in him as a colleague. Over drinks one night, Harding went further, becoming nearly paternal: "You may think that I've been an absolute devil this last year," he said. "You're quite right, I have deliberately. You'll find Millie a much nicer man than I am, but I trust you to serve him just as loyally all the same."

Despite the effects of malaria, Williams was happy. "I found myself at last accepted, and the acceptance was all the dearer because it had been so hard to win." That night, he tried to shrug off how sick he was. But after one marathon card game, he was spent. He was awakened at six in the morning by a cool palm on his forehead. He opened his eyes and saw Harding with a glass in his hand. "Drink that!" he said. "Champagne and stout. Do you a world of good." Williams drained the glass and went back to sleep. Although Harding would return after his leave, "It was the last order he gave me as my No. 1."

CHAPTER 9

SCHOOL FOR MEN
AND ELEPHANTS

———

I T HAD BEEN ONE YEAR. AMONG THE THINGS WILLIAMS LEARNED was that time in Burma was more cyclical than straightforward, measured by seasons rather than years. And the rhythms of forest life were becoming the patterns of his own.

There was the oppressively hot spring, starting in mid-February or early March, when the forest assistants did some of the toughest, most uncomfortable and arduous work—counting the hundreds of logs that were marooned in dry streambeds throughout their territory. The sand would get so hot that it was like walking through fire. In camp, Williams often shed his clothes entirely. The leaves fell off the trees, and any trickle of water was coated in green scum. Without cold, clear water running, all drinking water had to be boiled. For the elephants, it was just as sweltering, but the middle of March would bring their vacation—six weeks off to spend in rest camps, deep in the darkest, shadiest parts of the jungle where rivers still flowed. "All nature seems at a standstill, waiting for the life-giving monsoon to break," Williams wrote.

Next, around the end of May, the storms would come. "There is a violent clap of thunder," Williams noted, "and then, like a curtain dropping, down comes the rain. In a few seconds it is impossible to see across the clearing. Elephants, under the trees stand like statues as the rain splashes off their backs. In a few seconds they shine like ebony carvings." The rivers rose instantly, roiling "yellow and thick," as one forester said, "bringing down all the debris of nine months of dry weather." Within hours, what had been a trickle would become a raging, impassable torrent. The sleeping logs would come alive and "by their hundred go shooting past, twisting and turning in ever varying patterns." This was also the season of mosquitoes, sand flies, leeches, and every kind of biting thing. And Williams would find he was in for a punishing spell of malaria following any monsoon tour.

"I came to see the things to be afraid of were not wild beasts," Williams wrote, "but the climate during the monsoon season and the repulsive creatures that flourished in the rains: the black silent anopheline mosquito which carried malaria, the hookworm burrowing through the ankles and passing through the bloodstream to make its home in the upper intestines, the leeches on the dripping leaves and the tinea [a maddeningly itchy and pernicious fungal infection] lurking in the mud."

A watercolor scene Williams painted of a bungalow in the forest.

Late fall was the best time of year: Cool Novembers brought chilly mornings and days of good, hard work. Williams always had a bungalow of his own and a string of elephant camps to visit. Mornings were brisk when Aung Net would gently waken him with a cup of hot tea.

At night, after a curry supper, Williams carved little animals out of wood, sketched, and painted. He learned how to make jungle scrimshaw, etching animal images into small pieces of tusk and darkening them with India ink. When he put down his pencils and brushes and extinguished the lamps, he could sit with a last whiskey, listening to the sounds of the forest and the voices of the men. Looking at the light of the campfire dancing on the wall of trees around him, he saw the forest in the mystical way his uzis did. Perhaps it was the vastness of it, the way light and dark played tricks on the eyes, the eerie sounds of the night creatures, or the need to believe matters of life and death weren't so random. From the men, there was regular talk of ghost tigers and tree and water spirits. Williams himself often sensed that certain areas in the jungle felt hallowed, and usually he would discover that they were, in fact, holy places to the local people. To walk these forests, he noted, one had to accept phenomena that were beyond logic.

Williams loved to hear the men talk about ghost tigers and forest sprites. He believed in them, too.

And much of the mystery came directly from the nats. Though the uzis were Buddhist, they had no qualms about believing in these spirits. Nats had been worshipped for thousands of years, and when Buddhism became the country's state religion in the eleventh century, these beings and their animist cosmology were simply folded in. The nats, hybrids of humans and spirits, can be angelic or demonic. Most are ghosts of humans who died in some tragic way. Like Catholic saints, each one governs a distinct spiritual field. With their evocative names—Lord of the Great Mountain, Lady Golden Sides, The Lord of Five White Elephants, the Little Lady with the Flute, The Brown Lord of Due South—specific nats are propitiated at births, weddings, and deaths; for the prevention or relief of illness; planting or harvesting crops; and just about any aspect of life. In the jungle and in village homes, little wooden cabinets were crafted into simple altars where offerings of food (nats were said to be especially fond of coconuts) or even cheroots could be left.

Harding had warned Williams about giving credence to what the uzis said about the nats. "Let their superstitions get under your skin and you're sunk." But Williams was clearly receptive to the jungle creed, as proved by a visit by what was thought to be a ghost tiger. Once, during the rainy season, an uzi who was an atheist and did not respect the nat shrines was silently taken by a tiger in the middle of the night. Snatched right out from the middle of the row of sleeping uzis, who had not heard a sound. In the morning, huge paw prints in the mud revealed that the man had been dragged down to the creek. But there the prints disappeared. Not another mark on the other side or anywhere along either bank was seen for miles. It was as though the cat and the body he was carrying turned into mist. Everyone, including Williams, agreed it had been the work of a *nat kyar,* or spirit tiger.

WILLIAMS'S SECOND NOVEMBER IN Burma brought two pieces of good news: He had passed his formal probationary period, and elephant school was granted a trial run. Harding was still on leave when the verdict came in, but Williams knew the old man deserved thanks.

And the best way to show gratitude to the great taskmaster would be to succeed.

The faculty for the school was already chosen. Po Toke would be general trainer. Although this meant that for at least a while he wouldn't be able to keep an eye on Bandoola, the position was a triumph for him—an official acceptance of his theories and practices. Assisting Po Toke was a wonderful headmaster nicknamed U Chit Phoe, Mr. Old Lovable: a Burman with infinite patience, Williams noted. There would be two elephant handlers per calf, plus three twelve-year-old boys who wanted to be uzis. In traditional circumstances, these boys would have been trained by uzis using adult elephants, but now they could actually grow up with their elephant partners. The calves and boys would become experts together.

In Williams's new elephant school, young uzis and calves would learn together.

Along with the human headmaster came an elephant version, too: a patient, mature bull to keep the young ones in line. The designated "Koonkie" was a forty-five-year-old tuskless male who proved just how tolerant and even loving bulls can be.

The elephant students were selected from the company's ledgers, which listed females in possession of five-year-old calves. With only three students enrolled and a campus consisting of a clearing in the forest, it was a modest beginning.

Three triangular shaped corrals were constructed, each just big enough to wedge in an agitated calf. Despite the cruel-sounding term, "crushes" were designed to be strong but also forgiving. Huge logs were used, denuded of rough bark. Pig fat greased the interior, and wooden pegs, not nails, fastened the sides together to prevent any scrape or injury to the young elephant's skin. The camp was well stocked with everyday forage and favorite elephant treats, too: tamarind, sugarcane, sweet lime, and bananas.

That first session was filled with trial and error. Yet, right away, the baby elephants learned. They accepted training, bonded with their boy-uzis, and showed that they had the potential to be a great investment.

The bosses thought so, too. Bombine administrators approved the continuation of elephant school as long is it was kept on a small scale, though, eventually, the training system would become an established part of the company's structure. More and more calves were signed up each term, reaching a high of twenty-nine. The kinks were worked out, and elephant school quickly established its routine.

The company's regional camps held around five hundred elephants, and it was their calves who would become students. Scanning the roster, Williams would select all the five-year-olds, whom he called "my babies." The exact date was a matter for the nats to decide. Part of launching each new semester was lighting candles to divine the proper time to begin. A small thatched shrine was constructed to honor the jungle nats, and offerings of fruit or flowers were placed in it.

Then the mothers and their young would be summoned. "On arrival," Williams reported, "there was chaos, for although strangers, [the calves] were pulling each other's tails and romping within an hour." For several days, while the mothers were fed, the babies were free to do as they pleased.

The mothers were gentle disciplinarians. Williams observed what happened when one little male wandered a good quarter of a mile away on his own. The baby was gorging himself on some lush bamboo shoots as his mother began calling. The calf "listened with one ear cocked, stopped chewing, held the tip of his trunk in his lips as if sucking his thumb, and then satisfied that she was still about, he started stuffing his mouth again." The calling and ignoring went on for twenty minutes. But when the "tone of the mother's call changed to one of sternness," the calf turned tail, crashing through the jungle back to her, Williams said, like a clumsy fat boy. Upon reaching her, he was met by a thump from her trunk hard enough to knock the wind out of him. He kept close by her heels for the rest of the day.

The curriculum began with the young uzis getting acquainted with the babies. They flirted with them, Williams said, giving them "a tit bit in the form of some fruit or a handful of rice." One at a time, the calves were removed from their mothers. In the wild, separation would not come this early or suddenly. Males would spend more and more time away until between the ages of ten and fourteen they would be on their own.

If Williams felt a pang for the poor little animals, he could remind himself that ultimately this averted a cruelty, for many of the babies would have died if left to struggle near their mothers in a logging camp.

The calves didn't see it that way. One might be lured away with treats, another "frog marched" in by the Koonkie, or lassoed around the legs by a soft buffalo-hide rope. "There is a short struggle and yelling," Williams saw, "but provided the mother is near, the calf soon quietens down." As soon as a young elephant was in the crush, the gate would be closed behind him. "The calf rolls and struggles, but the grease inside the pen makes him only slither and slide," Williams wrote.

Then the bribery would begin. The little elephant would be showered with treats and praise from the handlers. Despite that, the calf protested—often too upset to even collect a morsel. "For about

2 hours it struggles and kicks, then sulks, and eventually takes a banana out of sheer boredom and disgust—the expression on its face can only be compared to that of a child who eventually has to accept a sweet from a bag," Williams noted.

Once an elephant started accepting delicacies, the real lessons would begin. Po Toke showed them how it had been done with Bandoola. A young elephant handler in training—the boy who would likely guide a particular elephant for the next forty years—would be suspended over the baby in a pulley block system. The calf would bellow, clearly signaling "Damn you! Get off!" The rider apprentice would be lowered and raised repeatedly, the elephant praised and fed a nice fat banana each time she permitted the rider on her neck.

Next, a heavy wooden block, padded with soft material, would be lowered to the point of putting pressure on the elephant's back. The Burmans would chant, *"Hmit! Hmit!"* or "Sit!" until the elephant, weary of the weight, would slump—hind legs kneeling first, and then the front legs folding downward. The moment she did this, she would receive handfuls of treats. The block would be lifted, and as the elephant would reflexively stand, the men would chant, *"Htah! Htah!"* or "Stand!" so that she associated the command with the action. Again, she would be rewarded with sweet treats. By sundown, a young elephant would be released from the pen having been stuffed with hundreds of bananas.

None of the mothers objected when the babies were first taken away, but over the following days, Williams heard them calling. By now he knew the cadences of elephant talk and he could distinguish between contentment or fear. These mothering calls seemed less about distress to him, and more a shouted hello to touch base. There had to be a great deal of unhappiness, though, and Williams knew it. The bond between an elephant and her calf is astonishing, and it lasts a lifetime. Even in camps where so many natural relationships were broken, in which calves were separated too early, elephants were resilient in their love. They never forgot one another and delighted in reunions. One of Williams's pack elephants, an eighteen-year-old male, bumped into his mother at a logging camp on their route. "As we entered camp," Williams wrote, "the calf passed his mother and they both chirped." They might have been arranging a rendezvous, for the moment they were released after work they would find each other, and they continued to do so every night they were able to.

Of course, the joyful pairings weren't limited to mothers and their offspring. Females, such as Williams's travelers Me Tway and Chit Ma, formed bonds with one another that were sometimes interrupted by separate assignments. When friends or relatives were back together, even briefly, they would greet each other with much emotion by vocalizing, touching, and making eye contact. They always seemed to make plans because the minute they were set free in the afternoon to forage, they would run to one another and keep together throughout the night.

Williams saw that his elephants were a lot like people when it came to the variety of friendships they formed. And scientists later would prove the point. Some Asian elephants act like social butterflies, keeping as many as fifty friends, while others prefer a smaller circle. Among those with smaller groups of friends, the bonds are usually strongest. The detailed sorting of these friendships is yet another sign of the high level of what modern scientists would say is the cognitive capacity of elephants.

At school, the best approach to helping the heartbroken young ones was to lavish them with love and to keep them busy. They were even taken on field trips. The Koonkie would be outfitted with a buffalo-hide brace around his neck, which was attached to another such collar on one or two young elephants. The big male would walk his students and make them heel—pulling them along or even cuffing them with his trunk if they lagged or struggled. Once the calves got the hang of it, Williams found that the Koonkie, like the nannies he had seen back home, could control the young ones with a look instead of a swat.

Working with Po Toke, Williams drafted an outline of an ongoing program. The calves, he proposed, should have about two years of this kind of coaching: learning to follow the instructions of the uzis—including the basics of foot commands behind the ear to turn right, or a movement of thighs commanding a left turn. At about the age of eight, they would go to work carrying light loads as traveling

Despite the restrictions on their lives, even working elephants managed
to form complex social bonds. Williams was fascinated by the subtlety
and strength of these connections.

elephants. At first it might be old kerosene tins filled with water and
the blanket roll of their uzi, or a small kah. This was elephant graduate school. On expeditions, they would teach the young elephants
skills they would use later in logging. Gathering logs for the night
fire was a natural. Their uzis would also teach them the names of the
pieces of equipment, having them hand—that is, trunk—up each
item as they learned to distinguish the words for ax or chain.

All the time the animals would be growing in height and bulk. By
the end of their traveling years they would be capable of handling
five-hundred-pound loads on their backs and ready to graduate to
logging work if it suited them.

For Po Toke, that inaugural school session marked the first time
in his and Bandoola's lives that the two were not together. He worried, and with good reason. The bull was entering a dangerous age
when males often feel compelled to fight with larger, more mature
opponents for mating rights. And Bandoola was sure to be one of
those tuskers who wouldn't back down from a challenge.

CHAPTER 10

DRUNK ON TESTOSTERONE

———

On a sweltering April afternoon in 1922, Williams, his bush shirt soaked through with sweat, was crouched down in the shade between boulders in a parched riverbed. He could almost hear the heat, not as sound, but as the absence of it—there was no whisper of wind; only silence from the narrow, slow trickle of water running beneath the granite rocks. Traveling with Kya Sine, a hunter hired by the logging company, he had hiked in what seemed like slow motion for five miles outside of camp, through forest and now along the rock-strewn bed. They were tracking Bandoola—missing, and, for the first time in the elephant's life, fully in the grip of a mysterious condition called *musth*. Bandoola was right on schedule, as the uzis found that most males began their musth cycles in their twenties. The yearly periods of musth were weaker in young elephants and intensified with maturity. The strength of musth also depends on physical condition, so the better fed and stronger a bull is, the more explosive his musth cycle.

Bandoola had been on the loose for five days, his uzi unable to capture him. The men in camp were in a panic. Musth bulls pick fights, and when one was nearby, no one was safe. The first precaution was to gather the rest of the elephants in camp. Next was to contain the bull.

As Williams and the hunter caught their breath, they considered their options. They had begun the day with no plan other than to find Bandoola. They had to see him to know how far along he was in the cycle and what his state of mind was.

Even though Williams had been immersed in the world of elephants, he had not seen any tuskers he knew well at the peak of musth—often described as "a form of madness or possession." Impervious to pain, intractable, and reckless, bull elephants in musth go berserk with their own virility. No handler, if he could help it, would get within trunk-length of these animals. In working camps there were methods of dealing with the condition—primarily keeping the animals chained, and starving them to reduce the length and power of the cycle.

Musth had been recognized in captive bull elephants for thousands of years. The ancient Sanskrit manual on all things elephant, the *Matangalila,* spoke of it in accurate terms: "Excitement, swiftness, odor, love passion, complete florescence of the body, wrath, prowess, and fearlessness are declared to be the eight excellences of musth." Combativeness, chemical signaling, overwhelming sexual urges. The old text got it right. Musth would be recognized in African elephants with scientific certitude only in 1981.

The term *musth* was derived from the Urdu word for intoxication—appropriate for this state in which a male is drunk on his own testosterone. During musth, levels of the hormone can increase to fifty, or even a hundred, times normal.

When it comes to sex, musth gives elephants an edge over rivals. It's not just humans who fear a musth bull—other bulls do, too. Bigger, stronger males not in musth will generally defer to a smaller one who is. Bulls have even been observed running in the opposite direction when just catching a whiff of a musth bull. Receptive females, on the other hand, are attracted to them.

The uzis, who made it their business to understand it, recognized four stages of musth: Initially there is a loss of appetite and an indifference to commands. The temporal glands swell slightly. Next comes what the men called "upper musth": the glands secrete a watery substance. The penis is erect a good amount of the time and occasionally jerks upward, touching the bull's belly. Then the temporal glands truly increase in size, and stream fluid. A whitish discharge drips from the fully extended penis. This is "lower musth."

Finally, the animal reaches what the uzis called "the musth drinking stage." Now the temporal fluid, which has taken on a strong odor, pours down the cheeks so copiously that it runs into the mouth. The musth bull also dribbles urine almost continuously, turning parts of the penis and sheath green, and scalding the inside of his thighs. The penis is fully extended, swollen, and hangs down to the ground. A musth bull is pungent, and because it warns other males and can attract females, he likes it that way.

The bull doesn't just smell different, his looks change, too. He stands tall, holding his head higher, with the forehead thrust forward, and the chin tucked in. Sometimes he presses his tusks into the mud of an embankment and the temporal discharge appears to drain faster and ease the sensation for him. This is full musth, an unmistakable state of mind and body. At this point, the uzis believed that even the nicest bulls were capable of charging and killing anyone in sight. It was as if they had been slipped a powerful, mind-altering drug.

Depending on the bull's age and condition, musth can last a few days or a few months. It is taxing to remain in this high-alert, intense state for long. One African bull, in musth for an incredible six months, lost more than a thousand pounds in the process. When musth ends, the bulls are exhausted and often in poor condition. Losing so much fluid comes at a cost. And the high level of testosterone circulating in their systems impairs their immune systems, making them vulnerable to parasites and disease.

In the teak industry, any time was too much for the biggest, best workers to be out of commission. When the uzis saw, smelled, or sensed the change in their tuskers, they took action. Securing them with strong fetters and tying them up with heavier-gauge forty-foot chains, they treated musth bulls like dangerous convicts.

Because Williams had not witnessed the phenomenon in full bloom, he could not argue confidently about whether it was the mating imperative he suspected it was. This would be his chance to gain some experience, and the fact that it would be with Bandoola added intrigue.

Williams and the hunter had been able to follow Bandoola's trail out of camp, but then it had grown cold. Past a certain point, they could locate no more footprints, not even any droppings. Finally, they saw a few trees badly mangled from the thrusts of sharp tusks. It had to be Bandoola.

There was no indication of where the elephant had gone from there, but treading quietly in the native rope-soled shoes he had taken to sometimes wearing, Williams instinctively headed toward the dry riverbed. He knew the animals well enough that, particularly if he was familiar with the terrain, he could intuit their movements. "I was sure Bandoola was nearby," he recalled. "I could feel his presence. I could visualize him standing perfectly still waiting to charge us."

Leaving Kya Sine and his rucksack in the shade of a boulder, he traveled alone upstream, like a dog on a scent, galloping forward as though a trail had been left for him. After an hour of bounding from one river rock to another, he scrambled to the top of a boulder, and there before him stood Bandoola, looking nothing like a murderous monster.

Still, the scene was curious. Bandoola had planted himself in the shade of a tree, facing a chunk of stone as big as himself. He was swinging his trunk from side to side, a movement which Williams knew the riders called *pa-ket-hlwe,* or "rocking the cradle." It was a motion that some believed to be a red flag for bad behavior. The bull also swayed his entire body, putting all his weight on his left legs, then his right, alternating back and forth, in a movement the uzis called "winnowing the rice." During the entire spectacle, Bandoola maintained an enormous erection—his engorged penis, S-shaped and weighing perhaps sixty pounds, nearly touched the ground.

Williams crept closer to Bandoola, fascinated. Now he could see the temporal glands clearly. They looked as if they were drying up.

The tusker's ears were set back, flat against his head. He appeared to be dreaming with his eyes open.

Williams wondered if Bandoola imagined the stone he was facing as a receptive female elephant. The man and tusker really did have a lot in common—even sexual frustration. "I was alone. I was young and fit. I was on musth," he wrote. The sight of Bandoola romancing a rock echoed his own longing writ large.

He dashed back to Kya Sine and filled him in, imitating Bandoola's movements. The hunter was relieved. *"Hmone aung byee,"* he said. "Musth has passed." Kya Sine would go check on him while Williams rested. In the heavy heat, the young teak man was only too happy to collapse in the shade of the boulder.

Sometime later, from a deep slumber, Williams became aware of the sound of Kya Sine's voice: *"Mmah!"* "Lift it up!" He opened his eyes when he heard a breaking branch. He saw Kya Sine atop Bandoola commanding him to clear debris in front of him. Without a word, Williams shook off his lethargy, gathered his things, and followed behind Bandoola back to camp.

Po Toke and Williams decided that for the time being, Bandoola would march as a pack elephant back to training camp where, as a safety measure, a small length of the bull's tusks would be sawed off and blunted. As common and painless a practice as it was, it seemed like a desecration when applied to Bandoola.

They loaded up and headed out for the march of several days. One night during the journey, Williams got a rare treat: He was able to observe two elephants mating in the forest. It was Bandoola and a recently captured wild female.

Sometime earlier, the two elephants had advertised their desires to each other through special low-frequency calls: hers saying she was in estrous, his that he was in musth. Then, when no one had seen him, Bandoola had investigated this female's readiness by smelling her and her urine.

The two might have gone through a refined courtship. Sometimes elephants about to mate will intertwine their trunks, walk together, or delicately touch and sniff each other. The male might also prod her with his tusks to guide her along to a location of his choosing, often away from other males. But by the time Po Toke had discovered them, they were past polite dating. He brought Williams out to watch. The two elephants mated again and again over the next several nights.

Williams was enchanted. The intercourse lacked the brutishness that he had witnessed in some other animals. With elephants, he observed, "two animals merely fall in love with each other and days if not weeks of 'playing with fire' is engaged in. The male mounting the female with ease and grace, remaining in that position for periods of 3 to 4 minutes. Eventually the marriage is consummated and the act lasts from 5 to 10 minutes," he wrote.

Watching Bandoola have sex, Williams thought, "almost with envy," that the big tusker "had lost his loneliness and found a mate."

When they finally reached training camp, Bandoola was in good humor. He placidly allowed the men to clamp chains on his legs and secure them to a massive tamarind tree, with large bushy branches that formed a bright green umbrella of shade. It was time for the tusk trimming. The men made sure the saw would not come close to the nerve ending, which was far back from the few inches to be "tipped." Rope was tied from one tusk to the other in order to protect the trunk from an accidental cut. A finger dipped in red betel nut marked the incision point, and then Po Toke took up the handsaw. After just a few strokes of the blade Bandoola objected—jerking his massive head hard enough to send Po Toke flying backward. The big male then "let out bellow after bellow of rage." Williams could feel danger in the air.

Po Toke shouted for Bandoola to stay still, but the tusker ignored him. The experienced elephant man calmed himself, then returned to speak reassuringly to the animal. Bandoola, Williams said, became "as silent as a coiled spring." Everyone stood frozen.

Po Toke picked the saw up from the ground where it had fallen and reached to grab Bandoola's tusk again. This time, the big male didn't even wait for the metal to touch ivory. He lunged forward, yanking the heavy chains taut. Po Toke's commands had no effect. The bull was in a frenzy. Bandoola reached his trunk for one of the chains, grasping it and pulling as hard as he could. When that didn't give, he threw all of his strength into lunging forward over and over, heaving his bulk against the iron fetters.

The heavy chains on his forelegs snapped in thunderous claps.

Men scrambled away, wild-eyed.

Bandoola now turned to the tree, many times larger than himself, and, placing his tusks high up, began to shove. He would step back for momentum, and then bully his way forward, rolling all his muscle into the effort. With each slam, tamarind fruit, leaves, and branches showered down. Then the impossible happened: The giant tree began to rock back and forth with the elephant. Branches fell with great snaps, whooshes, and thuds; roots beneath the soil broke off in muffled pops. Williams "watched appalled and yet filled with awe."

With Bandoola's next drive came disaster. His back legs were still manacled as the entire tree toppled right onto him. When the noise ceased and the branches settled, Bandoola was nowhere to be seen, buried under the weight and girth of the magnificent tree. As dust still choked the air, Williams feared what everyone else did: Bandoola was dead.

All ran to him. The great tusker was lying on his side, motionless, under the weight of all the timber. But as they snatched at the debris and reached down to Bandoola, they saw he was alive—his sides heaved with each breath he took. Everyone began to saw and hack at the boughs. They grabbed heavy felling tools in an effort to split the links of the chain securing the bull's motionless back legs. It took several blows before finally, with a metallic crack, the thick link broke open.

Bandoola slowly got to his feet. He looked stunned but seemed as gentle as a lamb. Not only alive, he was unharmed. Williams checked every inch of Bandoola's hide and discovered that except for scratches, the furious bull hadn't sustained any injuries. The matter of tipping his tusks was never revisited.

CHAPTER 11

MASTER CLASS IN TRUST
AND COURAGE

———

BILLY WILLIAMS WAS CHANGING. THE ELEPHANTS WERE EDU-
cating him in matters of character and biology. Within two years of
the elephant school's first sessions, Williams had established an elephant hospital at the same site. It wasn't a building with wards and
surgical suites; merely an area where good stores of medicine could
be kept, a place where sick elephants could recuperate in lush, safe
surroundings. Only the toughest cases went to the hospital. And
without a licensed animal doctor for hundreds of miles, Williams
worked on them all. His first four years on the job proved the equivalent of veterinary school. He did what he could: He read, questioned anyone with knowledge, consulted with the uzis, and learned
by trial and error.

He found that working elephants suffered from colic, or went
septic from tiger wounds. They fell victim to anthrax, tuberculosis,
pox, rabies, and tetanus. There were diseases of the heart, lungs, and
blood. They sustained punctures and gashes while hauling teak.
They had accidents—falling down slippery slopes, dragged away by
raging currents, immobilized by thick mud. They dropped weight.
They got pregnant. And most of all, they developed "galls," those
pus-filled abscesses just under the skin where their harnesses chafed
them.

As Williams got better at helping elephants, he realized they were doing him a favor also. Through the parade of sore feet, sliced skin, and upset bellies, they were conducting an emotional master class, educating him about love, courage, and trust. He saw that actions meant more to elephants than words, and he supposed it was the same with people, too.

Trust had to be earned and was granted only to those who could be relied upon. Once he gained their trust, they allowed him to do anything. They actually seemed to grasp that his procedures were "being inflicted for their own good." In fact, Williams said, "I know, without question, that an elephant can be grateful" for such medical care.

What made him so sure was a big girl named Ma Chaw, or Miss Smooth (a term for a shapely woman). After a night in the forest, the elephant had dragged herself back to one of the camps in Williams's territory with long and deep lacerations crisscrossing her back. She had been in a brawl with a tiger. "The most horrible thing an elephant might suffer was a wound from a tiger's claws," Williams came to see very quickly. Where the tiger had ripped her skin open, healing would generally be a straightforward process. But the raked patches, where the skin remained intact, were more sinister. When sharp, dirty nails puncture skin, bacteria is injected, which quickly forms life-threatening pockets of infection. Elephants' skin is so thick that often when there is a gash, only the outside layer will heal, sealing up a foul pouch beneath it. The concealed sore can quickly turn deadly as infection spreads throughout the body, causing organs to shut down in septic shock. Ma Chaw's wounds were so extensive that Williams had to suspend any touring in order to tend to her every day.

Sweet and gentle, but also a little bit of a ham, Ma Chaw would fuss and resist care for a few minutes before standing still. She had to endure several steps of a ghastly procedure in which Williams would slice open those hidden chambers of infection running under the skin of her back, scoop out rank-smelling pus, and then use a syringe to apply disinfectant. Because purified antibiotics wouldn't be widely available until 1941, Williams used what he could. One treatment he'd had some success with involved packing sugar into the wounds. It provided antimicrobial and even granulation-inducing properties, helping form the matrix of tissue that would knit together and heal.

Still, it took three full weeks of nearly around-the-clock care for Miss Smooth to make it out of danger. During that time, the two had shared moments of happiness. Williams gave her sweet tamarind balls, bananas, and sugarcane for being such a good patient. He learned where she liked to be rubbed on her trunk and forehead. He spoke to her quietly in Burmese. She expressed her feelings with low rumbles of contentment that he could feel in his chest, and sometimes she squeezed her eyes shut and produced high-pitched chirps of delight.

Finally, Williams left Ma Chaw in the hands of a reliable worker and requested regular reports on her progress until he could rejoin her two months later.

On arrival back at Ma Chaw's camp, he sat out in a folding chair in a clearing in front of his tent to have a cup of tea. The camp's seven elephants were being bathed in the creek, close enough for him to hear the ritual commands and the splashing and trilling of the elephants. When they were marched by afterward, Williams called out, "How is Ma Chaw's back?"

At the sound of his voice, his old patient rushed straight at him in a floppy trot. He patted her trunk and gave her a banana. When she had finished it, Miss Smooth did something odd: She lowered her rump to the ground, with her back toward him.

With her uzi looking on with amusement, Williams patted Ma Chaw's back and quietly told her to get up: *"Htah."* She did as she was instructed, leaving with her rider.

Williams had never seen such a display. Was it submission? Politeness? He thought it was gratitude. But he wondered if he was making too much of it. In any event, it was time for inspection. He drained the last sugary swallow from his teacup and headed for the line of elephants.

Ma Chaw was at the end. When it was her turn, Williams ran his hands over her wrinkled hide. Working her flesh, he discovered that though her back looked normal, it was not. As he pressed and squeezed some of her skin, he lingered at an area about nine inches long. There was heat and just the tiniest opening to signal the problem—one of her old wounds that had not healed.

She didn't fight him for a moment; in fact, she seemed to welcome his invasive treatment. It was as though she had asked for it. "I can never be quite sure that she came and showed me her back in order to tell me that it was still painful," Williams wrote with scientific caution. But, he added, "I am sure that she liked me, trusted me, and was grateful."

Like his counterparts back home, Billy Williams, as a young workingman, was learning to negotiate the adult world. But here in the jungles of Burma, elephant society was his model. He didn't emulate middle-aged bankers or scholarly old college dons. For him it was matriarchs and bulls. His bosses taught him some. The uzis, too. But mostly it was the elephants. And as their characters revealed themselves to him, he absorbed their wise lessons.

Particularly where mothers and their young were concerned, he witnessed an astonishing display of loyalty and bravery. There were two pairs of elephants who helped him form his own personal standard of courage, giving him the backbone, he later said, he never would have gained from fellow humans.

The first involved Bandoola's mother, and it occurred one afternoon just before darkness fell at the beginning of the rainy season. With this first downpour, the headwaters had built up and begun to sluice down the waterway, a fast and quickly rising tide. It was just what a forester wanted—torrents that would wash all the teak from the mountainsides so it could begin its route to Rangoon. Williams listened, hoping to hear in the distance the telltale boom of two-ton logs knocking into one another as they rammed their way along at high speed. He walked through the soaking rain down to the edge of the river. Here the riverbank was like a canal with twelve- to fifteen-foot shale walls. He could see that the waters, at a depth of about six feet, were gaining fast. Just then he heard the roar of an elephant in a tone that chilled him. He practically spoke their language by now, and he recognized this as a cry of terror. Along the opposite side of the river, about 150 feet away, he made out through the curtains of rain several uzis rushing around in agitation. He raced over to investigate.

There in the fading light, pummeled by the downpour and trapped in the torrent, was one of his favorites, the elephant who had given birth to Bandoola, along with her tiny three-month-old female calf. He didn't know how she got there or what had happened. But Ma Shwe was up to her shoulders and barely holding her own against the current. Using every bit of her strength, she pressed the baby against the shale with her whole body—keeping the calf's head above water and preventing her from being swept away. It was a life-and-death struggle. The current kept claiming the baby—setting her in motion "like a cork in the water." But Ma Shwe was just as relentless. Each time the calf was pulled off, the mother, with extraordinary strength, would use her trunk to grab her and reel her back.

The high, sheer banks gave her no purchase—no possible way out. Worse, Williams knew this river well, and he felt certain Ma Shwe did, too: Just below them, three or four hundred feet away, were deadly rapids. The elephants would be lost forever if they were pulled toward them.

As he tried to come up with a rescue strategy, there was, as is typical in monsoon, a sudden two-foot surge in the water level. With that swell, the calf washed right over her mother's hindquarters, bobbing downriver. Ma Shwe threw herself into the tide, frantic. She finally got to the little one on the same side of the river where Williams stood. Ma Shwe clutched the calf with her trunk and again pinned her to the bank. Williams felt helpless. He could do nothing but watch, and it seemed there wasn't much more Ma Shwe could do, either. Sooner or later, she would be too tired to hold on. Several agonizing minutes had ticked by when the exhausted elephant got her trunk around the calf's body, and she reared up out of the water. "Then as if with one mighty super animal effort" she lifted the baby as she would a log, stretching herself to the limit, placing her up on a narrow ledge five feet above the waterline, but still well below the top of the wall. With this last act of strength, Ma Shwe fell back into the river, which hurled her down toward the rapids.

There was only one spot before the falls where she would be able to exit. Given her intelligence and determination, Williams hoped she would reach it. But even if she did, she would then be on the opposite side of the river from her calf. Williams turned to the baby, who, on a ledge just wide enough to hold her feet, "stood, tucked up, shivering and terrified." Her "little, fat, protruding belly was tightly pressed against the bank."

How could he save her? He thought about attempting to raise her to the bank with ropes, but worried he would scare her back into the dark waters. After another half hour, Williams realized he was losing time and light. He might have lost hope, too, when he heard what he said was "the finest call of the wild I ever heard. Ma Shwe had reached her bank and was making her way back as quickly as she could, calling the whole while—a defiant roar—but to her calf it was music. The two little maps of India, the shape of the calf's ears, were cocked forward, listening to the only call that mattered, the call of her mother." Then, in the fading light and pouring rain, a figure that matched the gray dusk emerged from the jungle on the opposite shore.

As soon as Ma Shwe saw her baby, her voice changed. "She stopped roaring and began rumbling," Williams noted, "a never-to-be-forgotten sound, not unlike that made by a very high-powered car when accelerating." It was a "phut, phut, phut" sound that was the audible tip of one of those secret elephant calls too low for human ears. Williams could literally feel her joy.

But the drama wasn't over. Night was falling fast, and under near biblical rains, the two animals remained on opposite sides of a raging river from each other. For hours, in the pitch blackness, Williams heard the chest-rattling thunder of those deadly giant teak logs crashing into one another. He wasn't doing the elephants any good standing out in the rain, so he went back to his bamboo hut. But he could not change into dry clothes, nor even sit down, knowing Ma Shwe and her baby were still out there.

He grabbed a few things and ran back to the spot above the ledge. He shone the beam of a flashlight down and saw the poor baby still on her precarious perch. He went back to his tent and then again returned to check on the calf. The glare only seemed to disturb her, so he forced himself to leave. He could only hope that the elephants, as they usually did, would puzzle out the solution.

With the first dim light of day, Williams bolted back to the river and found a beautiful sight: mother and calf reunited; the boiling river reduced to a coffee-colored trickle. How had it happened and when? No one witnessed the reunion, but Williams had a hunch that Ma Shwe had gotten across the river and found a way to lift her baby out. It's something elephant mothers do.

Later, when the calf turned five, the traditional age for naming since their real personality would have emerged by then, the men christened her Ma Yay Yee. Miss Laughing Water.

Williams would come to see that the heroic love between mothers and babies was reciprocal. Often it was expressed in small gestures—a tiny baby threatening someone who approached his mother, for instance—but there was one case that stunned Williams and would stay with him. One November, a new class at school was convened, and all mothers with five-year-old calves were summoned for the new academic year.

Among them was a female in her midthirties named Mahoo Nee, or Fire Opal, whose extraordinary eyes "were of a rich dark brown illuminated by a flickering light, like flames." Mahoo Nee was leading her male calf over the many miles from her camp to the school grounds. Along the way, her uzi had been riding atop her as they waded through some dense vegetation. To make it easier for her and the baby, the uzi would reach down in front of Mahoo Nee's head as they walked, slashing at some of the branches with his knife. But in doing so, he inadvertently cut a type of vine that when broken open can burn and blister the skin.

When they arrived in camp Williams walked over to greet them and assess the new little student. But as he drew close, looking up into the gentle face of his old friend Mahoo Nee, he was horrified. Some skin was burned, and her eyes were covered with an opaque film.

He spoke with the uzi about what had happened. Her eyes must have touched the vines, the rider said. With a growing sense of alarm, Williams examined her. He wanted to find out if there was some vision remaining, any ability to distinguish light and dark or movement. "When I waved my fingers to within a quarter of an inch of her long lashes, there was no flicker of an eyelid," he said. She was completely blind.

The elephant hospital was nearby, but there was no salve to treat the damage, no hope that her sight could be restored. At least she would be safe with him, Williams thought. There was plenty of forage gathered for her, and she could be bathed in the cool stream nearby. The gentle elephant deserved a little pampering.

When the mother and calf were led away Williams noticed something extraordinary. "I saw the calf back his hindquarters towards his mother's head," Williams wrote. "When she felt him, she raised her trunk and rested it on the calf's back; and in this way they moved about the clearing. It was like a little boy holding his blind mother's hand and steering her down the street."

Generally, Williams had found calves at this age to be unruly. Able to feed themselves, they begin to wander off on their own and exert some independence. When they are close by, they tend to be nuisances to their mothers. He was surprised to see a sense of responsibility and maturity in the calf, he wrote, "until I remembered that human family relationships can alter enormously, if either parent or child is injured. Instinctively a sort of balance is struck and the normal instincts are modified."

The care of his mother "would give him the discipline which he would have had to be taught at school, a discipline of devotion, but all the stronger for that." Williams wondered if the calf would eventually tire of the burden and escape into the wild. Without him, Mahoo Nee would have to be hand-fed for the rest of her life.

Mahoo Nee and her son were sent together to a kind of elephant retirement village, called the "Old Crocks' Home," British slang for something broken down. It was near a river where the terrain was flat and the tasks easy (pushing stranded logs from sandbanks). Older elephants or ones with minor physical problems who could still handle light work were sent there. Even Bandoola had been employed at the spot once during a time when Po Toke was trying to keep the growing bull from strenuous work. Retired elephants didn't have to work at all; in fact, their fetters were removed forever, and they received extra rations of salt and tamarind fruit to help digestion.

Very quickly, the men in camp had a name for the new calf. They called him Bo Lan Pya, or the Guide Man.

At the Old Crocks' Home, the calf and his mother developed a routine: Mahoo Nee would work a regular shift, her rider directing her movements. In the afternoon when she was done, the Guide Man would come by. They'd have their daily bath and then "off he would take her to find the six hundred pounds of fodder which she needed as her daily ration," Williams wrote. "They would spend an hour feeding in the kaing grass. Then, trunk on back, she would follow her son to the bamboos for a couple of hours more, then off again for a few hours in creeper and cane brake jungle. Another hour or so, browsing and resting under a shady tree and then down to the water to drink."

The steadfast calf had all day to himself, but never even seemed tempted to run with a wild herd. Mahoo Nee and Guide Man were always together by choice. Their movements, and it even seemed their thoughts, became intertwined. An exquisite communication, Williams noted, developed between the two of them. Those infrasonic rumbles had special meaning to them. They spoke to each other in a way that the men couldn't hear.

Completely without sight, Mahoo Nee thrived. She worked, she foraged at night, she had joys, and she experienced intrigues. Her bond with Guide Man was a revelation. The calf doted on her. "The proof of his good work was Fire Opal's condition," Williams wrote. "For three years she was physically perfect." Williams went to the camp whenever he could to see her. Invariably he left in high spirits. Just seeing her happy life cheered him.

At the beginning of one monsoon season, he seized a chance to call on the blind elephant's camp. When he arrived, it was raining and the river was rising quickly. Mahoo Nee was among the several elephants pushing logs into the water, and he could see Guide Man on the far bank, roaming around but sticking close to home base.

For some reason Mahoo Nee looked unhappy, and since the current was picking up speed, Williams called for her rider to bring her onto the shore near him. As the uzi did this, the blind elephant called out for Guide Man. "I looked across the river," Williams recalled, "and in a moment or two I saw the grand little head of the calf appear out of the tall elephant grass about four hundred yards away. His ears were cocked forward. His little tusks stood out like toothpicks. He bellowed back, as much to say, 'Wait a mo', mum, I'm coming!' But the river bank at the point where he had emerged had a sheer drop of twelve feet."

Swollen, rapidly changing rivers during monsoon are dangerous, but what happened next was a freak accident. As Guide Man raced to find a gentle slope on the bank for his descent, he hit a spot that had turned into a precarious ledge—the earth below it scooped out by the churning water. The whole structure gave way under him. When he hit the water, more heavy mud came sliding down, trapping him.

Williams hollered for a canoe, though before it was even put into the water he realized it was hopeless. The little calf had drowned. It was agony enough for Williams, but then he looked over at the solitary figure of Mahoo Nee. She stood silently in the shallows of the river, straining to hear, as the waves slapped against her flanks and the rain poured down. Her uzi directed her to the section of the river where her son had drowned. She began to call out for him—bellowing over and over. Though Guide Man had not made any sound the humans could hear as he slipped under, Williams felt sure that Mahoo Nee knew what had happened. "It may have been my fancy," Williams wrote, but "in her calls there was no hope of answer." She seemed to be expressing shock and grief as she stood over the buried body of her son. She reluctantly moved away when commanded, crying out as she pushed against the current, crying still as she heaved herself up onto the shore. And all the way back to camp. By nightfall, she was silent. Heartbroken, Williams and the uzis hand-fed her all her favorite treats. She did eat some, but something was now terribly broken inside her.

Three weeks later, she was dead. Williams held no postmortem, though that was standard procedure in such cases. "The cause of death," he said, was "obvious."

CHAPTER 12

THE JUNGLE FAMILY
HAS NO WIFE

———

By the summer of 1925, Williams was a true jungle man—
not a spare ounce of flesh on his bones, hair buzzed down to a military minimalism, skin browned by the sun. He worked like a jungle
salt and played like one, too—keeping a polo pony or two at his regional headquarters so he could join in organized games when he
came in from the forest. He had made lifelong friends with some of
his colleagues, and admired others—men such as Colin Kayem, "the
bravest and maddest" forest man Williams knew; Harold Langford
Browne, as handsome as a matinee idol and beloved by the uzis; and
big Geoff Bostock, a highly respected teak man moving up the company ranks. Williams's satisfactions were enormous, and yet as he
drew closer to the age of thirty, he began to take stock of his life as a
whole.

He had been to England on leave once to find that most of his
friends were married, while he had hardly dated. He tried making up
for lost time there through an intense love affair with a beautiful
woman from a wealthy family. But he was soon back in the forest
alone. Sometimes he experienced such an overwhelming urge to
mate that he thought about quitting. His despair wasn't unusual.
Forest assistants like Williams spent most of their time in the jungle,
unable to meet Englishwomen at all, but even the fortunate ones

who did manage to become engaged would not marry till they ascended to the ranks of management. It was a well-established axiom that it took about ten years for a forest man to be in a position to wed. Currently at the halfway point, Williams began to wonder if he could hold out.

Williams was an avid polo player and kept a pony or two at his bungalow.
In this photograph, his beloved Alsatian, Molly Mia, trails him.

Though he recognized the beauty of the Burmese, he said, he did not want to adopt the colonial habit of using and discarding local women as needed. Instead, he would take the three-day river run down the Chindwin and then grab a train to visit the houses of prostitution or fleshpots of Rangoon. The writer George Orwell had been to such establishments in his time in Burma, in the 1920s, and described them as "dark & mean" places, with dying flowers on the front doors and rotten bamboo floors stained with betel spit within.

With a little luck, Rangoon could also bring the prospect of proper dates. It was a challenge, though, to swoop into town on little notice, and with hardly any pocket money, and then find an unattached beauty to squire around. More remote still was the hope of meeting a woman who would welcome a life in the jungle.

He wasn't having much success in finding a wife, or even a girl-friend, but he did begin to build something of a family around him of animals and people. It had started with Aung Net—their bond was instant and lasting. Williams would say, "No man ever knew me better and I knew him as I knew no other Burman. He grew up with me almost as my son." He was the first of many without conventional appeal that Williams brought into his fold, hiring the misfits and the unfortunate. There was his personal cook, Joseph, a half-Indian and half-Burmese Christian who spoke English, Burmese, and Hindustani. He was unflappable—nothing riled him, and however many guests showed up or wherever in the forest they were, he was always remarkably creative with the ingredients at hand.

There would be a gardener taunted by his peers as an idiot, and San Pyu, an orphan from the Shan region to the east. San Pyu was born with no thumb or fingers on his left hand. But he used his "stump," Williams wrote, "with devastating effectiveness," for tasks such as kneading dough.

Animals were part of his chosen family, too, though, except for the elephants, they didn't stay long. Wild creatures usually returned to their wild lives. An orphaned baby otter named Taupai was one. "She was a darling," Williams later said, "one of the most lovable pets I ever possessed." But after only about six months, she was gone. "She found her happiness," Williams wrote, swimming off with a group of wild otters.

Dogs would be with him for a few years at a time. The jungle life was hard on them, and rabies, leopard attacks, or accidents would take them long before they reached old age. He would have many: pariah dogs; a bull terrier named Sally; Cobber, a Labrador retriever; a springer spaniel, a cocker spaniel named Rhona; a black chow named Bilu; German shepherds Karl and Molly Mia; there were more, and they often overlapped.

In fact, this tumultuous year was the one in which he lost his very first dog in Burma, Jabo. Always an independent spirit, Jabo had chased after a female in heat and then tried to catch back up to Williams by hopping aboard a passing canoe. The men on board hit him with an oar and drowned him. Williams was heartbroken. Though he didn't find out the truth about Jabo's end for years, the dog's disappearance added its weight to what was becoming a period of "tremendous restlessness," one that led him to consider resigning. Ultimately, he would stay put. He needed the elephants and they needed him. Especially, as it would turn out, Bandoola.

Williams was in Po Toke's camp the morning the tusker returned on his own, bleeding profusely, his skull and shoulders covered in gore. It was a nightmare vision, the huge bull elephant staggering into the clearing, blood running down his gray hide, seeping into the soil around his feet. The men shouted and Williams ran out to Bandoola. Williams quickly ordered water and disinfectant and began to delicately clean away the blood to reveal the actual wounds. Most of the injuries were superficial. Still, he knew he couldn't afford to miss an abscess. So once Bandoola was well scrubbed, Williams carefully examined every inch of him. The bull was stoic. Cut by cut, Williams's fingers probed and explored their way over the elephant's forehead, eyes, cheeks, trunk, ears, and neck. All seemed good. But when he made his way to one of Bandoola's shoulder blades, he found trouble. What looked like a nick on the surface turned out to be a deep, penetrating gash the width and length of a typical tusk. Here was the answer. Bandoola had fought a bull elephant. And since all the camp's own male elephants were accounted for, it had to have been a wild one. The wound was serious; Williams knew his beloved elephant had come within inches of losing his life. Only the bone of the shoulder blade had prevented Bandoola's heart or lung from being clipped.

Williams syringed the big wound with disinfectant and patched all the other lacerations. It was time to gather food and water for Bandoola and to let him rest. But Williams couldn't help wondering: What damage had Bandoola done to the other guy? After washing up, he headed out to investigate. The fight had taken place nearby—trampled vegetation and blood spatter marked the spot. One blood trail led back to camp; another pointed in the opposite direction. Bandoola's foe was clearly mortally injured—since wherever he had paused in his flight there were bloody droppings. Pools of coagulated blood showed that Bandoola had thoroughly trounced the animal. This wild bull must have sustained serious head wounds, Williams deduced, because leaves that were skull height to a tusker were marked with red along the route.

Following the trail, Williams came to a forest of tall elephant grass. It would have been suicidal for him to follow a stricken tusker into the dense sea of vegetation, so he stopped; he knew already what the ending would be for the poor creature.

Back at camp, Bandoola's lacerations were looking better, but a systemic infection took hold. "His whole blood-system became affected," Williams reported. "He developed abscess after abscess, sinuses and fistulas." All of them received aggressive care. Through the painful procedures, Williams found the tusker to be "the most wonderful patient I have ever handled, man, woman or animal."

Williams changed his schedule to focus on Bandoola, and for the first time, he was closely involved in his everyday care, bathing, feeding, and doctoring him. There were times when every step forward seemed to be followed by a step back, and a few points at which Williams thought he might lose the tusker for good. Through it all, it seemed Bandoola felt shamed by the erosion of his magnificence. Months went by before the elephant was able to eat normally, walk without soreness or weakness, and keep weight on. Even then, Williams couldn't quite bring himself to let the animal out of his sight, so he recruited him as one of his travelers. It seemed a little beneath Bandoola's dignity, but he got to know the other pack elephants. It would take an entire year for the tusker to fully regain his health. Perhaps Williams was being overly cautious. Or maybe he just enjoyed the elephant's company. But eventually, when there was no denying Bandoola was restored to his physical magnificence, he was returned to logging work. And the two friends said a temporary good-bye.

CHAPTER 13

"THE MURDER OF ME"

———

IN 1926, WHEN WILLIAMS WAS SETTLED IN AT ONE OF THE LOGGING camps, an itinerant worker named Aung Kyaw showed up. Williams knew him well, having watched him grow from a teenager into a young man working and living on his own. He stood out: first, because he was handsome, athletic, and so much taller than the rest— about five-ten—and also because of his natural magnetism. He was an extraordinarily able forest worker with particular knowledge of jungle life and medicine. But Aung Kyaw was also attracted to trouble in the bigger towns along the railroad line. Only when he needed money would he go back to the camps—to grab temporary jobs as a follower with the elephant men. He had a reputation for disappearing before his full term was up. "He was the New Year's Resolution," Williams noted, "bright, fervent but not lasting." Perhaps he was even unstable. Because of this, Aung Kyaw had been blacklisted with the company. Though Williams was officially prohibited from employing him, he felt the directive was inherently unfair—any officer could ban a worker without explanation. This kind of random authority irked Williams, and he often enjoyed flouting it. Aung Kyaw was hired.

At first, everything was fine. In fact, Aung Kyaw worked diligently, so when the camp was in need of eggs and live chickens for an impending trip to a valley near the Chin Hills, Aung Kyaw and another man, San Ba, were sent off with fifteen rupees each. But San Ba returned alone, reporting that Aung Kyaw had left for another village. Williams was annoyed. He assumed that was the last he would see of Aung Kyaw.

Williams went back to the paperwork that had been preoccupying him—hashing out the details of a complicated fifteen-year teak extraction plan. The calculations were tedious, and he spent hour after hour with papers spread out over two camp desks. Exhausted by the end of each day, he looked forward to quiet evenings—a nice dinner, a few pegs of whiskey, and reading the weeks-old periodicals that had arrived in the mailbag.

There were enough things to keep Williams's mind so full that he had nearly forgotten Aung Kyaw when a week later, it was announced that he had returned empty-handed—no chickens, no eggs, no money. Williams summoned him but did not glance his way as he arrived at the tent. Aung Kyaw had to wait, squatting on the rug, while his boss deliberately ignored him, slowly checking some of the timber figures in front of him. Finally looking up, Williams questioned Aung Kyaw, already knowing the answers: How many chickens did he get? How much money was left over? Aung Kyaw had nothing in hand and no explanation. He looked ashamed, muttering vague answers.

Williams admonished him—he swore mildly in Burmese, saying Aung Kyaw must have spent the money on liquor and women. "My language was not violent," Williams would later write, "but I did use every Burmese jungle expression at my command to tell him what I thought of him as a man."

Even during the exchange, Williams would regularly disengage from the conversation to peer down at the paperwork, tallying sums to show Aung Kyaw his contempt. And then he'd ask questions again. Aung Kyaw's mortification seemed to redouble, but he stayed silent. A full minute went by. Finally, Williams lost his temper. He told the worker to leave. Rather than using the polite phrase in Burmese, he barked a demand as an insult: *"Thwa like!"* or "Clear out!"

As soon the words came out of Williams's mouth, he regretted them. "It made me almost ashamed to have insulted Aung Kyaw so deeply," he said, "and I looked down at my papers so that he could go away without further humiliation."

But Aung Kyaw didn't go away. He defiantly remained in place. The longer he ignored his boss's order, the more Williams lost face. So Williams whipped around in his chair. Just as suddenly Aung Kyaw stood, reaching for a sheath tucked into his waistband at the small of his back.

Williams was incensed. "You dare draw a dagger at me?"

Aung Kyaw held the weapon in his right hand—a brutal eight-inch-long knife with an ivory handle.

They glared at each other. As Williams lunged forward, Aung Kyaw raised the knife. They struggled. Williams landed a solid punch to the face, which sent his adversary backward, bleeding. Then, Aung Kyaw came forward, "crouching like an animal," lashing out with the knife. Williams dove at his attacker's knees, lifting him "like a rugger tackle."

The brutal embrace was intimate. "For a moment," Williams would write later, "I felt the warmth of his body against mine." As Williams prepared to throw his assailant to the floor, the knife struck his arm and then plunged into his left side. "There was no pain," Williams recalled, "but a sound like a stone being thrown into water and I groaned with the blow." Now Williams got Aung Kyaw to the ground, pinning him. It was victory of a sort, but even as he gained the upper hand, he saw the blood flowing down the knife blade toward the handle and realized it was his own. On the verge of black-ing out, he yelled for help. Aung Net came running to the rescue, heroically snatching the dagger from Aung Kyaw's hand. Williams was afraid that Aung Net, driven by his loyalty, would kill Aung Kyaw. But very quickly, half a dozen men appeared.

Williams stood up, "feeling rather strange and seeing round specks revolving before my eyes." With everyone tending to Wil-liams, Aung Kyaw ran off. The camp men chased after him.

Williams assessed the damage. A cut on his arm was bleeding pro-fusely, but the real devastation was to his ribs. Blood saturated his shirt and streamed down to his socks. The sodden garment was tugged off, revealing a gash. He prayed his lung had not been harmed.

After being bandaged, he rightly figured a whiskey would only increase the bleeding, so he asked for tea. Lighting a cigarette, Williams took his first long drag. It hurt like hell but made him realize his lung was not punctured.

He needed a tetanus shot, though because of the bleeding, he could not be moved quickly. There would be five painful days in camp. Shortly afterward he arrived at headquarters in Mawlaik near the border of Manipur. Aung Kyaw was already there, having surrendered in remorse.

Williams was having similar feelings. Over the three weeks it took for him to heal and for the days he waited for the trial, he constantly ruminated about what had happened. The pain that lingered in his ribs did not spark a desire for vengeance. Instead, he came to feel that he had mishandled the meeting entirely. Put simply, he said, "I asked for it."

Aung Kyaw was the first and last Burman he ever hit, he wrote. He blamed himself for having been belligerent and contemptuous from the start. Things would have gone quite differently if he had been more humane. When the dagger appeared, Williams felt, he should have made an effort to calm, not provoke, Aung Kyaw. He could have called out to the camp workers to intervene before anything started. But he had felt his manhood challenged, so he had escalated the tension. A better man would have risen above the misunderstanding, not stooped to it.

Williams had an epiphany: "If I had shown Aung Kyaw the sympathy and understanding that I prided myself on having for elephants," he wrote, the stabbing would never have occurred. He realized that the emotions of men in trouble mirrored those of the animals he loved. He had forgiven elephants for killing men if what the elephant had done seemed justified. There was a lesson in that. "One thing certain," he wrote, "was that in those jungles no one including myself ever thought of destroying an elephant for killing a man." He let that thought guide him now.

As the trial date approached, Williams reframed the incident with Aung Kyaw in a characteristically honorable way. "We had very nearly committed a murder together," he reasoned, "the murder of me. I was thoroughly ashamed of my own part in that affair, and I thought Aung Kyaw was ashamed of his." Aung Kyaw's life was at stake, and he alone would pay the price, Williams wrote, "for what was in some measure my crime."

Williams entered the District Sessions desperate to help Aung Kyaw. When their eyes met, he saw the accused's face break into a genuine smile. The horrible incident had forged a strange bond between them. "If only the judge could have ordered him to say that he was sorry, I felt that justice would have been done and Aung Kyaw and I would have left the court friends for life," Williams said.

It was too late for that. Aung Kyaw wore a red jacket that marked him as criminal facing a charge of attempted murder. His legal team did not appear competent, and Williams saw the courtroom was packed with Burmans employed by the British (Bombine and government clerks) to side against the accused. The odds didn't look promising.

Despite the fact that he was a witness for the prosecution, though, Williams was determined to be Aung Kyaw's advocate, knowing he might be his only one. The accused looked bewildered as the proceedings went forward in English. He could not understand a word.

That gave Williams an idea. When motioned by the elderly Anglo-Indian judge to come forward and testify, Williams surprised everyone with a request never made by foreigners: Speaking in Burmese, he asked to take the Burmese oath after he had done so with an English Bible. "As the witness pleases," the judge said, "but all evidence and proceedings will be taken in English."

Williams was passed a pungent bundle of palm leaves bound in red cloth. Before a hushed courtroom, he held the frayed Kyeinsa over his head and kissed it. This abridged version of the Book of Oath, or Book of Imprecations, promised an unceasing hell for anyone falsely testifying.

The courtroom hushed as Williams told his story. The lawyer asked if Aung Kyaw had come to the camp with the intention of murdering Williams. Williams thought of all the times elephants had killed. It was never, he believed, premeditated. It was always "a spur of the moment reaction followed by remorse." He answered no.

Aung Kyaw took the stand. Speaking through an interpreter who translated his testimony into English, he told an implausible tale about Williams brandishing a revolver and then falling onto the knife. When the prosecutor rose and began questioning Aung Kyaw, the story fell apart. Finally, Aung Kyaw recanted and asked if he could simply tell the truth. He then corroborated Williams's version.

Aung Kyaw was given a light sentence of three years. A year later, as it turned out, he was out of prison and living with his family when Williams went to visit. "I saw his dear old parents," he said, and they called for their son. "As soon as he entered he just fell on his knees and cried asking pity and forgiveness." That had already been given, Williams said.

Making peace with the other beings in the forest wouldn't be so easy.

CHAPTER 14

BANDOOLA: HERO
OR ROGUE?

―――――

Bandoola had just saved Billy Williams's life, carrying him sick and unconscious across the raging Yu River. Though delirious through most of the trip, Williams, in flashes, remembered the tusker's Herculean effort, his slow and careful search for footing in the boulder-strewn waters, and the animal's stamina. Williams recalled, too, the sensation of the river water washing right over the basket he was riding in. Their safe crossing was a miracle.

Now they were on the opposite bank, but still only halfway to the medical help of the wilderness station on the Chindwin. Williams's eyes were rolling back in his head again, and Aung Net and the other camp worker who had ridden across with them knew they had to get him out of the rain. The men first set Bandoola free to forage, and then pulled Williams up a set of ladder stairs into a dank, sturdily built hut, raised up on stilts. Aung Net toweled Williams down, got him into clean clothes, and tucked him into a cot.

Under normal circumstances, getting to the Chindwin would have been straightforward, as the Yu fed into the greater river. But one section of the waterway, dangerous even in good weather, had been rendered impassable in the rains. In fact, Williams knew of no one who had even attempted the rapids at this time of year. His only choice was to ride Bandoola through miles of virgin forest to reach the Chindwin below the chute. But, now, even that seemed beyond him. As his condition worsened, Williams feared he would not survive the lurching ten-day trip.

The thigh-high mud of the rainy season carried a sometimes
deadly fungus that the men called elephant itch.

The torrential monsoons of 1927 were conspiring to kill him. He was experiencing a cascading series of maladies, including malaria, and the effects of a sometimes deadly fungus that thrived in the thigh-high mud of the rainy season. The men called it *tinea sin wai,* or elephant itch. Wherever the sludge touched, the skin would erupt in little pustules. "I knew the course this hideous thing would take," Williams wrote. "Ulcers developed in some places on my calves. In sympathetic reaction the glands in my groins had swollen to the size of fists. It was impossible to stop scratching for a moment, impossible, even with the aid of whiskey to gain any sleep." In his torment, the onset of malaria was nearly a blessing, for at least it regularly knocked him unconscious.

But, of course, he didn't stay asleep. Waking in the hut, and in agony again, Williams called for Aung Net to fill an old kerosene can with boiling water. Aung Net helped steady his shaking hands, as the two lifted the heavy tin and poured its contents onto Williams's legs. It was torture, but it helped. "The discharge from the sores oozed down like black treacle," he wrote, "and the relief was such that I was able to endure the pain in my groins for as long as a quarter of an hour before collapsing on my bed again."

The rain was as relentless as his illness. After two days, Williams's condition worsened. Delirious and weak, he gave up. He hoped to simply die in his sleep. Over the years, he had spent enough time stopping in this place, which was on his regular circuit, to have cultivated some favorite flowers and shrubs. It was all too possible, he realized now, that the bougainvillea bushes he had planted would soon mark his own grave.

Eventually the rain paused just enough to allow some of the other men carrying supplies on elephantback to reach him. For Williams, though, there was no relief. The rains resumed. Then, a second miracle took place. Three dugout boats arrived, the last piloted by Colin Kayem, the Bombine man whose bravery was legendary.

As soon as Kayem stepped off the boat, Aung Net ran to inform him that Williams was near death. The two scrabbled up the ladder. In the lantern light, Kayem found his old friend delirious, soaked in sweat, and gaunt. Gently pulling the sheets back from where they stuck to Williams's weeping legs, Kayem saw the devastation. He got to work, spending the entire night draining the "venom" from the drum-tight ulcers.

Somehow, this time, it worked. By morning, Williams felt the best he had in more than a week. Sitting up weakly in his cot, he even joined Kayem in a cup of tea.

Over the din of the rain hammering the roof, Kayem announced a decision. "We're getting out of this bloody hole," he said. "I'm making up a crew of three volunteer boatmen to shoot the rapids." It was just what Williams had worked so hard to avoid. And yet his friend somehow made it sound easy.

"I don't mind," Williams responded. "Anything you say."

Kayem organized the strongest men and loaded supplies into the boats. He secured his patient into a chair in the bow of one of them and had a canopy draped above him. Aung Net would be at his side. Bandoola and the rest of the elephants stood in the pummeling rain as the camp men waved good-bye. The boats pushed off, paddling right into the center of the fast-flowing rain-pocked waters. For hours, they battled their way down, nearly capsizing again and again through the surging current and whirlpools, and around the sharp rocks. Kayem was finishing what Bandoola had started. Once past the worst of the rapids, he called to Williams, "Don't worry, old boy, you'll see Paris again."

And he was nearly right. Williams would at least see Rangoon again, where he was hospitalized for an extended stay. Only months later, by Christmastime in fact, was he fit for the jungle again.

AT DAWN THE DAY after Christmas, Billy Williams woke up hung over aboard the fancy company-owned stern-wheel paddle steamer anchored in the Upper Chindwin River. Harding, long back from his leave and now set to retire shortly, gently woke him: "You had rather a thick night, partner," he said. "You'll probably need this to see those elephants across." He was holding a glass of "black velvet"—a potent half-and-half mix of champagne and stout. Williams came to groggily. He could hear the soft lapping of water against the sides of the boat.

There were four of them onboard—Williams, Harding, Millie, and Tony, a young man flirting with the idea of a life in the jungle— and they all had been drinking for days. The night before, Harding had passed out in such a state of torpor that his friends thought he was dead. During a late game of cards, he had suddenly slumped forward in his chair. Williams saw that the sunburned bald patch on the top of Harding's head had lost its color and now "looked as white as a bladder of lard and as cold." It made him realize that he "deeply loved" the old man.

At dawn the tough bird had been the first to rise, tenderly waking Williams with a little hair of the dog. Williams drained the glass and got up into the chill to look out at the blanket of mist covering the water. He could see just a few of the taller trees on the far bank reaching above the fog like a dream.

This was the big day, and though two of the men aboard—Harding and Millie—were more experienced, it was Williams's job to lead. And not just his job. It was his calling. He was now clearly better with elephants than men who had decades on him. And it took a true elephant man to supervise a river crossing. Thirty-five working elephants were assembled on the shore, ready to ford the mile-wide river to a new logging site. Love it or fear it, to all elephant men, a crossing this vast was a colossal event.

If the passage were to be successfully accomplished, it had to be on the elephants' terms and timing. This wasn't a matter of superstition or sentiment; there really was something mystical about the whole endeavor. It took one elephant to lead, her identity unknown. When she emerged, it would be as though she had been anointed in a secret ceremony. No observers could detect how her rank had been sorted out. It was a baffling event that pointed to the sophisticated nature of leadership, at least as it is conducted among elephants.

Crossing a wide river, even this one with its long sandbar in the center, was challenging. Although they could pause on the shoal, the elephants still faced two long swims on either side of it. With the river current and the number of elephants making the crossing, Williams knew they would all end up scattered on the far shore—some drifting a half a mile downstream.

Alone, Williams left the steamer on a native dugout at ten to meet U San Din, the head elephant man. It would take time since the animals would be loath to enter the water before the chill was out of the air. As the dugout cut across the surface of the water, Williams was struck by what he saw in front of him—bright sun, a layer of lingering mist, the far bank of sand and tall grass, and dozens of elephants gathered in a jagged queue, ears flapping, sinuous trunks snaking, feet shifting.

They were vocalizing, too. By now it was familiar talk that Williams could parse. Low rumbles to make close contact. Full-throated roars for longer distances. Short squeaks signaled unease; longer squeaks, joy. Earsplitting trumpets announced a charge. And then there was that odd, metallic boom created by the trunk knocking on the ground when an elephant was unsure of something.

It pleased Williams. Despite the inherent risks in the mission ahead, he was touched just looking at them in formation. He felt connected. Even more so when his eye was drawn to the handsomest among them—Bandoola. Though Bandoola was with the other males, held back away from the front line of females, his size made him easy to spot. No doubt Bandoola was aware of him, too, if not by sight, then by the sound of his voice, or his scent in the air.

Using dugouts and canoes, the families of the elephant riders, along with the dragging gear, were ferried to the far shore. By two o'clock, the air was warm. The riders mounted the elephants and tested the beltlike ropes fastened around the girth of the animals. The uzis would be hanging on to these straps when the elephants joyfully submerged themselves occasionally during their swim.

It was time to ask the elephants to cross. Williams gave the order for silence among the riders. All was still. Everything was left to the animals. They were free to enter the river. U San Din climbed into a dugout canoe to monitor things from the water. He and other paddlers in canoes would act as shepherds, rallying the elephants straight across if they began to let themselves drift downstream with the current.

Everyone waited for the as-yet-unidentified leader to start. In the wild, hierarchies are well established—family groups are led by older females. Even in zoos, elephants work out their pecking order. Their chain of command is a matter of both competition and subtle cooperation. In logging camps, the natural ranking is dismantled. Leaders don't emerge in that setting for one simple reason: They are rarely allowed to lead. If there's a power structure, it asserts itself when the elephants are released into the forest at night.

Here on the bank of the river was another of life's lessons from the elephants that could be applied to people: Dominance is not leadership. From animals, Williams said, people could learn about taking "authority without being a bully." The big tuskers could splash into the water but no one would follow them. What was needed was confidence rather than bravado. In fact, years of experience had taught the uzis that the leader would not be a male. The notion of the wise matriarch remained alive among them. So the riders had marshaled the bulls at the rear.

The fog had burned off, but mystery still hung in the air. Who would go first and who would the others follow? The men were fascinated and on edge. There was stillness and quiet in the waiting. Then the silence was broken.

With a whoosh of water displaced by their huge bodies, eight females waded in, "as casually as if they were going for their daily scrub." Five more entered. But they stalled out. This was recreational, a dozen elephants enjoying a soak. No leader yet. It was almost as though the vote was still being tallied. The elephants casually stood about as the tension among the men grew.

Williams heard a commotion from the shore: Finally, a young female with an uzi on board pushed her way to the front and darted into the water. No hesitation. She progressed into deeper and deeper water, lunging directly toward the channel with purpose. She even submerged. "For a moment she disappeared, rider and all," Williams said, "then she rose with the buoyancy of a cork. She was afloat, swimming steadily towards the shingle island in mid-river."

Maybe it was her confidence that caught the other elephants' attention. Maybe they had chosen her to begin with. Whatever the transaction, one by one all the other females convoyed behind her. They swam strongly, occasionally dunking their riders under, but always popping back up to the surface. It was such a thrilling sight that from the bank, where they had gathered together, Williams, Harding, Millie, and their young guest Tony all spontaneously rose in a silent standing ovation. "There are few sights more delightful than to see a powerful young elephant swimming in deep water," Williams wrote.

The makeshift matriarch let the current carry her clear from the sandbar. She didn't seem to want to rest. She just kept swimming for the far shore, with all the other females in tow. "For this migration," Williams wrote, "the elephants, who worked in teams and as individuals, suddenly became a herd as in the wild state, following the females."

With the girls well on their way, it was time to release the tuskers. Williams watched Bandoola enter the river like a handsome frigate, plowing the water before him in great waves. Even when most of him was underwater he was magnificent—his great head above the surface and his exposed skin shiny purple with wetness.

All the elephants were in the water now. The uzis rode, but they gave no commands—the animals were dictating events now. Captive elephants had transformed into wild ones, becoming just a little more majestic for it. It was enough to keep the human audience on their feet.

It took a few hours before all the animals made shore. Not an elephant or uzi was lost. Everyone would eat and rest now on the far bank. Williams saw them off and returned to the steamer, looking forward to celebrating. But no sooner had he arrived than a dugout made its way to him carrying a horrible message: Bandoola had killed his rider.

CHAPTER 15

A MURDER INVESTIGATION

———

I T SEEMED IMPOSSIBLE. WILLIAMS WAS TOLD THAT AFTER THE CROSS-
ing, the great tusker, just like all the other males, had been tied to a
tree. When his uzi, Aung Bala, bent down in front of him to adjust
the chains on his legs, Bandoola had run a tusk through him, killing
him with a common technique—using his head to crush the man.
He had then tossed the crumpled body away like a broken toy.

While these deaths were infrequent, they were a risk any rider
accepted readily. Elephants were so valuable that even the rogues remained employed. They would be placed in the care of experienced
handlers who received extra hazard pay, and would often be guarded
by a spearman. An elephant who had killed would always wear a
metal bell, instead of the wooden kalouk, to mark him as deadly.

Bad elephants, Williams always said, were as rare as truly wicked
men. But even normal, good-natured bulls could turn into homi-
cidal brutes when in the grip of musth.

Bandoola didn't fit either category. He was no rogue, and he was
obviously free of musth. "If the killing of an uzi when on musth was
justifiable homicide, this looked horribly like murder," Williams
wrote. He left the other revelers on the paddleboat to investigate.
Should the report prove true, Williams wasn't half the elephant man
he had thought himself, nor Bandoola half the elephant. He mulled

it all over as the men paddled him to shore. Aung Bala, the dead uzi, was a known opium addict, but addiction was fairly commonplace and did not hinder other riders. And with Po Toke supervising the animal's care, there should not have been a problem.

When Williams arrived, the uzis and their families met him. The sorrow in camp was palpable. As he walked forward, he saw something he had never thought he would: Po Toke, the icon of gentle training, spear in hand, guarding the shackled and disgraced Bandoola. A second spearman stood at attention, too.

Williams took a hard look at the tusker. He believed he had witnessed nearly every human emotion in elephants, including shame. In fact, many elephants who kill humans appear very remorseful afterward, even trying to pick their victims up and get them on their feet. But Bandoola looked unrepentant. If anything, the attack seemed to have given him an appetite. There were great mounds of fresh food all around him—sugarcane, plantain trees, and bamboo— and he was tucking into it all with an astonishing greed.

It didn't make sense. And the answer would not be straightforward. Williams would have to play detective. The first step was to rule out any physical cause for a problem. Williams confirmed what he already knew—Bandoola certainly was not in musth; there were no fluids staining his cheeks.

So had someone beaten the elephant? Since there were no conspicuous wounds, he looked for hidden ones. He told Po Toke to carefully pull Bandoola's ears forward. If an uzi were going to mistreat an elephant, he would target this sensitive skin behind the ear. Williams saw nothing. Bandoola was unmarked.

The more Williams studied the scene, the more nervous Po Toke became. And then one peculiarity suddenly stood out to Williams: There were no droppings near the chained elephant, and no sweep marks in the sand indicating their removal. The elephant simply had not defecated for hours.

Williams asked Po Toke who had brought Bandoola's banquet, and he said that Aung Bala had. Now that just didn't seem likely: The man had been dead for hours and there was too much food still there, particularly for an elephant eating so ravenously. Williams thought he had figured it out: Bandoola had been starved. Williams said nothing about his hunch, but told Po Toke to walk the half mile to the village with him to view Aung Bala's body.

All along the route they passed the other elephants who had made the crossing that day. The little clearings in which each group of elephants stood were in contrast to the scene of Bandoola's incarceration. For the rest of the elephants, there was hardly anything left of the evening meal and plenty of evidence of digestion: piles of droppings where the elephants stood.

U San Din, who had led the river crossing, was waiting at the headman's house. When Williams confided what he thought, U San Din looked relieved. He had not wanted to be the informer. Now he didn't have to be; Williams had solved the mystery. U San Din filled in a few details. Yes, Bandoola had gone without food, and not just on this evening. For at least three days he had been given nothing, and restricted from foraging on his own. Unlike most other nights when the elephants were released into the jungle, the days before and after a big swim, they were secured in order to keep them close. Bandoola's rider, the "opium eater," had been too high to care properly for the tusker. He should have been reprimanded by Po Toke, but Po Toke had also neglected Bandoola. Po Toke's own emerging domestic drama had distracted him. He had taken on a second wife, a teenager. The unhappiness of his first wife and the demands of the second kept Po Toke too busy to look after Bandoola.

Days without a real meal and then the extreme physical exertion of a wide river crossing had exacted their toll on the tusker. He was famished and exhausted, and yet still compliant when his uzi ordered him to stand near a tree for shackling. After that, however, he had grown impatient. Standing there alone, with no food, he had protested by stamping his feet and heaving himself side to side. His chains tangled and knotted. When Aung Bala approached him, it was to straighten the fetters, not to give him food. "Then the captive elephant saw red" and killed the man, Williams wrote.

Po Toke had attempted to conceal his culpability by quickly stacking heaps of vegetation around the hungry animal. There was plenty of blame to go around, and Williams shared some of it. Yes,

Po Toke and Aung Bala had abused Bandoola. But Williams had been drinking his way through the last several days. Not one of the three men in Bandoola's chain of command, he felt, had come through for him.

Williams returned to the boat. Harding heard the story and told him that he would leave disciplinary decisions to him. Both men agreed that Bandoola was not a killer and that to label him as such would only turn him into one, with fearful handlers who would subject him to jabs of the spear on a regular basis. The killing would not go down in Bandoola's official record, nor would he wear a metal bell.

Po Toke was a trickier matter, but, ultimately, Williams could see the bigger picture. This was the first time the old elephant man had ever failed Bandoola. Williams knew he was heartbroken over it. He demoted Po Toke but did not reduce his pay.

This did not settle the matter. Something larger was happening with Po Toke, but what exactly, Williams couldn't say. A short time later, when Po Toke tried to quit his job, Williams was able to persuade him to take a leave of absence instead. But Williams continued to be mystified by Po Toke, and, it would turn out, he had no clue about what the master mahout was plotting.

CHAPTER 16

REBELS AND REUNIONS

———

L ATE IN 1928, WILLIAMS WAS PROMOTED AND REASSIGNED. HE would be a forest officer now, with several assistants in his charge, working out of headquarters in Pyinmana, about 390 miles southeast of Mawlaik. Considered at the time to be one of the most valuable woodlands in the world, it was turning into one of the most dangerous for Europeans, an incubator for rebel activity. The men who were labeled as "rebels" were often nationalists—people who wanted their country back. Coincidentally, or maybe not so coincidentally, it was also where Po Toke was taking his leave, the place of Bandoola's birth, and the home village to Po Toke's in-laws.

Throughout the country, these years were troubling ones for the British government and its citizens. There was a clear desire among the Burmese for self-rule, and, at the very least, activists wanted more control of their country's affairs. A point of contention was the forests themselves. They were administered by the British with the result that the big timber leases were granted to European, not Burmese, firms. A few years earlier, there had been a strategic concession. A position was created for a Burmese forests minister. Though it was a step forward, the minister had limited powers, and the authority to allocate the all-important teak leases remained in British hands. In addition, there was widespread unrest from peasants living near forest reserves who were blocked from their traditional gathering of firewood and bamboo.

The response was a rising peasant militancy. Generally that took the form of illegal timber extraction, but it eventually went so far as the murder of a forest official. There was, in the words of the chief conservator, "an expression of general lawlessness closely connected with political agitation." One of the biggest political agitators was Saya San, a Buddhist monk, medicine man, and politician. In the late 1920s, he began to encourage nonviolent disobedience in a campaign to grant free wood and bamboo to peasant families. Soon enough, Saya San went further, organizing armed insurrection. It was a complicated movement, fueled by elements that included legitimate nationalist desires and rejection of taxation policies, as well as resentment over the restructuring of education in the country, which had been traditionally managed by the Buddhists. Too much was in British hands—not just in terms of power, but in simple acreage. By one tally, Burmans themselves owned only about half the land in the rich rice-growing provinces.

Williams's new assignment was in the heart of the area where discord was growing, and he arrived just as it began to take root. Getting to know new workers amid such political turmoil was difficult. He didn't have the lay of the land yet and hadn't established relationships with the men. He was aware that working for a British firm made him a target. No one knew if a handful of recent crimes was connected to a larger political scheme, but there were stories of Europeans having been murdered in the jungle—a forestry worker killed by uzis in Williams's area south of Mandalay, and a Catholic priest slashed to death down south in the delta region, among them.

Williams relied on the camp staff and traveling elephants he brought with him, and he felt optimistic about the workers he would meet. He completely trusted his own men, yet he understood that even with them a divide must exist. "Though I had learnt Burmese and took some trouble to understand the men who worked for me, I knew that I only understood a small fraction of what was going on in their minds," he wrote. He was aware of what colonialism meant

Williams completely trusted his own men, yet he understood that
in this colonial world, a divide existed.

to the Burmese: "I though the employee of a private company, was
the Government, they were the governed."

This was particularly true since he worked for Bombay Burmah.
The corporation had had a hand in establishing British rule in the
country in the first place, in the third of what historians describe as
three distinct chapters in the British takeover of Burma.

The First Anglo-Burmese War was precipitated in the 1820s by
the great Burmese general Bandula's acquisition of Assam—too close
to British-held India for comfort. That war resulted in Burma's ced-
ing land in the Arakan, or southwest region, to the British. At mid-
century, the arrest of some British nationals on suspicion of murder
offered pretext enough for the Second Anglo-Burmese War. This
time all of the coastal provinces, including Rangoon, came under
British rule. Finally, in the late 1800s, a number of factors converged.
The country's monarch, King Thibaw, was perceived as unfriendly
to British business—right at a time when France was solidifying its
grip on the neighboring territory that would be French Indochina
(Vietnam, Laos, and Cambodia). So when Thibaw's government
fined Bombay Burmah for tax evasion, the British had their excuse

for the Third Anglo-Burmese War, which ended with Britain abolishing the Burmese monarchy and taking over the rest of the country. The royal couple—Thibaw and Queen Supayalat—were exiled to India, their palace in Mandalay converted into the military compound of Fort Dufferin. Denied the respect of being a separate colony, Burma was administered for many years as a province of India. The British took control of timber exports, among other lucrative businesses, and Indians were recruited to fill most of the civil service jobs. The colonialists considered the Burmese lazy, and thousands of Indian workers were welcomed. During Williams's time, 53 percent of the population of Rangoon was Indian. Millions would immigrate to the country over the decades, where they would be bitterly resented by the native population.

Still, at the start of his new job, Williams's strategy was to simply do the work and become acquainted with the men by visiting the logging camps in his jurisdiction. He got on with it, traveling from camp to camp, paying the men, examining the elephants, and mediating any problems.

This was a brand-new population of elephants, each with his or her idiosyncrasies. Williams quickly grew to understand them. In quick order he memorized their names. He treated their illnesses, galls, and tummy upsets with assurance. He had learned by now that swelling in limbs could be reduced by standing the animals in cold streams. If an elephant became hard to manage, Williams knew to swap out an inexperienced uzi for a more sophisticated one. Pregnant cows were given reduced loads and hours. They were fed better.

Williams even inoculated his elephants with a new, experimental anthrax vaccine. The infectious disease, caused by a type of bacterium, was a terrible scourge, weakening and killing scores of animals.

In Pyinmana, he had a chance to do something about it. But he had to accomplish it using a large-bore needle that the elephants didn't like. Even with elephants he knew well, this would be a dangerous undertaking, and in this new place, the animals were unfamiliar to him. He found, however, that he was experienced enough to take it on.

Still, life with elephants was risky. That was alarmingly clear one

Williams eagerly inoculated his elephants with a new, experimental anthrax vaccine. The infectious disease had killed scores of animals in his care.

day when Williams was hiking in the forest far ahead of the travelers with one of his camp workers. In the checkerboard patches of dark shade and blinding sunlight, something seemingly impossible happened: An elephant had become invisible by doing nothing more than standing still. Unaware of her presence, Williams practically bumped right into her. When he was within feet of the elephant, she roared to life, stretching her ears out horizontally in alarm, bellowing in fury. It was swift and volcanic. She charged without a second's hesitation. Instinct pulled Williams and his worker in opposite directions. As he bolted, Williams turned his head to see where the worker was. The man was safe, as the angry elephant had naturally beaded in on only one of them, and that one was Williams.

He ran in the direction of a nearby village, able to distinguish as he did so the sound of the clanking of metal—two different pitches, in fact, which brought both good news and bad. The elephant was clearly fettered with chains around her ankles, which fortunately would slow her progress—important since these creatures can reach short bursts of eighteen miles an hour, easily overtaking most men. But the other clanging was unmistakable: Instead of the usual teak bell around her neck, she wore a metal one. The cold, insistent sound made him shiver. It meant only one thing: The elephant on his heels was a killer.

In that instant, he knew not only what she was, but because he had worked hard to learn the names of all the elephants in his new territory, he also knew who she was. Taw Sin Ma. So mean-tempered that even as a youngster she had earned her name, which meant "Miss Wild Elephant." She was the most dangerous animal in his territory.

Williams weaved and dodged around trees and finally made it into the camp. By then, Taw Sin Ma had given up her chase, probably because she didn't want to be caught by her uzi, who lived nearby. Without fanfare, her rider headed into the forest to catch her.

Williams went back to rounds. But there were more surprises.

In the middle of a terrible hot spell, his elephants did something remarkable. It was a day with no wind, and the men had been complaining "It's hot," or *"Ike thee."* Williams was wandering among the elephants as each was set free to forage in the jungle for the night. It wasn't an official inspection, but he passed his hands along their bodies for a quick check and a dose of that kind of serenity that is passed wordlessly from an elephant to a man who loves them. Then one by one, with a kind of dignified exhilaration, the elephants entered the wall of vegetation surrounding the compound, their hind ends disappearing behind the curtain of green.

A meal was quickly prepared. As Williams sat down to eat, suddenly all six elephants marched back into camp. It was unheard of. They never returned during their time off. Not only that; they were rejecting the shade to stand "right out in the open under the blazing sun." Normally a mass of motion, they were strangely still, "as if lost in thought." It was eerie.

Things became more curious. A hot wind tumbled the dry litter of the forest floor, and when it stalled out, the world hushed. The heat intensified.

"I stood up as a most peculiar sensation came over me," Williams wrote, "as if I was not wholly land-borne and yet not wholly air-borne. From very far away—perhaps from India it seemed or from Tibet—came a low rumbling."

Suddenly everything was swaying—the treetops, the house, even the elephants. The forest seemed to groan and creak. Branches snapped. He felt the sensation of being on a boat "coming into a swell."

"Then the earth shook like a wet spaniel shaking its coat," Williams wrote. Dead tree limbs and a ticker-tape parade of leaves fell to the ground.

After the earthquake, when the footing was solid again, the riders shouted with relief. "The elephants," Williams noted, "as though they had finished attending some solemn ceremony, left the clearing and re-entered the jungle to make up for lost time."

Williams wondered if another shudder or aftershock was possible, but the men assured him the elephants said no, and they were never wrong. So he calmly went back to his table.

AT ONE OF HIS logging sites, Po Toke surprised Williams with a visit. He was taking his leave of absence nearby and was worried, he said, about a rumor that Bandoola was missing from the old camp on the Upper Chindwin. Williams's antenna went up. Harding's words "Watch him as you go" came back to him. He felt sure the old elephant rider, who hated to be apart from his prized elephant, had had a hand in Bandoola's "disappearance." But it would have taken some doing since there were hundreds of miles and the great Irrawaddy River in between the two locations.

Despite his concern, Williams could not drop everything to track Bandoola—after all, if Po Toke had not engineered the escape, it was unlikely he was anywhere near the region—so he continued his regular rounds in the forests.

With so much talk of rebellion brewing in Burma, Williams for the first time felt vulnerable when traveling in isolated pockets of forest. He even received a threatening anonymous letter written in Burmese warning him not to work in the area. Though he might have been scared, he wouldn't be scared away. The best thing to do, he thought, would be to get a bodyguard. Currently without a dog, he soon acquired one: a cross between a bloodhound and a feral dog, with a rich chocolate-colored coat, heavy jowls, velvet ears, and "small, neat, sure-footed paws." His tail was curled, like a chow's. He had been chained in a barn and neglected. "He was marvelous," Williams wrote. "He bayed at me with the voice of a hound. He twisted his tail almost out of joint, begging for another home and yet another chance."

Williams's friends thought he was crazy to trust the brute. But he read something in the dog, and was glad to have such a courageous animal with him as he traveled through rebel territory, carrying a great deal of money for an elephant contractor.

Over the next several days Williams found the dog he called Ba Sein, named for the region where this breed was common, to be one of the most extraordinary he'd ever known—protective, intuitive, and perpetually on high alert. Even at night in the tent, he did not seem to sleep. "His eyes fascinated me: as warm and brown as his short coat, they seemed fixed on something deeper and beyond anything I could see," Williams noted.

All was well until they arrived in the very next camp, a forlorn, deserted village, where Ba Sein was somehow poisoned, found in the throes of a seizure, and dead within minutes. Williams suspected the anonymous letter writer had killed his beloved dog. He immediately called the men together to pack up and head out. "My camp was never broken quicker," Williams recalled. "The elephants were loaded, the last one carrying the cold body of Ba Sein wrapped in a blanket."

It was rare to move camp after sunset, but this time it was necessary. At about midnight, the group reached the largest town in the area where there was a colonial presence. The civil police were out in force, one officer telling Williams, "The whole damned countryside's in the hands of rebels."

It was the start of a months-long shutdown of work and an especially bad time for teak firms in the aftermath of the Wall Street crash, an event that affected finances even in Burma.

For safety's sake, European timber men were ordered to be quarantined and were forbidden to travel among their camps. That meant Williams would not be able to check on about a hundred elephants under his care. As hard as this was to accept, he felt that at least they would be well cared for. No matter what the political leanings of the uzis—and Williams realized he was not privy to them—they would never abandon their elephants.

Of course his men couldn't discuss civics with him. It would be too risky. Under British rule, political activity was banned. Activists had discovered a way around this, though. Religious organizations were sanctioned, so nationalists found they could advance their cause through Buddhist associations.

In India, Gandhi promoted civil disobedience, but in Burma, Saya San wanted action. By combining elements of Buddhism, astrology, and magic, he had created a popular movement and was on his way to counting three thousand soldiers in his army. By December 1930, Saya San had abandoned any pretense of simple religious activity. He wanted to rule the country. Six forest department employees were killed during this time, though it was unclear whether they were murdered by Saya San's followers.

In response, the British amassed eight thousand soldiers, most of them Indian, to fight off the rebellion. Williams and his traveling elephants were among the forest men conscripted when armed posses of British citizens were formed to scout the forest.

During these tense tours, the traveling elephants were kept chained along the perimeter of camp at night instead of being released. The men could not go out searching for the animals in the morning, as was the custom, because they would be vulnerable to capture.

As it turned out, Williams's party didn't run into any rebels, but they were harassed by a different kind of nighttime prowler. A free bull from the forest was slipping into camp in order to visit the tethered elephants. It happened several times and didn't let up even when they had moved camp ten miles during the day. The men were the first to tell Williams about the stalker, then the agitated elephants did, by making that distinctive metallic banging sound with their trunks during the night. When the sun came up, Williams could see large elephant footprints around the border of the clearing. A bull had not only visited them; he was actually trailing them.

The next day, the group assembled and went out on their rounds, hiking single file into a sort of jungle tunnel—a track worn through the wall of dense forest vegetation by men and animals. As they neared the Palway Creek, the entire column came to a halt as the riders called out: *"Taw Sin! Taw Sin!"* Wild elephant. Williams, who had been marching toward the rear of the train, squeezed his way to the front to assess the situation. It could be dicey to deal with an animal like this in close quarters. The reaction of the working elephants to a wild stranger was unpredictable. When Williams reached the intruder, he saw a massive male in peak condition. The bull had beautiful gray skin freckled with pink, and tusks that curved like dancing girls.

It was Bandoola. Hundreds of miles from his work camp.

The tusker had recognized the pack elephants, his old mates, and when Williams called his name, he certainly knew him. Bandoola had been on his own for about a year. And as much as he liked Williams, he preferred his freedom. He trumpeted, turned, and hurried off, exposing the brand on his backside.

He didn't go far. Instead, he played a game of hide-and-seek with the line of familiar men and elephants. Throughout the day as they marched on along the track, they caught glimpses of him. He was tagging along.

Williams figured he could use Po Toke in this situation, but Po Toke was missing, too. He was supposed to have reported back to duty at the old camp up on the Chindwin, but had not—curious, especially since he had last been seen in an area where rebel activity was strong. Williams gathered his riders. From what they had seen, they all felt that Bandoola had become wary of humans during his year of wildness. Would anyone volunteer to try to catch him?

It was suggested that they use a traditional method for capturing a wild elephant—*mela shikar*—a strategy in which two "full-grown female elephants of a steady temperament" are ridden right up to the wild elephant and positioned on either side of him. Each elephant carries two riders so that once in position, one of the men can shift onto the back of the wild elephant.

Two solid females—Shan Ma and Yinzin Ma—were selected. They were ridden straight into a wall of elephant grass higher than their backs where Bandoola had last been sighted. Williams scrambled up a tree to watch, tracking Bandoola only by the swaying of the tops of the grasses that parted as he moved below. The camp elephants were easy to spot because the heads and shoulders of the men who stood on their backs, acting as lookouts, were visible above the tall grass. These scouts whispered their directions to the riders who sat below, blinded by the wall of vegetation even as the elephants pushed their way through. The operation was carried out nearly silently and in slow motion. True to their natures and unafraid of Bandoola, Shan Ma and Yinzin Ma calmly munched everything in their path, pulling up and eating the succulent grasses as they moved, while slowly being guided to approach the hidden male.

They were close. "Then suddenly," Williams wrote, "when they were within a stone's throw of one another, the silence was broken by a chirp, a chirp I somehow associated with this lovable great animal Bandoola. . . . It is a signal of contentment and joy." The girls chirped back and then all three rumbled, not a deep chest rattler, but a reassuring one "like the noise of a Rolls-Bentley," Williams noted. The animals might not see each other, but they were conversing. All was well.

A rider delicately transferred to the big male, stepping carefully with bare feet onto his back. Soon Williams saw a happy little column of three—"First came Shan Ma with one rider only, then Bandoola, whose rider had merely stepped off Shan Ma's back on to his new mount, and finally Yinzin Ma with her two riders." Williams was touched by these men whose "friendship with animals had not been broken by civilization."

Here, so far from the Chindwin in the middle of rebel territory, Williams was surrounded by the elephants he loved most. He was in no hurry to transfer Bandoola back. The tusker remained touring with him until the rebellion was put down. Although working as a traveler was a demotion for Bandoola, Williams made a point of never dressing him up as one. It would have wounded his own pride as well as Bandoola's to see him again in the pack saddlery of the transportation elephants rather than the dragging gear that marked the big, powerful working bulls.

In the meantime, he inquired once more about Po Toke. The great elephant man apparently had been placed under suspicion by the police and restricted from leaving his village. Eventually released, Po Toke made his way to Williams. He looked awful. Williams would never know for sure, but his instinct was that Po Toke had, indeed, joined the rebels. More than that, he suspected that the elephant trainer had arranged Bandoola's great escape.

As enlightened as Williams was generally about basic human dignity and freedom, he would not support the nationalist movement over his own country. He assured himself that the empire was helping the Burmese. But he also chided himself "for taking [Po Toke] to be a simpler character than he actually was." The man who had taught him so much was complicated. He had a life that he would never share with any Englishman, including Williams. Ultimately there was a breach. "The trust which had once existed between us was shaken." Williams wasn't single-minded enough to write his mentor off, though. "I couldn't deny that Bandoola could not be in better hands than Po Toke's," he wrote.

He kept the elephant and his trainer together, but sent them packing back up to the Chindwin forests far from where Po Toke might have connections to any insurgency. The rebellion would be eliminated fairly quickly anyway. Saya San had been hiding out in a monastery north of Mandalay. When he fled east toward the Shan Hills, he was captured, tried, and hanged.

In the meantime, in Pyinmana, Williams had been able to prove something to himself. Far from his Burmese home base in the west, with little contact from his mentors, he had taken on a novel assignment, a new population of elephants, and he had succeeded. Reaching a level of expertise that he had dreamed of for a decade, Billy Williams was finally, unmistakably, an elephant wallah.

PART TWO

LOVE AND
ELEPHANTS

CHAPTER 17

TIGER HOUR

———

By 1931, at the age of thirty-three, Williams was ready to give up on love. Resigned to his fate, he headed back to his regular rounds in the forest with his latest dog, a smart, loyal Alsatian named Molly Mia.

During one of his marches, he bumped into the chief conservator of forests, Stephen Hopwood, in the Bwetgyi drainage where he was fishing in a stream. Williams was eager for the chance to talk to the jungle salt. In his early fifties, Hopwood was taciturn as all hell, but a decent man. He had been in Burma his whole adult life except for a stint in the army during World War I, when he served as a field gunner in France. Wounded in action, he was awarded the Military Cross for gallantry. He was said to know more about the Burmese forests and their inhabitants than any other living soul.

Hopwood had not always been so gruff. It was the tragic death of his wife, Helen, that had turned him. She was with her husband on forest rounds when a fever turned deadly. Hopwood had made a heroic effort to transport her to the hospital in Mandalay, but it was too late. When she died, he disappeared into the forest and cut off contact with friends. Search parties eventually located him, but the old jovial Hopwood was gone forever. He would never even be able to bring himself to say Helen's name again.

Hopwood told Williams to go on ahead to the site, but to be sure his elephants, the "travelers," were released downriver since his own were loose upriver. It would be easier for everyone if they stayed separate.

Dogs, including Molly Mia and Karl, were among Williams's closest companions.

Along with Molly Mia, Williams hiked over to the area Hopwood had described. As he crossed the river, he could see the camp on the high bank—a nice open space surrounded by tall trees. Oddly, there were two tents instead of one. Williams felt a small pang of disappointment. He wanted to talk with the conservator about an upcoming project. If someone else joined them he might not have the old man's ear. Maybe he should just skip the whole thing and keep hiking farther along the drainage.

Just then he caught sight of "a tall, slender girl in the clearing."

She saw him, too, and waved. In greeting, Williams raised his Terai hat, the exact replica of Harding's, modeled after the one worn by Gurkha soldiers in the British and Indian armies. He had loved that hat till this moment, when he suddenly felt insecure about it. "As I crossed the clearing, it occurred to me that it might appear slightly ridiculous. I felt, I confess, rather shy."

The woman had just woken from a nap in the sun and was surprised to meet anyone else in the forest, never mind an Englishman. She noticed first how tall Williams was, and, as he drew closer, his kind and good-humored expression.

Not only was Susan Rowland pretty and unmarried, but, Jim Williams was happy to learn, she had a love for animals as he did.

She was twenty-eight years old, five foot seven, slim, and pretty, her gray eyes setting off her dark brown hair. Her khaki safari outfit flattered her. It should have, for she had purchased so much clothing for Burma that her family had christened her "Lady Rangoon."

She spoke first. "I'm Susan Rowland."

"I'm Billy Williams of the Bombay Burma Teak Company."

He asked if he and his men had startled her, and he assured her they were not jungle bandits. He was charmed by the fact that she seemed as self-conscious as he was. "Perhaps she was embarrassed at an unwelcome stranger?" he wondered. And then he laughed to himself, "Or was it just my hat?"

He told her that he had just talked to Hopwood, who had not mentioned that she was there. She thought with some amusement, "How like Uncle Pop to have forgotten my existence." Still, she was "delighted to see someone young and so obviously lively."

She noticed Molly Mia at his side, and Williams introduced her. "I'm afraid I have the most unfriendly dog in the world," he told her. "She is extremely good-natured, but like all Alsatians is very single-hearted and I can't make her take any interest in anybody but me."

Williams realized suddenly that as he spoke, Molly, the most devoted dog he'd ever had, was no longer next to him. She was rubbing herself against Susan. Williams had never seen the dog approach anyone else before.

Susan felt a surge of pleasure. She reached down and stroked Molly. The silences in their conversation seemed to disappear. "What a lovely dog," she said. She'd even heard of Molly Mia; the forest assistants had spoken of the dog's extreme devotion to Williams.

Susan offered him a drink and they sat down together. She hadn't told him why she was in the area and filled him in—she was in Burma to care for her uncle as a succession of other female cousins before her already had. "I don't care who you are," Williams said to her, nearly giddy in the moment. "It's just the greatest fun to be sitting down here having drinks, so unexpectedly, alone with a pretty girl."

Williams told her a little of himself—that he was from Cornwall, working in Burma as a teak man. And they were soon lost in conversation. Eventually the sound of kalouks brought them out of their trance. Williams said his travelers must have arrived, and he would go and inform the men of what the plan was.

Seeing the interest in Susan's eyes, he asked, "Like to come over and have a look? I'll tell you about them." He had shared the bare outline of his life, but it was at this moment, she said later, when introducing her to his elephants, that he was transformed from a charming man to a remarkable one.

The lead elephant, a bull, emerged from the forest. He was breathtaking—"a magnificent male elephant with gleaming tusks," Susan said. Behind him were fourteen others in every shape and size.

Williams pointed to the tusker. "The fine chap leading is normally a 'worker,' not a 'traveller,' but he's convalescing."

Williams walked up to the elephant, speaking to him in Burmese, looking into his eyes, and explaining to Susan why this was the protocol. She watched him communicating with this bull, first verbally and then in some way that seemed almost magical. Williams made physical contact—spreading his big hands across the elephant's rough hide. Without a word passing between them, the animal lifted his trunk to allow a full view of the front of his chest. Williams examined an innocuous-looking white spot, rubbing and prodding it. He glanced at the rider, pleased. The tusker was ready to go back to dragging work soon.

Behind the big male were three old girls in their fifties. For them, Williams said, life on the road was a kind of semiretirement. They carried light loads and would mostly be free to forage and commune with other camp elephants or wild ones.

Susan looked beyond the old dignified cow elephants to where the action was: with all the younger elephants, ranging in age from eight to twenty-one. They could hardly keep still or silent. She saw eleven trunks snaking around in the air—catching her scent, touching one another, or grabbing leaves to stuff in their mouths. In anticipation of what was coming in minutes—their freedom for the night—they chirped and squealed, their faces puckering, their cheeks pulled in to produce amazing high-pitched sounds. Their joy, she found, was contagious.

Williams casually mentioned that the younger ones were either in school or had just "graduated." Susan had never heard of such a ridiculous notion—elephant academy?—and a look of skepticism crossed her face. Williams caught it. "I'm not joking," he told her. "It's true." He explained the system he had worked so hard to put in place. His pure, innocent enthusiasm, his gentleness, and his compassion, all mingled with such authority, was disarming her. She realized the devotion he had for his animals. The blend of reverence and intimacy seemed the very definition of true love. What love should be, anyway.

Just then, Hopwood marched triumphantly back into camp with supper, a ten-pound mahseer—a savory game fish that the British sometimes called "Indian salmon." He invited Williams to stay for dinner, then disappeared into his tent to bathe and change into fresh clothes, observing, as was the custom, as much formality as could be managed.

At least they wouldn't be eating the usual fare. Susan had grown more than tired of the safe, bland menu that "Uncle Pop" preferred. He relied on good British canned goods from Barnett Bros. in Rangoon: "tinned soup, tinned vegetables and tinned fish, which he liked unadorned," she wrote later in a memoir. His beloved horses back in Rangoon ate only hay and oats shipped to him from England.

They all needed to freshen up. Susan went into her tent and Molly followed. Williams was incredulous, but he simply set about seeing his own tent pitched. When they emerged, it was dusk, a time, Susan wrote, when "an eerie light seems to fall over the jungle." She had heard it called "tiger hour."

A large log fire was built. Hopwood's staff served drinks. Molly settled in, wrapping her sable-colored body around "Susan's shapely legs." There was much to question Hopwood about: forest conservancy in Burma and the troubled global economy, which was seriously affecting the teak business. But Hopwood began with tales of his exploits. Very quickly, Williams forgot all about what he had wanted to discuss with the conservator. It wasn't the old man's stories of big game hunting that rattled him; it was Susan.

At midnight, Hopwood stood, saying, "I'm off to bed, goodnight both of you," and he was gone.

Williams and Susan privately breathed a sigh of relief. Immediately, however, the young suitor was again stricken by shyness. He could charm most women, but there was something different about Susan. "I wanted to be with this young woman but I couldn't think of anything to say," he remembered. So he spoke from his heart. He told her that he had always loved animals and that since starting with the company in Burma elephants had become the center of his life.

As she listened to him, she sized him up: "Handsome, tall and powerfully built, warm, twinkling brown eyes and fair, curly hair." In the firelight, the tiny raised areas on his cheek—embedded buckshot from a gun accident when he was a teenager—were just visible. She also noticed his "beautiful hands." She was amazed by his kindness, his "fund of jungle knowledge," and his wonderful and witty storytelling.

Williams excitedly told of his upcoming mission for Bombine: He would travel to the heavily forested Andaman Islands in the Bay of Bengal, working with a crew of local convicts to see if there was enough edible vegetation to support a herd of working elephants. The company was investigating the possibility of timber extraction on the mysterious archipelago.

Susan was shocked by how stung she felt. Why should she care so much about this newcomer's plans to leave? Especially when there were so many attentive men in her life. Aside from forest tours, she had spent the past year in a stately residence with Uncle Pop in Rangoon. The social whirl began every day before breakfast, when she rode a handsome English hunter named Perfection along the city's riding paths. Every week, practically every day, there was swimming, dancing, and tennis. Horse races were attended on Saturday afternoons, in "ankle-length frocks and picture hats." She had membership in all the top colonial clubs: Gymkhana, Pegu, Sailing, and Country Club. Weekdays, while Uncle Pop was in his office at the secretariat, she bought groceries, picked out new things from grand department stores such as Rowe & Co., or had clothing and shoes made to order from little boutiques, all on limitless credit. Everywhere there were young Englishmen interested in her.

Yet something was missing. It was true that unmarried girls from home were in the minority in Burma, and she had had her pick of Rangoon's expat bachelors. But no one had intrigued her as Williams had.

When they said good night, she went off to her tent distressed at the thought of his imminent departure. "I was surprised, almost angry with myself," she wrote, "to find how miserable I felt at the thought that this young man, whom after all I had only known for one day, was going away and that I should probably never see him again."

In the morning, Susan uncharacteristically insisted on joining the men for their day's work assessing the trees in the area. As they hiked, she was pleased that "Molly, was very much on my side; she made a tremendous fuss of me the whole day, and even came and lay across my feet when we stopped for a rest."

Whatever thoughts Billy Williams had had about a quick departure were now erased. That night, following colonial jungle etiquette, Williams reciprocated the dinner invitation.

Freshly bathed and in her best travel clothes, Susan walked the few feet to Williams's camp. When they all sat down in canvas chairs at the collapsible table, she was astonished. Joseph the cook, wearing a black fez atop his gray hair, had outdone himself. "We had a meal which I found it almost impossible to believe could have been produced in the jungle," Susan wrote. They started with chicken soup, then moved on to a roast duck served with green peas and fancy duchess potatoes—potatoes mashed with eggs and cream, shaped into rosettes and baked till crisp on the outside, all followed by fresh mushrooms on toast.

This time, Hopwood understood he was a third wheel and took himself off to bed especially early, nine thirty, leaving Williams and Susan alone with the bulk of the night still ahead. By now, they felt more comfortable with each other. The Burmese jungle was a backdrop as romantic as any, with the exotic, insistent calls of nocturnal birds, and in the clearing, out from under the jungle canopy, the stars were nearly blinding against the dark sky.

Williams's familiar black label whiskey helped put them both at ease. Susan loved Billy's stories, and she was touched that he was so curious about hers, listening attentively to what she called her "outpourings."

She and her five siblings had lost their mother in the 1918 influenza pandemic, and were raised by their paternal grandmother. Susan had been trained as a children's nurse, or nanny, because her father dismissed her real desire to go to gardening college as "too hard work for a girl." She wanted something different for herself, though she wasn't sure what, and the offer from Uncle Pop had been a thunderbolt. He was a stranger to her and Burma a mystery, but she leaped at the chance. "I was like a newly-hatched butterfly, whose wings were still a little damp and crumpled, but nevertheless wings."

Hopwood, "Uncle Pop," was her father's first cousin. He had sequentially brought a number of nieces over to Burma to run his household, calling each in her turn "Miss Poppy" so he would not have to learn their names.

It was just the sort of thing she and Williams laughed over this night. As Williams amused her with his own self-deprecating stories, Susan felt an attachment growing between them. And she began to think of him as "Jim," as his family called him, rather than "Billy," the name used by his peers.

"The more Jim talked the more his tremendous zest for life came over to me," she recalled. This man had a rare personality—he was warm and laughed easily, but he also "gave a sense of solidarity and strength, and inspired a deep trust." He believed in an inherent goodness in people and exuded that quality in himself. It came off as confidence without any conceit—a trust that he could handle anything and it would be all right.

Susan asked what would happen to Molly while he was away on his expedition. Williams told her this was his biggest worry. His nomadic life in the forest made him feel especially close to his loyal companion. She was without question the most intelligent dog he had ever had. He had always had small cots, raised up off the floor, for all his dogs to sleep in, but Molly was the only one who knew how to adjust her own mosquito net, tucking herself in at night. He could send her ten miles back to camp to retrieve an item and count on her to do it. He was certain that he didn't even need to speak to her, or be near her, to communicate with her. He would think of a command, such as "sit," and even without hearing it, Molly would obey. That inspired him to experiment with their ESP from longer and longer distances. On the occasions when he left her behind in camp, he felt he could continue to see her in his mind—not a memory, but a real picture of her in that moment. He was certain he could silently "call" to her from miles away, and she would find him. He even coordinated a test. He commanded Molly to stay in camp, and then asked Aung Net to note the exact time if, in fact, she left her post. From four miles away at precisely noon, he silently beckoned Molly. Aung Net told him later that at that exact moment, Molly Mia, suddenly alert, dashed off into the forest, running directly for Williams, whose location she could not have known in advance.

Molly Mia, left, was the smartest dog Williams ever had. He felt certain she could read his mind, and she did things, such as tucking in her own mosquito net at night, that none of his other dogs ever did.

"We have got so attached and dependent on each other's company," Jim told Susan, "that I don't want to be parted from her." In addition, he couldn't imagine her being able to adjust to a temporary owner.

Susan pointed out that the dog didn't seem to "dislike me too much." And then she said, "Oh, do let me look after her for you, I have wanted a dog so much and I am sure Uncle Pop won't mind especially as she is such a lovely dog." Molly, who must have picked up on Susan's excited focus on her, wagged her tail.

In the flickering light Jim looked across at the beautiful woman and made an extraordinary offer: "If you'd like her, Susan, I'll give you Molly Mia." He was thinking of the dog's feelings, figuring that if Molly became attached to Susan it wouldn't be fair to yank her away again when he returned. He told Susan that her care of Molly "would solve everything."

It would solve a few things for me, too, Susan thought. By sharing Molly, she would gain a solid connection to Jim. They demurely said good night. To Williams's astonishment, Molly Mia trotted right behind Susan to her tent.

In the morning, after tea and breakfast and packing, Williams prompted Susan to leash Molly in preparation for his departure. "I said good-bye to the dog, rather furtively hoping that there might be a bit of a scene," he admitted, "but Molly merely wagged her tail. When I had gone about half a mile from the camp, I waited, listening for the sound of the Alsatian crashing after me." It became clear there was no such desperate escape, and Williams laughed to himself, thinking: "If she's got Molly Mia when I get back, the only way I'll get her back is to marry the girl." Still in camp, Susan had similar thoughts. Even though their time together had been short, "some sort of unbreakable link had grown between us." And she had, in Molly Mia, a "hostage."

BACK IN RANGOON THE next week, the courtship resumed, with a few complications. When Williams phoned the house looking to take Susan out to dinner, Uncle Pop answered. The old man completely mangled the message, reporting to Susan that "that chap Williams" was looking to visit to talk about deep-sea fishing with him. He didn't think it was a good idea as it would only upset the dog, but he had agreed to close Molly off in a separate room if Williams came for dinner. It wasn't what Williams had said at all.

The next night, Jim pulled up to the fancy house at 25 Windermere Park, in Rangoon's most fashionable suburb, intending not to dine with Uncle Pop, but to have a date with Susan. When Hopwood trundled off to his own meal at home, Susan realized that her uncle had planned this surprise all along. Before she left for the evening, she went into the dining room. "My heart went out to poor old Uncle Pop as he sat there, straight as a ramrod, alone at the dinner table," she wrote. "In the elation of the moment, I decided to give him a kiss. He looked puzzled and rather horrified—I never attempted it again."

Jim and Susan spent every moment together that week, sightseeing, dancing, and socializing, often with Molly by their side. Susan discovered what all of Jim's colleagues already knew about him: His stamina was boundless. He "never seemed to tire," she said. And she was charmed by Williams's popularity. "The more I went about with him, the more I was drawn to his magnetic personality and tremendous sense of fun," she said. "We danced and laughed and talked about everything under the sun, and by the end of the week I knew I was in love with him and, what was more important, I felt that he loved me."

She was right, but Williams had a lot going on, notably a complicated expedition. When he wasn't courting Susan, he was negotiating the politics of the Bombay Burmah Trading Corporation and making preparations. An employee he had regular contact with was an assistant to one of the executives. The man was a playboy, who, Williams wrote, had been nicknamed "He Man" by the others at the firm.

He Man offered to take care of Molly Mia, but Williams told him that job had gone to Susan. "In that case," He Man replied, "I suppose I shall have to look after Susan."

A FEW DAYS BEFORE his departure, Williams threw a formal dinner party for twelve, with linens, china, and printed menus. Joseph was the chef. As Williams was frantically packing and making lists, it was only natural that the theme was "What have you forgotten?"

When Susan arrived, all dressed up and walking Molly Mia beside her, Jim thought she looked like Diana the Huntress. Unfortunately, He Man appeared, too, and while Williams grabbed the spot to Susan's left, He Man claimed the right, swiftly taking center stage. He "impressed the girls by biting the side out of his champagne glass and chewing it like a wafer biscuit." Though the women were astonished, Williams was appalled. Flirting with Susan, He Man then grabbed her glass next and bit down. To Williams's glee, blood poured from his mouth. One guest warned, "Look out, He Man, or Molly Mia will start chewing you."

Sophisticated and attractive, Susan Rowland (right) drew attention in Rangoon.

Throughout the evening, the guests teased Williams, taking bets on how he would meet his demise: whether he would starve to death or be fattened by cannibals and cooked in a pot. Soon, jokes about which body parts would be the most edible turned bawdy.

Williams came up with a useful game: Everyone would turn over their homemade menus in order to jot down important items he might have failed to pack for the trip. As the others set about scribbling suggestions, Susan quietly placed a note into his hand. She had written one word: Susan.

Williams looked into her eyes, smiling. "No, I haven't," he said to her, "and shan't." He tucked the paper into his pocket.

On Williams's last night in Rangoon, Hopwood invited him for dinner. The old man gave him a box full of very good, but very tangled, fishing equipment, including shark hooks and a harpoon gun. Uncle Pop, who liked to appear unaware of the courtship, suggested that Susan help him straighten out the gear, and then he went off alone to smoke a cigar. The couple slipped out of the house.

Brimming with ardor, Williams took her to the most sacred place in Burma. In the warm tropical night, they walked around the massive gold-domed Shwe Dagon Pagoda and its complex of pavilions, temples, and religious relics. The thousand-year-old Buddhist shrine has a bell-shaped stupa that had been replated in gold by the faithful over such a long time that the best guess was that it now weighed one hundred thousand pounds.

So commanding by day, it was "luminous with floodlights by night," in the words of W. Somerset Maugham, "a sudden hope in the dark night of the soul." The pagoda was alive with people, the flickering glow of many lamps, the song of the cicadas, and, most of all, the tinkling of thousands of gold and silver bells. Susan breathed in the sweet air—filled with the perfume of heaps of flowers that had been left behind by daytime worshippers—lotus, jasmine, and marigold.

The mysticism of the Buddhist faith resonated with Jim because, he said, he came from a corner of Cornwall where it was believed that "Ghoulies and Pixies still exist." He was attracted to the unknown in spirituality and also the generosity, the gentleness, and serenity it seemed to bestow among its followers. He believed that it was the Buddhist "belief in the community of all living creatures" that had fostered the loving relationship between humans and elephants in Burma.

Alone together on the eve of his departure, the couple conveyed their deep feelings for each other, with talk of marriage. But Jim and Susan would each recall how that transpired quite differently. Jim noted that their communication was wordless—that they had an unspoken understanding. He wrote, "We neither of us declared our feelings outright. It was not necessary." He mentioned to Susan that after the Andamans he'd be off to England. The implication being that they would marry there. He merely kissed Susan on the forehead to say good-bye, reserving his exuberant emotion for his farewell to Molly Mia.

Susan would always remember a heart-to-heart talk in the dreamlike light of the pagoda. "On that last evening together," she said, "when the thought of parting seemed unbearable, we agreed that if we both felt the same way when he returned in three months' time, we would get engaged."

CHAPTER 18

THE
CANNIBAL ISLANDS

———

THE MISSION TO THE ANDAMANS WAS AN ADVENTURE BILLY WILliams had been spoiling for. And yet he couldn't focus entirely on it, because he was leaving behind those dearest to him: his elephants, his Alsatian dog Molly Mia, and Susan Margaret Rowland.

He had reason to worry on all counts. The elephants, whom he had doted on for ten years, were in the hands of a new recruit, capable but untested. Molly, the jungle-trained dog who had never been apart from him, would now be staying with someone she hardly knew, and in the crowded city no less. And Susan. He knew by now that she was the love of his life, but he had to trust she felt the same way. He had seen far-flung tuskers converge on a tiny patch of jungle, drawn by a receptive female, and the human equivalent was happening in Rangoon in his absence. Susan had been the target of attention from other Bombine men, and, most unsettlingly, from He Man, who had promised to look after her. That thought, more than the heaving ocean, had the power to sicken him.

Would he have a soul mate, a dog, or even his platoon of elephants in four months? With all of those unknowns, he wasn't sure what he would be returning to. And that was assuming he would return, which not everyone at the time would have bet on.

The Andamans, consisting of 550 islands, had for centuries unnerved outsiders. It was a mysterious archipelago surrounded by shark-infested waters. Harboring hostile natives, terrible disease, huge monitor lizards, and mangrove swamps, this was a corner of the world in which explorers could vanish without a trace. Some of the islands were no more than rocks jutting up from the water. Very few were inhabited; fewer still had ever been seen by Westerners, but all were feared. Ptolemy called them the "Cannibal Isles." Williams's Burmese friends referred to the place as "Kalah Kyan"—the Black Islands, the Islands of No Return, or the Disease Islands.

He would have three young assistants for the work: Geoffrey W. Houlding, of Bombine's Rangoon mills, Max Christian Carl Bonington, and a young man named Bruno. "I had no briefing for the adventure," Williams wrote. "I was merely told that since the competition of Pacific hardwood timbers was so affecting the prices of teak markets of Burma the company which employed me were considering entering the field. It was believed that the forests of the North Andaman Islands might offer supplies. My work was to explore them, cruise them, enumerate sufficient trees and sample areas of what I found and report."

The only timberwork that had been done there previously was on narrow coastal plots, so the quality and quantity of wood in the interior were unknown.

Most of all, Williams's personal contribution would be assessing whether elephants, so necessary to hauling logs in the jungle, could survive on the available vegetation. In preparation, he had followed one of his female elephants for three days and nights, getting little sleep himself, in order to identify what and how much she ate. If he was going to look for adequate elephant forage he wanted to know it when he saw it. Geoff, "a Forest engineer with expert knowledge of timber milling," would determine if the forests contained timber worth harvesting.

The most remarkable part of the trip—the fact that his colleagues found repugnant—was that Williams would be employing a crew of forty-eight hardened criminals. He had always viewed Burmese prisoners in the mold of Robin Hood, not Western thugs, and had no qualms. The convicts would be given the utmost courtesy. He believed now, years after the stabbing incident with Aung Kyaw, that treating others with the respect he gave his elephants could, often enough, work miracles.

The deal made with the convicts was a good one: They would have a year shaved off their sentences for good behavior, they would receive payment in cash at the end, plus, at Williams's insistence, they would be issued new shorts and vests—or light button-neck undershirts—and a blanket. Burmese knives, or "dahs," used during workdays, would be returned each night.

MOSTLY, THE JOURNEY WAS what Williams had hoped it would be. There were natural marvels awaiting him: emerald green islands, white breakers, and thousands of varieties of coral, including fire and staghorn. The archipelago was home to massive saltwater crocodiles, sharks, cobras, geckos, deer, and robber crabs—the largest crabs in the world, big and strong enough to crack open and consume coconuts. He even came close to a dugong, a marine animal that is a near twin of the manatee, and may be the inspiration for mermaid tales.

The work in this "richly timbered, but very difficult country" was punishing, and the crew members felt they were hacking their way through an inch at a time. When Singapore-based RAF Supermarine Southampton flying boats arrived to take aerial photos for the expedition, Williams scrambled into one of them. From high above, without the slow work of cutting paths, he was even more amazed at the beauty: seas "in every shade of blue," dotted with pinks from coral beds below or "blotches of dark seaweed" waving like cornfields, and mangrove swamps patterned like "dark green oriental carpets."

The planes not only rendered a heavenly vision of the islands, they would, before they left, provide his one chance to correspond with Susan. He had been eager to stay in touch, but now, quite suddenly, he felt seized with doubt—not about his own feelings, but hers. Back down on the ground, he wondered if during his exile he had exaggerated the depth of the connection between them. "I did not know how to write to Susan what was in my heart. Perhaps the sympathy which I thought existed between us, unspoken, was all my fancy. My letter might arrive between one date with He Man and the next. I had not the trust in my own love. I was afraid of making a fool of myself."

Perhaps it would be best to write nothing, "preferring the certainty of not being hurt to the possible joy that a letter might give." But he had a book by John Still, *Jungle Tide,* lying open on his camp bed. And he copied out longhand one of the poems that had resonated with him. It seemed a safe way to take a chance. The verse was an ode to nature, all the things that Williams cherished—mountains, jungles, the sea, and "wild things that wander there." But it kept coming back to the refrain "All these I love with a love that possesseth me / But more than all of these I worship thee." He placed it into an envelope unsigned, sealed it, and gave it to the pilots returning to Singapore. He wouldn't know her response for weeks.

In the meantime, the islands provided a moment of tenderness. While exploring a wooded area with one of the men, he saw a spotted deer stag leading a small group of females. The male strolled directly toward Williams, his movements "full of grace and quite without fear." He waggled his tail and cautiously approached to within inches. "His long neck stretched out and the twitching nostrils of his velvet muzzle were close enough for me to touch." The buck extended his neck another inch and gently licked the salty sweat from his hand. "It was an extraordinary sensation," Williams said.

Throughout the expedition, Williams saw ample evidence that the islands could support elephants. In fact, he was excited to discover proof that one single male elephant, shipped down here decades before, was still on the loose, island hopping. But by this time, Williams already knew that Geoff's report would not be favorable and would kill the project's prospects. There was plenty of timber—a variety of species including highly prized padauk, marblewood, and soft woods used by the match industry in India—but Geoff believed there were too many potential hazards in extracting it from the remote islands, which had no infrastructure in place.

Everything the party had done, Williams felt, had been useless.

The worst of it was the fate of the prisoners, who had been so hard-working and conscientious. Williams had hoped to hire them as free men when a logging operation started up. "Never were my heart-strings so torn," he wrote, as on seeing the men loaded aboard the boat to return to prison, where he knew they would sink back into their "sheep-like lethargy." They had turned out to be "good and honest and reliable."

He had climbed aboard the Rangoon-bound ship looking like a bearded "pirate," wondering what lay ahead for himself, his elephants, dog, and girlfriend. Clean-shaven and upbeat by the time of arrival, Williams eagerly scanned the waiting faces on the docks. Susan wasn't there, but the last person he wanted to see—He Man—was. In fact, the cheeky bastard had already spotted him and was grinning and waving madly. He didn't even wait for the gangway. Always a show-off, he sprang from the dock and heaved himself over the railing, bouncing in front of Williams with an exhalation of breath. Did this mean he was engaged to Susan and breathless with the news?

As it turned out, Williams had nothing to worry about. He Man told Williams that Susan had been delayed in Mandalay but would be back in Rangoon the next day. He carried a cable from her. Williams ripped it open and read. She had booked herself on the ship back to England that she thought Williams would take when he went on leave in a couple of months, the *Staffordshire*. Her intention was clear, but he would cable her back immediately: "You're on the wrong ship. If you are coming home with me it's the *Shropshire* you should be on."

Along with the joyful news came a terrible report. In Williams's published writing, he maintained that the note read, in part: "Molly Mia sends apologies not meeting you, but we are delayed a day in Mandalay." Susan Williams's own memoirs concur. But the truth was more painful. In his private papers Williams wrote of a terrible "heartache" on learning that Molly Mia had "died as a result of an accident whilst I was away." He didn't say what exactly had happened; it was his habit to bury the most painful events of his life in silence.

In a cable from Mandalay, Susan Rowland made her feelings clear to Williams, whom by now she was calling "Jim," as his family did. She was in love with him.

The next day Susan arrived, and even in grief, Jim found "there was an understanding between us." There wasn't much time for romance; Williams had a detailed report to write in the week before he was to head up-country. But it helped keep his mind off Molly. "Like most heartaches I have had in life," he wrote, "it was good for me, for only by keeping going full out can such things be lived down." Something else would comfort him, too: elephants. As luck would have it, he was about to be immersed in them. Before taking leave, he was scheduled to head north for the satisfying task of inducting fifty newly purchased elephants from Thailand into the Bombine ranks.

The animals and their riders had been making their way to Upper Burma for the past year. The elephants would stay, and the men would be returning to their homeland, handing their charges over to a set of new riders.

Out of Rangoon and returned to the forest, Williams was back in his element, marching for miles every day in the corner of the world he knew best. Williams's new recruit, "Edward," had been up-country all this time—in charge of hiring the new men and coordinating the rendezvous. The camp he had chosen was a fine clearing framed by massive tamarind trees that provided desperately needed shade in the hot season, and a wide creek bed offering the only trickle of water available for miles.

IT WASN'T LONG BEFORE Williams, so starved for the company of elephants over the past months, heard the symphony: the sound of fifty teak kalouks approaching. Then, the hot, hushed forest came alive with the unmistakable presence of giants. Williams was on his feet. Out from the wall of vegetation and into the clearing walked an incredible sight—the first regal tusker. The massive bull was clearly in musth—his temples darkened in streaks with the flow of his glands. He was ridden by a mahout and flanked by two spearmen. After him, one after another after another, came the colossal convoy. One out of every four was a tusker. Atop each squatted a rider, bare-chested and wearing loose black trousers as if they were in regiment uniform.

"Never in my service had I seen such a parade of magnificent animals," Williams thought. They were stockier than his own Burmese animals. And despite a year of marching, "their condition was superb."

Williams, with Edward and his lead elephant man, walked the towering line, taking the animals in one by one. Feeling nostalgic for his own start in Burma, Williams turned to Edward and echoed his old taskmaster Harding, who had entrusted him with his first four elephants twelve years before: "There are fifty of the finest elephants in Burma. They're yours, and God help you if you can't look after them."

Williams now raced to his up-country headquarters in Mawlaik, where he had been transferred once again, for some quick tying up of loose ends. This was where he had spent most of his service as a young man, and further, it was Bandoola country. He was about to head off on home leave and would instruct the man who would fill in for him there. Edward had his work cut out for him: settling the fifty elephants and riders into several new camps with about seven animals per camp. They would not actually start work just yet, since this was the beginning of their hot weather season rest.

It was a whirlwind, but by May 1932, Jim Williams was aboard the Bibby liner *Shropshire* with Susan by his side for a six-month leave. Hopwood had given his blessing to their union. Old Uncle Pop had said, with characteristic restraint, "He really is a man, Miss Poppy."

Williams was, in fact, a real man now. And the realization of it as the ship cruised by the Andaman Islands prompted something surprising—what he called a "confusion of feelings." He had survived more than a decade in the jungle and was reaping the rewards that company lore had always promised him—a promotion, a wife, a sense of destiny fulfilled. But beginnings brought endings. Molly was gone, and his dream of the Andamans, too. In addition, he was, quite clearly, leaving something significant behind. "Looking back," he would write, "I date this as the end of my being a young man."

CHAPTER 19

SUNLIGHT AND SHADOW

———

"IT WAS A GLORIOUS MORNING, ONE OF THOSE DAYS WHEN THE sun chases the shadows over the hills," Susan would remember. At 9:30 a.m., September 9, 1932, she and Jim were married at the All Saints Church in the picturesque old market town of Evesham at the edge of the northern Cotswolds. They had waited till the very end of his leave so that their honeymoon would not rob his parents of time spent with him.

Jim had secured a shiny, powerful black AC Six sports car, with a red racing stripe and a specialized high-performance clutch. It was the beginning of what would turn out to be a lifelong lust for fast cars. The two-seater kicked up gravel as they left the church in a roar—they had no set plans as they tore vaguely toward Wales, munching fresh-picked apples from Susan's family garden. "We purred along," Susan remembered, "the car seemingly as happy as ourselves." On her hand was a sapphire ring they had purchased in Ceylon.

By the middle of October, they were back in Burma, reunited with Jim's Eastern family. Standing on the wharf when their ship docked was Aung Net, Joseph the cook, and Po Lone, a newcomer to the group who spoke English. There was a busy week in a borrowed brick company house in Rangoon—just enough time to shop for "tinned and bottled luxuries" that would be unobtainable in the outpost villages—and then it was off to headquarters in Mawlaik, on the Upper Chindwin, close to the border of Manipur. They began at the chaotic and colorful train station in Rangoon, grabbing the Mandalay mail train and riding first class in a comfortable, breezy compartment with access to the well-stocked saloon car. (In the packed third class, hundreds of Indian and Burmese passengers would be forced to stick their feet out the windows in an effort to stay cool.)

They had time to visit Mandalay, on the banks of the great Irrawaddy River, the country's second largest city. And then they were off to Monywa to catch the company boat for a three-day river romp up the Chindwin. Headquarters in Mawlaik, the riverine station, would now belong to Williams. It was a large town and a big responsibility.

The couple arrived just before sunset, their little luxury boat emitting two shrieks from the siren as it pulled up to the jetty. On the high sandy bank Susan could see the bullock cart waiting to take their luggage, and behind it, several wooden shacks.

In their new home in Mawlaik, Susan (left)
could watch Jim play polo.

"Here, besides the firms," Susan wrote, "were stationed military police, civil police, Forest department, etc." A little hospital, nothing more than an insubstantial bamboo hut with matting walls, was run by an Indian doctor. The rustic social club managed to include a tennis court, polo grounds, and "a hazardous nine hole golf course." And while there were no fancy shops with English goods, there was a sizable native market selling local produce and offering spectacular orchids for a dime a dozen.

While their possessions rode in the wagon, Jim and Susan walked a mile to the house. By the time they arrived, they were covered in the fine red dust of the road. It was November, "the loveliest time of the year in Burma," Susan wrote. "The beginning of the cold season when every day is like a perfect summer day." Their new home, enclosed by a white picket fence and set high up on a hill with a view of the town and river below, was constructed entirely of teak, with white painted eaves. A breezy veranda, used as an open-air living room with some old cane chairs, rimmed the first story. The pretty yard was filled with brightly colored bushes and flowers—purple bougainvillea, imported yellow allamanda, and red and yellow cannas, which were visited by delicate hovering hummingbirds. Susan immediately made plans to add a vegetable garden in which she could grow chili peppers "to give a bite to Jim's breakfast buttered eggs."

The interior was spacious and handsome. Just inside the entrance, there was a large dining room (where the table legs were set in tin lids filled with kerosene to discourage ants) and a sitting room. An elegant, twisting teak staircase dominated the center. The furniture, chosen by the company, was solid and formal. The stuffiness could be relieved, however, by floor-to-ceiling hinged shutters, which opened the rooms to the outdoors.

The bedrooms were ample, and each contained two baths. Despite the presence of faucets, the big zinc tubs were filled not by modern plumbing but by servants hefting jugs of hot water. A glazed earthenware "Pegu jar" containing cold water was always within easy reach. The toilets were emptied by a lowly Indian worker who had his own sweeper's staircase from which he could silently and invisibly remove what would be flushed in a modern bathroom.

As eager as Susan was to settle in, it would have to wait. There wasn't time to unpack boxes from England, as the couple were about to embark on their first jungle tour together. This is what Jim had been dreaming of for a decade: his life among elephants shared with his true love.

He wanted Susan to have everything he did, including his clothes. He designed a feminine version of his own field wardrobe for her, starting with an Australian bush shirt, customized with four big pockets, tailored for a woman, and hemmed at knee length. Beneath this, Susan would wear fine smooth-cotton lisle stockings, woolen ankle socks, and canvas hiking boots. She loved it.

Their journey began that first cool morning just after dawn. Jim's rank and marital status now entitled him to a large entourage. Twenty traveler elephants—tuskers unsuitable for logging work, adult females, and even a teenager—appeared from out of the ring of forest that surrounded the house. The animals were led to the rear veranda from which servants loaded them up with luggage, light-weight Burmese baskets, and gear. It was expertly organized—tents and poles on one elephant, and beds, suitcases, tables, chairs, and radio set distributed in a systematic fashion on the others. Po Sin, Joseph the cook's kitchen elephant, carried not only all the pots and pans, but in cane plaited baskets, the live chickens and ducks who would ultimately end up in them. (Susan eventually insisted on pardoning two ducks; the two birds were carried all the way home where they lived out their natural lives as pets.) They also brought Rhoda, a little buff-colored cocker spaniel; Gipsy, a wirehaired fox terrier; and one cat, a Siamese named Tigger. When everything was in place, they set off.

After four hours of steady marching, they reached their campsite, which had been cleared by some of the logging staff. A large open dining room with woven bamboo walls and thatched roof of jungle grass had been built that very day. Most of these camp dining rooms contained a bamboo table for the radio and a tray for drinks. Wherever foresters went, little buildings were put together fresh, and rarely used for more than two days. The jungle quickly reclaimed everything before it could ever be occupied again.

Soon after, Susan heard the sound of the kalouks and looked forward to watching the elephants as they were unburdened. Within a half hour the tents were up. Installing the "wireless" set involved a lengthy process, because the battery had to be secured in a basket of hay for travel to avoid spilling the acid. Once the antenna had been fixed high in a tree, if the conditions were right in the hilly terrain, Susan could listen to the chimes of Big Ben from London over the calls of jungle birds. Though they were far from Westminster, "This made us feel nearer home," she wrote. The connection was so deeply felt that on the occasions that "God Save The King" was played on air, both Jim and Susan would rise from their canvas camp chairs and stand at attention.

In the couple's tent there was one large area in the center for the raised beds, theirs as well as those for the dogs. Mosquito netting was draped over all of them. There was even a bathroom inside, partitioned off by canvas and containing a tub. Discarded kerosene tins were filled with water from the nearest stream and heated over the massive campfire. Susan would enjoy a hot soak nightly before dinner. For fun, she sometimes played fortune-teller and read Jim's future in the leaves at the bottom of his teacup. They would then go off to sleep, cocooned in wool blankets.

IN THE EVENINGS, AUNG Net set the table with linens that he kept spotless. Cocktails were poured. Joseph prepared fresh bread, pickled pork, or roast chicken. How different this was, Susan thought, from "the very austere and comfortless touring" she had done with Hopwood, where all the meals were "dry as dust."

At sundown, the jungle came alive. Williams often kept a large reflector lamp burning all night to discourage wildlife, particularly leopards, who were known to snatch dogs right out of tents, away from sleeping owners. One of Williams's colleagues lost a large Labrador retriever that way.

In the morning, Susan was up first because "the boys" could not enter the tent until she was dressed. During the day, while Susan oversaw domestic tasks, including pressing clothes with a heavy charcoal-heated iron, Jim caught up on paperwork and met with contractors and logging camp workers. People in the vicinity, curious to meet Jim's new wife, would come by to pay their respects and bring offerings—"half a dozen eggs on a plate, a pineapple, bananas, sweet limes, oranges. No one ever came empty handed," Susan wrote. She was overwhelmed by the warmth she was shown. The people embraced her, and she found their culture and customs to be reassuringly kind and family oriented. In the bigger villages, she loved the sounds of Buddhist ritual: the children chanting, the gongs summoning monks to prayer, and later, the chiming of pagoda bells in the night air.

At all of these places, Jim pulled out his big medicine kit, for he was not only an elephant doctor; he had become a bit of an MD, too. With his company-issued medicine box full of quinine for fevers, suture silk, needles, ointments, pills, and bandages, he was on call with the villagers. Life was too harsh in the forest for him to be reticent about treating the most horrifying diseases and wounds: the woodsman whose run-in with a sun bear had left his eye dangling and his scalp torn from his skull; women with breast abscesses, which were treated with maggots to clear away dead tissue; and many others suffering from malaria, dysentery, smallpox, goiters, and nutritional deficiencies such as beriberi. Williams knew he might kill a patient with his amateur doctoring, but to refuse care would be a sure death sentence. Susan watched Jim during his field clinics, and started to pitch in, eventually acting as nurse.

Soon they would pack up and be back on the trail. Jim brought Susan to the area that had been his headquarters when he started in 1920. The great joy of the reassignment in Mawlaik was that Jim was once again in Bandoola's backyard. In just a couple of weeks, he'd be able to introduce his wife to the tusker who had saved his life.

For the Williamses this wasn't just a jungle tour, it was a honeymoon, and they made love often. Or often enough to be noticed. Settling in to a campsite, Susan came to Jim asking him to investigate a strange odor radiating from her bed. Williams stripped it down and discovered that the leather strapping that tightened the canvas had been coated with fat from a roasted wild pig. When he confronted the servant in charge about what was going on, the man grinned and said it helped stop the creaking.

Susan took to the life with remarkable ease and eagerness, and Jim felt profoundly happy at having found someone who loved the forest as much as he did. "I had previously enjoyed my loneliness in the jungle despite all the longings for companionship which at times assailed me. I enjoyed it because it brought me private joys which I could not believe that anyone would ever share with me. The discovery that Susan could not only share my pleasures but also enlarge them was the perfection of my happiness," he wrote. He also reveled in the fact that even though Susan had toured the forests of Burma with Hopwood, she had never really seen them, not the way she could with him. Hopwood was a hunter; he wanted to kill creatures. Now with her husband, Jim said, "she came to enjoy all the living things of the jungle: the birds, the beasts and the flowers." It was their Eden.

"The wonderful beauty of the Burma jungle at dawn is something never to be forgotten," Susan wrote. "The deep green faintly tinted with pink as the sun was coming up, the mists in the river beds. The spirals and faint smell of wood smoke from the newly stirred camp fire. The call of the doves or the longer cry of the Burmese imperial pigeon. A pleasant nip in the air, the occasional squeal of an elephant being harnessed. Sitting down muffled up in a warm woolly sweater and scarf, sipping one's first cup of tea, smoking the first cigarette. The wonderful beauty and sensation of it all was only fleeting, but in those moments life was good."

Susan and Jim hiked the forest together, sometimes ten miles at a stretch, starting on paths that were wide enough to drive bullock carts on, but then usually narrowed into tiny game trails made by wild animals. They would walk along, sharing their favorite pack food, such as slabs of plain chocolate or rye crackers, and point to signs of wildlife or jungle flowers in bloom. Jim might sit down on a boulder with her and blow on a blade of grass held between his thumbs to mimic the mating call of a barking deer. Occasionally, one of the small creatures would venture to poke a red head out of the vegetation.

They visited the logging camps, where Jim greeted the elephants like the old friends they were, and Susan could see the very best of him. The first time, Susan was sitting in camp when Williams came striding up. "Come on, Sue," he said, "the elephants have been brought over from one of the elephant camps for me to inspect; they are being bathed just below here in a pool in the creek." He had been an elephant man for more than a decade, but this moment still filled him with excitement.

The uzis scrubbed the elephants' skin with a
vine that lathered up like soap.

They walked down to the banks of the creek. A dozen elephants—females, tuskers, babies—splashed in the cool water. The big ones were on their sides, their uzis atop them, crouched down and scrubbing their skin with a vine that lathered up when soaked. Many of them lazily sucked water in their trunks and noisily sprayed it into their open mouths. They would do this over and over, sometimes plunking their trunks underwater and breathing out—sending a sizzle of bubbles to the surface.

As Jim and Susan continued their tour, they finally met up with the one elephant he had spoken so often about: Bandoola. Reunions with this tusker were always emotional, and though Jim never would have quite let on, Susan by now could read him. How could Jim not betray his excitement?

She felt it herself. Jim had not exaggerated—here before her was the finest tusker she had seen. No matter how long he had been separated from the elephant, Williams greeted him in the same way. He spoke to Bandoola in Burmese, rubbed his cheek, and presented a sweet hidden away for him. Susan instantly grasped Bandoola was the very embodiment of determination, an animal of the highest "courage and cleverness," just as Jim had said. In fact, all the virtues he attributed to this elephant had reminded her of Jim himself. No man could rival Jim in her mind, but maybe an elephant could measure up.

Po Toke wanted to make a good impression, and he often liked to show off a few of Bandoola's tricks: how he could pick up any tool asked for, tie a knot, untangle a chain, or move a boulder. Almost thinking aloud, Jim said, "He's a wonderful animal." Susan smiled and took his arm. "You're quite paternal about him, aren't you darling?"

"Am I?" Jim said. "Yes, I suppose I am." Susan hoped she would see more of Bandoola in the months to come. Jim would make sure of it.

As they continued touring, Susan discovered the armies and air forces of biting and stinging insects. And everywhere leeches. Jim warned her that in deep jungle they came not by the hundreds, but by the thousands, and they were famous for embedding themselves in any orifice available. Susan had her fair share of them—"silently hummocking over the leaves" and attaching themselves to her skin, where they would bloat up on her blood till touched with a lighted cigarette. They, of course, made meals of the dogs, too, and the elephants even suffered the indignity of having them slither up their trunks.

It didn't happen often as they traveled these great stretches of forest, but part of Jim's job now was checking in on his assistants. They were all lonely young men hungry for English-speaking company. One day, they rendezvoused with a young assistant, Gerry Carol. He was like most of the others, tough and self-reliant, friendly and obliging. He was a favorite of Jim's.

Gerry served Jim and Susan a meal with his best stores of food and liquor. And the next morning, he and Jim set about tending to the elephants. They made plans to travel together for a week. Gerry had been such a grand host, Susan was looking forward to reciprocating. But on their first night of travel, over dinner, Gerry wasn't himself. Early in the evening he apologized, saying he thought he had caught a chill and needed to turn in. It was a red flag to Williams. He knew how precious this kind of companionship was to a lonely forest assistant, particularly one as gregarious as Gerry. If he went to bed early, something was very wrong. Sure enough, by morning Gerry was in the grip of fever. This alone was not a matter of concern, malaria being as common as a head cold for forest men. But throughout the day none of the usual remedies—including trebling the quinine—helped. By evening, his temperature had climbed to 105 degrees and Gerry was delirious. "I don't like this, Sue," Williams told his wife. "We must get this chap in to hospital."

It was typhoid fever—transmitted when the feces of someone infected with it contaminates food or water—and it was outside Jim's by-now capacious field medicine playbook.

That night there was nothing to be done but to take turns in Gerry's tent, sitting on a cane stool, trying to make him comfortable with cold compresses and soothing words. By the light of a hurricane lamp, Susan looked into Gerry's blue eyes, which seemed to stare without seeing. She wrote later, "an awful feeling of helplessness came over me." In the morning the race would be on for the railway, a good thirty miles away, over "some of the most difficult hill country in Burma." They packed as quickly as possible and carried Gerry on a makeshift stretcher—a long camp chair supported by two poles—marching for seven hours. It was torture for the stoic assistant, who even in his wakeful periods never cried.

By the time they reached a village, he was in a steady stupor. They rested him in the shade, ministering to him even with the knowledge that nothing was helping. The next day they had a stiff, jolting bullock cart at their disposal, which would transport them over a bruising twenty-three-mile leg of the journey. Williams tried to fabricate a makeshift suspension system under Gerry's stretcher, but seeing that it did little good, Jim lay beside him as a human harness and cushion in one.

It was two grueling days and nights for the sick young forester, and a huge relief for the Williamses when they reached the railway—"We felt we had won," Susan said. They lifted Gerry aboard. "It was pathetic to see the look of relief which crossed his face when he felt the firmness of the railway carriage seat beneath his aching body," Susan remembered.

They traveled all day. Gerry woke just as a beautiful sunset emerged. Williams tenderly held his shoulders and eased him up to look out the window, "You must look at this, old man. It's wonderful." Gerry saw the warm colors shimmering across the horizon and reflected in the waters of the Irrawaddy. He managed to smile and to whisper to Williams, "Billy, you're the best doctor a man ever had—you knew just what seeing that would do for me."

They got to a modern hospital where Williams handed over the patient along with a meticulously kept day-to-day log of the illness. Treatment began immediately. The Williamses were assured that "enteric" was "dangerous, but not incurable." No antibiotics were available. Within three days Gerry was dead. "I don't think in all our married life I have ever seen Jim so deeply moved and depressed," Susan would say later. The spell of their magical honeymoon was broken.

CHAPTER 20

INTO THE CAULDRON

———

As a boss, Williams did not have to tour during the height of the hot season. But the heat sought him out at home. Even after sundown, there was no relief from it. Back in their big house, Jim and Susan wandered from room to room during the night flopping down on rice-mat beds, searching for cooler spots. "It was nothing out of the ordinary," Susan wrote, "for me to wake up in one part of the house and Jim in another."

There was no electricity. In the evening the pressure lamps became so hot that often darkness was preferable. Overhead "punkahs," or wide, slow-moving fans, were powered by "punkah-wallahs," usually the children of the servants. They would sit outside during the day with one end of a string attached to a toe, the other to the fan. By rhythmically tapping a foot, they kept the blades circling.

As bad as the monsoons were, Susan now looked forward to them just as a reprieve from the swelter. But when the rains returned, Jim would go back out on tour, and she would stay home. It was company policy that monsoon travel was considered too dangerous for wives.

In May, when the rains bucketed down, Williams waved goodbye to Susan from the back veranda as he left with his parade of elephants, all of them swallowed up by the lashing storm and the undulating green wall of the forest. He would be gone a month.

In the house, Susan found an incredible transformation: Every surface was sticky with humidity, and "winged creatures came alive by the million." She was already accustomed to the bugs and lizards that cohabitated with people in Burmese households. She remembered her introduction to them in Rangoon with Hopwood: "Dinner that first night was a nightmare. Insects fell in the soup, crawled on the fish, and ran down the back of my neck." In Mawlaik, in addition to the winged hordes, there were ants by day and scorpions by night. The scorpions often hid under pots or tins in the kitchen, and Susan discovered that their sting "could give one fever for a week." They were so prevalent that she welcomed the little lizards who came from nooks and crannies and from behind pictures at night to hunt them down.

But there were more surprises in the dankness: Furry mold grew on her shoes, laundry wouldn't dry, and when the occasional breaks in the rain came and the sun emerged, steam would rise skyward from the earth. Kipling had seen the poetry in this, describing "the blinding warm rains, when all the hills and valleys smoked."

With Jim gone, she was alone in the house with Po Lone, the servant who spoke English. And she had English neighbors to visit. She was invited to dinner at friends', and usually made her way there and back by strolling behind lantern-carrying servants who were on the lookout for snakes. At home she had the wireless to keep her company. The delivery of news could ignite a paradoxical sensation: feeling connected to the wider world by hearing of events as they occurred, but also more isolated by being so far removed from them.

For Williams, "jungle touring was grim." This season in particular, the monsoons were heavy. As if that wasn't bad enough, mail was not reaching him, and several of his men were ill. He was buoyed by one event—he was able to reach the camp where Po Toke kept Bandoola. Despite the conditions—driving rain that turned game trails into quagmires of boot-stealing mud—it was wonderful to see his favorite tusker.

In the hut one afternoon, Aung Net climbed the spindly bamboo ladder up to the doorway, announcing *"Sar yauk byee."* The mail had finally arrived. The mail carrier, San Pyu, was right behind. He had brought the correspondence from home in Mawlaik. The two men left, and Williams greedily sorted through letters from Susan, home mail from England, a bundle of newspapers, and work documents. But when Aung Net returned and began nervously tidying up what didn't need tidying—a little "jungle apology" of a dressing table, which contained a mirror, comb, brush, and framed photographs of Susan and Molly Mia—Williams asked what was the matter. Aung Net knelt before him, saying, "I fear to tell you." But then Aung Net did tell him: San Pyu apparently believed that Po Lone, the man left behind because he spoke English, was trying to poison Susan. As proof, San Pyu when brought back in, presented a small homemade envelope. Williams unfolded the wrinkled paper and found "a grubby pill about the size of a Beecham's," the British laxative. One of these, he was told, was added to every drink that Po Lone served to Susan.

With alarm, Williams asked if she had already become ill. San Pyu said she had not. Williams sampled a bit of the small pill. It seemed to be composed of dirt. But he had no idea what arsenic or any other poison tasted like. The first priority was to get word to Susan. While his impulse was to run to her, he knew there were young camp workers who could negotiate the night jungle faster than he could. It was decided that Bandoola would take a particularly fleet young Karen spearman, Saw Pa Soo, across the swollen, dangerous river. Then the runner could make the rest of the way quickly on foot. Jim, himself, would follow in the morning. He quickly wrote a note of warning for Susan and handed it to Saw Pa Soo. He told the spearman to put the note into Susan's hands, and that there would be a promotion waiting for him if he traveled fast enough.

As dusk quickly approached, Jim walked alongside Bandoola, who carried Po Toke and Saw Pa Soo. At the bank of the river, Jim stood watching in the rain as the big tusker disappeared into the deep water and the darkness. Bandoola to the rescue yet again. Po Toke would return with him when they had dropped Saw Pa Soo at a high ridge to start his journey.

But it seemed impossible to just do nothing. When Po Toke and Bandoola returned to camp, drenched, Williams couldn't settle himself. He had to go himself, and he had to do it now. For the trip, he had Aung Net grab a tin of biscuits and bottle an odd elixir: strong hot black tea and whiskey in equal measure. Aung Net, as always, would accompany him, along with another servant, the camp messenger, San Pyu. Miraculously, the rain abated, and the water level had fallen by the time Bandoola ferried them across the river.

The men traveled for three days nearly nonstop, pausing only to receive a bit of rice or travel suggestions from the workers in the camps they encountered. The journey was arduous and there were many miles of track in which the mud was three feet deep. Finally, on the third morning, they reached Mawlaik. A break in the rains allowed them to travel on a real road, though by this point Williams could barely stand. Struggling along, he heard hoofbeats ahead, and around the corner came a very healthy Susan riding a polo pony. Behind her was the groom on a horse called Little Me. Jim waved them over, ecstatic.

The runner had arrived, the police had already been notified, and all was well. The groom gave up his mount, and Jim climbed up onto Little Me. When he got home, he fell into a deep sleep. By evening he was down with fever. Attempted murder could not be proved, but the police suspected that Po Lone wanted to get rid of Susan. The servant feared that his services might become unnecessary now that there was a woman running the household, so he had picked up some so-called magic pills from a questionable village priest. He was fired immediately.

As sick as he was, Williams sent word for Po Toke to bring Bandoola to headquarters. Po Toke had been demoted a few years back, and now, in gratitude for his help with getting to Susan, Jim restored Po Toke to his previous position. He would once again be *singuang,* the man in charge of the camp. Further, Williams would make sure that the old man would never again be assigned to a different camp from Bandoola.

When all the dust had settled, Jim discovered that not only was everything good, it was grand: Susan was pregnant. The larger world began to intrude immediately, though. The ripples of the Great Depression took their staggering toll on the teak market. Forest revenue for Burma, which was nearly 22 million rupees for 1926–27, plummeted to only 8 million for 1933–34. And the government went so far as to slash its forest administration staff. Williams didn't have to worry about losing his job, but Bombine was making other changes to save money. After a little more than a year in Mawlaik, in November 1933, Jim and Susan received orders to relocate to a new district. Shwebo, northwest of Mandalay, on the eastern side of the Chindwin, was a dry forest, about a hundred miles away. Not very far, but it wouldn't be a quick transfer. They had to move themselves, and Jim was required to check in on several camps along the way. It would be a five-month journey on foot, part of it during the hot season: impossible for most pregnant women, but not for Susan. She was in love with forest life and as fit as an athlete. She insisted on hiking with her husband, not traveling by boat and train on her own. "As long as we were sharing life together," she wrote, "it seemed good wherever it was. For me [Jim] was the perfect companion."

The transfer meant that Jim would be separated once again from Bandoola. He didn't know then if fate or the nats would bring them together again, just as they had once before.

By the end of the month, Jim and Susan began their journey on the east side of the Chindwin. Their first bit of excitement was running into a python—seventeen feet long and as big and muscular as a man's thigh—as they hiked through a gorge. Jim shot it, fearing it had swallowed a village dog, but when they cut it open, they discovered the folded body of a little barking deer. He sent the snakeskin away to India to be cured, and Susan would keep it rolled up in her cupboard throughout her life.

They soon hit their first roadblock, arriving at a section of forest in which the flow of a river had altered, leaving what Williams estimated to be ten thousand logs stranded in deep mud, tall grass, and pools of stagnant water. Sidelined logs were the teak man's constant nightmare. Colleagues had been injured and even killed in the effort to free them. His good friend Colin Kayem had nearly died swimming for hours through a pitch-black cave, which had trapped thousands of logs beneath a curtain of overhanging rock. Seven men would eventually be killed using explosives to open that jam up.

Williams wasn't about to take chances. "When I contemplated my rough survey map," Williams wrote, "I realised that a herd of a hundred elephants would not be enough to drag every log to the channel." He didn't have one hundred elephants at his disposal anyway. What he could do was conscript a group of forty heavy elephants, mostly tuskers. This meant that a reunion with his favorite elephant was coming sooner than expected. Bandoola would be at the top of the list. He was, by now, a colossal bull in his thirties, nearing nine feet in height at the shoulder and weighing more than four tons. Williams would have the elephants drag as much as possible downhill. Hopefully, their work would create grooves in the muck, and when the monsoon rains came they would wash what was left down to the river.

The operation turned a lonely corner of forest into a crowded workplace. Rough workers, or coolies, were hired from nearby villages to hack lanes through elephant grass. Pairs of timber-dragging buffalo were drafted. It went on for a full month.

Of all things, early on, there were muttered complaints about Po Toke and Bandoola not shouldering their fair share of the work. This seemed implausible to Williams. Perhaps it was a problem with the rider. The next day he hiked down to the section of forest his old friends had been assigned. He informed Po Toke of the accusations, and said it might be best if Po Toke rode Bandoola himself. But Po Toke told him the rider wasn't the problem. It actually was Bandoola himself. The rumors were true. Bandoola could travel through mud, but he hated working in it. The master mahout reminded Williams of a story he had told him years before: As a calf, Bandoola had gotten stuck in mud, and the experience had frightened him. Williams considered: "It had happened over thirty years before. Bandoola was massive. He was full grown. He was the prime elephant of the Burmese forests. But he was shy of mud."

Williams thought of elephants in general and Bandoola in particular in human terms. "Very few men or women reach maturity without some scars of childhood, some secret fear or weakness. If that was true of humans, why should it be different with animals?" Bandoola was dismissed from the crew without prejudice, and the other elephants kept working. Williams was sorry to see his favorite tusker go, but he stayed put to see the project through.

Not long afterward, while he was still bogged down in work with the logjam, there was yet another reunion with Bandoola. But this time, it was frightening. Williams received word from Po Toke that Bandoola was "down." Elephants can and do lie down to sleep, but only for short periods. When sick elephants lie prostrate and won't or can't get up, it could mean they were dying.

Williams rushed away, reaching Bandoola's camp in daylight. Striding over to where the men had gathered, he saw the tusker on the ground. The sight was terrifying. The great elephant was lying on his side; his body looked misshapen, his parts misplaced. The worst of it was that Bandoola's abdomen was distended and visibly increasing in size. His eyes were wide open and fixed in a stare; his trunk lay snaked out in front of him along the ground "like some prehistoric reptile."

The night before, he had broken into a godown, or supply shed, siphoning out an untold amount of dry rice with his trunk. When satisfied, he had strolled down to the stream to drink gallons of water. Then everything expanded in his gut.

Williams stood close to the prostrate elephant. How could he possibly "make an elephant belch? Or vomit? Or break wind?" he wondered.

Whatever else he might do to relieve the pressure, he knew the first concern had to be forcing the big bull up on his feet. Earlier, Po Toke had tried a common and painful incentive for raising an elephant—rubbing chili juice into Bandoola's eyes. The animal was already in such agony he didn't even stir.

Williams had an idea from a story he'd heard about two wild African elephants using their bodies as supports to keep a third elephant from collapsing to the ground. Wild elephants have been observed working together to lift or steady another elephant, and they will even feed sick or injured companions when they have lost the use of their trunks. Williams needed two big bulls to pull off the job. "Send for Poo Zone and Swai Zike with dragging gear," he said. "If we don't get him up, he'll be dead in half an hour."

When the tuskers arrived, Williams had them led up to Bandoola's spine and ordered to use their tusks to lift him as they would a log. The animals bent down, placed their tusks like forklifts under the barrel of the prostrate body, and heaved. They got him up just a foot and couldn't seem to raise him any higher.

If they couldn't get him on his feet, at least, Williams thought, they should try rolling him over to his other side. It might bring some relief. Chains were attached to the underneath front leg and the underneath back leg—those that were flat on the ground—and the chains were looped up and over his body. Now Poo Zone and Swai Zike were backed up to Bandoola's spine facing away from him. The chains were hooked to their harnesses, and they were ordered to walk forward. "Together the two tuskers took the strain, dragging breast to breast, so even and so gentle in their combined action," Williams said, "that I felt sure they understood the delicacy of the action." They probably did.

As they pulled, Bandoola's body began to roll over. Slowly, the two tuskers walked forward until Bandoola was on his back and his legs were pointing skyward. Frighteningly, his head remained down in the same position. Williams feared his neck might actually snap as the body continued to twist. But suddenly Bandoola mustered the strength to turn his huge skull. He groaned with the effort. It was a beautiful noise. Bandoola might be in pain, but he had fight still in him. His trunk waved, and his mouth opened, gulping for air.

Instead of being flipped over onto his other side, though, Bandoola had different plans. As the distended side of his abdomen seemed to deflate, Bandoola struggled under his own power to a standing position. The men rushed to remove the chains, and Williams ordered the other two bulls placed on either side of Bandoola, "like two friends trying to support a drunk between them."

It worked. Poor Bandoola was up, if just barely. He looked wobbly.

His digestive tract was so broken that with the change of position, stringy undigested bamboo emerged from his backside and "hung from him in strands." His gut had been stopped up to the point where it couldn't even properly expel waste.

Williams didn't hesitate. He had two men hold aside Bandoola's tail while he buried his arm deep into the animal's rectum. He began to clear away the fecal matter, pulling out handfuls, and purging as much as he could grab. "I emptied as far as I could," Williams wrote, "plunging in my arm a dozen times as far as the armpit." Gas, gloriously free now, was making its way out through the cleared passage. For Williams, hearing those first rumbles of a functioning digestive system made him happy. They were signs of his recovery. Bandoola was up, and, Williams said, "My job of elephantine plumbing was over."

With that, and his return to camp, Jim could pick up Susan and continue the journey toward Shwebo. The travel was long and exhausting. More than that there seemed to be a dark cloud chasing them. First there was news that Jim's father had died. Then there was Susan's first glimpse, in early March 1934, of their new home. "A desolate compound," she wrote. There was no garden, its only flora a few poor trees, stunted and sickly. After the riot of blossoms they had lived among in Mawlaik, her first impression here was "dirty, dry and derelict." The place was an old military compound: The major's bungalow would be their house, the old crumbling barracks sat empty, and the mess hall was made into both Jim's office and bachelor quarters for his assistants in from the jungle. The servants' accommodations were in the worst shape—shabby enough that Jim had them demolished and rebuilt. A cemetery behind the lot added to the atmosphere. It was dotted with the tombstones of youthful British soldiers who had succumbed decades before to tropical disease.

As if to underscore the malignancy of the place, Susan would come across her first Russell's viper—among the most deadly in the world, with venom stronger than that of a cobra, it was a snake even snake hunters fear. Marzah Khan, their night watchman, killed it with his stave.

The couple settled in, though their surroundings would always be unsettling to Susan. By summer, their son Jeremy was born. He was a chubby, bright-eyed healthy boy. It should have been a time of sheer joy, but just then Jim became sick with fevers, chills, and aches. More important and uncharacteristic, he was also unhinged with fear. A round of dengue fever, a virus transmitted by mosquitoes, seemed to be the last straw for his embattled health. "His constant bouts of malaria and other diseases, had caught up with him," Susan wrote. Not only was he ill, he was increasingly certain that he had contracted rabies from one of his beloved dogs whom he had to shoot. He had not been bitten, but he easily might have had contact with the sick animal's saliva. He understood that his extreme grief at losing a dog had probably just ripened into an unfounded anxiety. But just the same, he couldn't stop worrying—and anxiety itself can

Williams always said that being surrounded by the elephants helped him get through the constant battles with malaria and even dengue fever.

be a sign of rabies. The incubation period is extraordinarily variable: anything from weeks to years. At every turn were the sharp little pricks of fear that he was showing symptoms of hydrophobia.

No one had ever seen him like this, and an urgent medical leave was issued in the fall of 1934. In November, he, Susan, and their nanny, Ma Kin, packed Jeremy up and by the twelfth, they made the port at Colombo, Ceylon, eagerly headed for home. As soon as they arrived on English soil, Jim was admitted to the Hospital for Tropical Diseases run by the Seamen's Hospital Society in London. He was fed, hydrated, and treated with the most modern medications available. And yet there was no quick fix. "It was a psychiatrist in England," Susan wrote, "who eventually cured him."

No sooner was he on the mend, though, when tragedy struck. Jim was still in the hospital when little Jeremy died of pneumonia. The baby seemed quite healthy but "picked up a virulent flu germ, and died quite suddenly," Susan wrote. He was buried in the plot next to his grandfather's in the local cemetery. Just as he had done with his memories of the war, Jim Williams never wrote about the event himself, but Susan described the loss as "a terrible blow to him."

The unhappiness of their year at home was exacerbated by the fearful news coming out of Germany. After Winston Churchill's warnings about a potential threat, it came to light that in defiance of the Treaty of Versailles, Germany had built up a substantial air force, and Adolf Hitler announced his intention to increase the strength of the army. It seemed the führer's lesson from the Great War had been how to win next time. And it wasn't hard to imagine that next time might come sooner rather than later.

In September 1935, the couple returned to Burma and their dreaded bungalow in Shwebo. Susan poured her energies into creating a garden in the desiccated compound and, as would become a lifetime habit, she memorized the Latin names of all her plants. For the next two years, Susan toured with Jim whenever possible. The house in Shwebo might not have felt like a home, but the forests always did. As long as the rains held off, she'd rather be in the field next to her husband.

While not reliable, wireless reception was good enough for them to hear the drumbeat of news about the increasing militarism of Germany. Over the next year it grew louder, and even Japan seemed to be following suit. Italy annexed Ethiopia. And Great Britain made plans to beef up its navy. In the forests of Burma there was peace, but Jim sensed it was only temporary.

In the meantime, there were changes for them closer to home. For Burma, there was a step up in colonial status. In April 1937, the country emerged from the umbrella of India's administration, becoming its own stand-alone territory. It now would have an independent senate, though the senators would be handpicked by the British governor.

An especially happy development was that Susan discovered she was expecting again. In the fall, she developed a bad case of malaria, but still on December 12, 1937, their son Treve was born. Jim and Susan were nearly silly with joy around him. They thought they could discern a real intelligence in his eyes. "We both felt inordinately proud of him," Susan wrote. Despite the loss of Jeremy, or perhaps because of it, the couple was determined to raise a robust child. Unlike other nervous mothers in the teak trade, Susan decided to gather the whole family on tour as soon as possible. Their only concession was that they waited till Treve was fourteen months old before turning him into a full-fledged member of the touring crew. Susan heard murmurs that some of the other wives thought they were "foolish and running unnecessary risks by taking our child with us, so far away from medical help." She dismissed them, feeling that the risk was worth it. They kept a nanny, a pretty Karen girl named Naw Lah. On long treks, Treve, wearing a miniature pith helmet, or topee, was carried in a bamboo jungle version of a palanquin, which Jim had designed to be crib, "carry-cot, and playpen all in one." By the age of three, Treve was trusted with a jungle knife, or dah, and rode his own prancing brown-and-white pinto pony. Aung Net taught him how to make small, hard balls from mud and fire them from a slingshot. Susan wrote, "The jungle nats were on our side and he never came to any harm."

Though Treve had not yet met Bandoola, the elephant was a hero to him. The tusker was so completely woven into the fabric of the Williams family life view and lore that when the little boy was faced with a challenge, he would ask his father, "Could Bandoola do it?" and Jim would respond, "Yes, he would have a good try."

Jim missed Bandoola dearly, but he presumed there would come a time when they worked the same forest again. It was something to hope for. And for now, his life was what he had always envisioned: loving wife, child, elephants, and the magic of the forest. Both Jim and Susan hoped this was the beginning of several years of idyllic forest life all together. But world events increasingly threatened. In the spring of 1938, Austria became a province of Germany, and Czechoslovakia was ready to fall. The Williamses received home leave and were gone from April to October 1938. With war imminent, Jim considered staying to enlist. But then, feeling certain that Japan would enter the fray, he figured he'd be of more use returning East.

Jim Williams adored his son Treve.

Back in Burma, his work went on as before. But in September 1939, when Britain, France, Australia, and New Zealand declared war on Germany, Jim again felt conflicted and thought about sailing home to join the army. Ultimately, he decided that with the war effort, "teak would be as important as steel" and that's how he could best serve. As it would turn out, he wouldn't need to go find the war; it would eventually find him.

But at the moment, the colonial government, from the top brass down to the lowliest office clerks, lived in a bubble, confident that, despite the fact that Japan was at war with China, there would be no Japanese attack in Burma. To Susan, and most of the other British citizens, the country seemed a safe place. Jim thought otherwise. At HQ in Shwebo, he erupted during a dinner party, upset over the complacency of those around him: "I tell you here and now that we shall all soon be deeply involved."

Treve was a capable little boy. By the age of three, he was trusted to ride his own pony and carry a jungle knife, or dah.

THAT YEAR, WHEN THE HOT season arrived, the Williamses de-camped for a house in Maymyo, forty miles from Mandalay. Called the "summer capital," it was a tony hill station and the closest thing to a slice of Britain in all of Burma. British officials relocated to May-myo from Rangoon as temperatures climbed. At an elevation of nearly four thousand feet, it was shady, cool, and filled with flowers. "To be lifted from the airless plain into the soft breezes and cool air of the hills breathed new life into us all," Susan wrote. The Williams-ses' cottage was surrounded by cherry trees in full bloom, and Bom-bay Burmah's well-liked and respected manager Geoff Bostock lived nearby in a grand house called "Woodstock," with his wife, Evelyn, and sons, John and Hugh. Jim would be working in the nearby Shweli Forest. Here, Susan felt, "the war seemed further away than ever."

In the spring of 1940, Jim's young niece and nephew, the children of his brother Tom, came from India to live with them for about a year and a half after their mother's death. Three-year-old Diana was inconsolable from the loss and sick with dysentery. Michael was still a baby, just under a year. In this happy home, they would soon be calling Susan and Jim "Mummy" and "Daddy." The family of five was sheltered, but the war was growing by the minute. Japan made things official in September 1940, entering into a pact with Germany and Italy.

Susan reveled in the cool air of Maymyo where, she wrote, "the war seemed further away than ever."

Burma didn't seem so secure anymore, and in November 1941, Tom Williams arrived to collect Diana and Michael. He argued that Susan and Treve should go along to the safety of India also, but Susan refused to be parted from Jim. As the house emptied, Jim, Susan, and

Brothers Tom (left) and Jim Williams were very close, but they disagreed about sending Susan and Treve to India.

Treve prepared for what they did not know would be their last jungle tour.

It started off well. The weather was still beautiful, and everything they could need was carried on the backs of the elephants, who formed an enormous line of more than twenty. The forest was their constant home, no matter which forest it was. The three were happy to be together, and they still shared life with their wider family circle of Aung Net, Joseph, and now Naw Lah.

Jim, who had spent a decade on his own, never took his new life for granted. As his family marched together in the uneven forest light, the sound of the kalouks behind them, he felt blessed. In the evenings, he and Susan would retire to a quickly constructed hut for cocktails and news on the wireless. It was a treasured routine. But one early December day, deep in the jungle, Jim had gently turned the tuning knob until a broadcast from the BBC World Service materialized. Drinks in hand, he and Susan listened to a horrifying report: Pearl Harbor had been attacked. The Japanese had also landed in British Malaya, not so far from Burma. The next days brought more developments. The United States, Britain, Australia, New Zealand, the Netherlands, the Free French, Yugoslavia, China, and others declared war on Japan. Then the HMS *Repulse* and HMS *Prince of Wales* were sunk as they defended Singapore, killing nearly a thousand men. Together, Jim and Susan tried to make sense of the news, what it meant for their country, for Burma, for them. Regular mail continued to reach them, and, as far as Jim knew, he was to continue his duties extracting teak. For most of December, that's what he did.

But before Christmas, the war hit home. The British evacuated an airfield in the southern tip of the country that was targeted by enemy planes, and the Japanese began air attacks on Rangoon. On December 23, 1941, air raids sounded in the capital, and about a thousand citizens were killed when they spilled out to the streets to watch the battle in the skies. Though no formal evacuation had been announced, that night refugees began to abandon Rangoon, the Indian workers and civil servants the city depended on among them.

The Williamses spent a disquieting Christmas acting brave and cheery for Treve, but feeling the weight of the world pressing in. Back home, friends and family had suffered through the Blitz, much of Western Europe was in the hands of the Nazis, and that night the crown colony of Hong Kong surrendered to Japan.

Finally, in early January, the telegram they dreaded but assumed was coming arrived: The family was to return to Mandalay immediately. Considering that the dispatch had taken more than a week to reach them, they knew the situation must have worsened since it was sent. As the elephants were quickly loaded, and their journey began, the family had no idea what they would be facing when they came out of the forest.

PART THREE

WAR ELEPHANTS

CHAPTER 21

FLEEING BURMA

———

THE BOMBINE MAN WHO MET THE WILLIAMSES WHEN THEY ARrived in Mandalay provided a grim assessment. The Japanese were, indeed, bombing Rangoon. And on January 20, 1942, the Bombay Burmah Trading Corporation had ordered that wives and children of all employees be evacuated immediately. They were the first of the European companies to do so, and some thought it premature. Jim had already missed his chance to get Susan and Treve on the first contingent of evacuees up the Chindwin.

An exodus of biblical proportions out of Burma had begun, and the Williamses were caught short—recalled from forest tour, they had none of their important possessions with them. Jim hurried back to Maymyo. The company would allow one piece of luggage and one bedroll per person. Photographs, books, diaries, gifts, and clothes were abandoned. Horses and pets were left in the care of hired locals, though many of their fellow evacuees shot their dogs, thinking they were better off dead than in the hands of the Japanese if it came to that. Many of their neighbors had buried valuables in their gardens and transferred cash out of the country. Hardly thinking things were so dire, Jim grabbed a few essentials for travel—one small suitcase each for Susan and Treve and a grip for himself containing a clean shirt and a few toiletries.

The family was directed to travel by rail and boat to Mawlaik, their old headquarters on the Chindwin. If necessary from there, they would receive orders to march about 170 miles by foot to a rail station in Manipur, India. Susan was skeptical; the very notion of a march seemed alarmist.

But the Japanese were advancing rapidly. They had begun their invasion of Burma from bases in Siam, or Thailand, and were now infiltrating in the south of the country. During January and February 1942 they poured into Burma in strength—moving forward more quickly than anyone would have dreamed, pushing the ill-prepared, ill-equipped, and poorly supported British forces farther and farther back. The Seventeenth Indian Division dug in at the Sittang River, hoping to make a stand against the onslaught, but after heavy fighting they were outflanked, as they would be again and again.

Burma was an objective of the Japanese, not so much because of the country itself, but for its strategic location. It blocked an overland supply route for the Allies to China, Japan's bitter enemy. Along the famed Burma Road came ammunition and fuel. Later, Burma was seen as a stepping-stone to India, part of the ever-growing ambitions of the Japanese. It was not far-fetched considering that there were plenty of Indians tired of British rule. At one point, Japan would count forty thousand Indian soldiers on their side, many of whom believed this would be their path to independence.

In Burma, the British began to see that their confidence was misplaced. The Williamses had some hard decisions to make. Who should come along with them? They perceived several so-called servants as members of their family. But were they better off staying in their own country? The Japanese were after the British, not the Burmese, and so many people in Burma appeared to have no political allegiances.

Burma was full of many different ethnic groups. And when it came to loyalties during the war, there was no one national reaction. For the most part, Burmans, who were in the majority, hated colonial rule and longed for independence. For many of them, there was the prospect that the Japanese might just turn out to be liberators;

after all, they promoted an attractive ideal with the slogan "Asia for the Asiatics." A large portion of the Karens (one of the country's largest minorities who had largely converted to Christianity), Kachins, and Shans sided with the British. Some in Burma fled to the jungles to avoid the Japanese, some welcomed them, some fought alongside the British. About eighteen thousand nationalists joined the Burma Independence Army, which was allied with the Japanese. Of course, later, some who had hoped for liberation encountered only occupation and "Japanese racism and brutality." A report at the time found that 10 percent (mostly minorities under the thumb of the Burman majority) were pro-British, 10 percent anti-British, and the vast majority "lukewarm, assisting whichever superior forces they are forced or persuaded to."

Jim and Susan gathered together a few of their closest workers to discuss what to do. It was decided that Aung Net, Joseph, Naw Lah, and San Pyu would all be safest sticking with the Williamses. Others in their group had families at home who needed them. This seemed like the right decision, though they had no idea what would happen when they reached the border of Manipur.

THE PARED-DOWN WILLIAMS GROUP took a train to the river station of Monywa. Jim would stay long enough to see them safely onto the company launch, then, while they traveled up the Chindwin to Mawlaik, he would return to the men and elephants he had left behind in the forest near Maymyo.

When they reached Monywa, they discovered they weren't so far behind the rest of the company's families: The second group of evacuees from Bombine was still there, in limbo with no information, as they waited for the launch. The company, now nervous about sending women and children off on their own, took advantage of the arrival of Billy Williams. He was ordered not to return to Maymyo on his own but instead to escort the entire group of more than fifty as far as Mawlaik. Williams argued with his superiors, desperate to return to his own forests to pay the riders and to secure the animals at home. But he was overruled.

Then the company launch arrived. Originally built to provide luxury for half a dozen people, it was now nearly swamped by the crowd. The open deck became a dormitory, with women and children sardined from one end to the other. Behind them, a little boat containing a quarantined family with measles was towed along. Williams had arranged this setup to keep the other families safe, and he was surely thinking of Susan—who they had just discovered was pregnant again.

When they arrived in Mawlaik, the rugged little river village Jim and Susan knew so well, the anxiety of the other travelers deepened. The town was remote and rustic, far from what was considered civilized, and had no access to any kind of major transportation. To be herded to the very edge of the country's borders and pressed up against a mountain range made it clear that the British had lost control. If Rangoon and Mandalay weren't safe, what was?

For British refugees in particular, the logging companies and the tea plantations in India would be a godsend, providing supplies, basic shelter, and help. The tough, knowledgeable employees would be invaluable to the British Fourteenth Army, too. As one high court judge wrote at the time, "It was an affair of 'tea' to the rescue at one end and 'teak' to the rescue at the other."

There was a great deal of fear and confusion as everyone waited for a directive from the company. Williams put the time to good use by organizing supplies, equipment, and elephants in case the women were to march toward Manipur on foot. Wisely, everyone was inoculated against cholera.

Williams's friend and boss Geoff Bostock had already been gathering emergency supplies, and halted all logging work so the elephants could be available. To Williams, this was the beginning of elephants entering the war. It was February 1942. The animals were conscripted to carry supplies, to ferry the sick and elderly, and even to widen paths where possible. The company quickly established rest camps, though their administration was soon taken over by the government.

The news continued to be dire. Singapore, Manila, and Kuala

Lumpur had fallen to the Japanese. Tokyo was relentless, even dropping bombs on Australia.

Jim understood what this all meant for the families stranded in Mawlaik. They had to get to the safety of India. A march on foot was ordered. The evacuation plan wouldn't have a chance if not for the elephants who could carry the fresh and tinned food supplies, bedding, and tents. The group would be hiking from Mawlaik to the Burmese village of Tamu, on the border with the state of Manipur, a trip of about six days. This would serve as a staging area to prepare for the next leg: up and over the treacherous mountains that loomed behind Tamu, and then to the Imphal Plain.

The past few weeks had galvanized the foreign population of Burma. By now, countless refugees were fleeing for India. With the larger roads packed, Williams judged it best to keep to the smaller paths. The elephants simply could not contend with such crowds, and where great masses of people were concentrated without access to toilets, conditions were already becoming dangerously unsanitary.

The company evacuees—40 women, 27 children, and 110 elephants—were divided into two groups. Williams and Bostock would be in charge of the first, which consisted of 22 women; 15 children; 83 men, riders, servants, and bearers; plus about 56 elephants, including 18 tuskers. Evelyn Bostock and Susan organized the larder into a meal plan for the journey. The women were Bostock's responsibility; the elephants were Williams's. Since this was his old headquarters anyway, Williams even knew most of the animals, though Bandoola was not among them. The elephants were to be used for carrying supplies, not people. Coolies, the lowliest laborers from the nearby Chin Hills in northwestern Burma, were hired to bear makeshift stretchers for the littlest of the children and the infirm.

They left Mawlaik on Monday, February 23, 1942, at 10 a.m., the beginning of the hot season, when each day would become much more stifling than the last. Many of the wives were novices, having never accompanied their husbands on a jungle tour. They did not have proper clothes or shoes for such a journey and were dressed like parishioners heading out for Sunday services. Their city footwear in particular often fell apart in the rough terrain, and to walk barefoot could be a death sentence as blisters and cuts invited infection.

Behind the families and ragged coolies in the caravan came the long line of elephants, unhurried, regal, and laden with luggage, camp equipment, and food, including one hundred chickens and sixty ducks. The experience was new to the elephants, too, who were unaccustomed to seeing so many strangers—particularly white ones who smelled different and even behaved in a different way from the other humans in their lives. At least their familiar uzis were with them.

From the start, the group established a routine. They woke each day at about five thirty in the morning, dressed, and had breakfast— a cup of tea, porridge, and thick slices of bread with marmalade. Within an hour, after organizing and packing, they'd set out on the day's ten-mile walk. Williams would stay behind, organizing the loading of the elephant packs. Once the elephants were ready, he would double-time it past the human group, scouting ahead for a suitable place to spend the night. He was relieved to find much of the route rich in fodder—plenty of vegetation for the animals, and almost always good sources of water.

The first leg of the journey was fairly flat, which helped condition the least fit among them. Everyone was able to make the marches without complaint, though Treve, much to Susan's shock, became balky. Accustomed to hiking on his own, he railed against his imprisonment when he was forced to ride in a canvas hammock carried by coolies. He had inherited his father's independence and stamina.

In the afternoons, when the intense heat set in, the group would stop for the day, and each family could enjoy the privacy of their own tent. The food stocks were plentiful—chicken stew, cheese and biscuits for lunch, pudding, bread and jam at teatime, and a three-course meal for supper. A pleasant feeling of community took over; Williams wrote, "The spirit of the women was remarkable, as every one of them had had to leave a comfortable home and abandon all her possessions at a few hours' notice." As time went on, there were inevitable tears in the social fabric. Late in the afternoons when campsites were chosen, several women would vie for the shady spots, which were at a premium. Susan did not participate, because Jim, a group leader, made a point of taking the worst patch for his own family.

Stress was not limited to the humans; the elephants felt it, too, as Jim was acutely aware. This was a new world for them, one in which none of the normal rules or rhythms applied. Gone were their old daily schedules—morning roll call, work, afternoon bath, release into the forest for the night. Here they were marched for hours, deprived of the afternoon scrub, and then chained till morning. Being unable to forage at night was hard on them and on the uzis, too, who had to gather hundreds of pounds of bamboo, grass, and branches.

Williams worried about how the strain would express itself in the sensitive and complex animals, especially as the days grew hotter. At the beginning, they were somewhat irritable and restless. Within days, though, their unhappiness was more palpable. Each night the elephants looked for any lapse in the riders' attention to run away, though they were always quickly recaptured. Finally a mass breakout occurred one afternoon. A few elephants began to bolt, and in the chaos they caused, the rest were able to escape, too. With dozens of elephants stampeding for the thick of the forest, the men flew into action, racing to grab their trailing fetters, and the women and children sought safety behind big trees. The elephants complied quickly, but "it was lucky no one was killed," Williams wrote.

That luck didn't hold.

ON MONDAY, MARCH 2, 1942, at the height of the hot season, they reached the border village of Tamu. It was a madhouse. The large outpost, with perhaps a hundred homes, a courthouse, and a telegraph office, had been a sleepy place. Now, it was "a congested bottle-neck, filled with thousands of refugees, mostly Indians, all wondering how they would negotiate the next fifty miles, along a rough bridle-track, and over mountains five thousand feet high," Williams wrote.

It was hell in the making, a place of chaos, filth, and fear. Very little had been organized. There were no sanitary facilities. And as bad as things were, everyone knew worse was to come, for after Tamu, there was nothing but mountainous wilderness.

Hardly a refuge for humans, this was no place for elephants. Restraining the animals had been problematic for Williams during the whole trip, and now he felt he was in charge of a ticking time bomb. No matter what, Williams decided, he would send the eighteen tuskers back to Mawlaik. The more even-tempered females would stay with them for the rest of the crowded journey.

Just outside the heaviest traffic of the village, Williams brought the elephants to a halt. While the women and children went to see what was happening in town, Williams and the uzis began to unload the elephants. Packs would have to be reorganized and redistributed as the number of elephants was reduced. In fact, some items would have to be jettisoned altogether.

It was unbearably hot and dusty, and everyone felt exhausted. The riders were handing down the parcels one by one to camp workers on the ground: tents, luggage, cookware, the wireless. Williams walked among the animals, making an inventory of gear and trying to gather things into some semblance of order. For some reason, one small scene caught Williams's eye. Ten yards away, atop a big tusker, one of the uzis was handing off a particularly colorful "air-travel suitcase," the kind covered in labels from the Taj Mahal, the Sphinx, and the Eiffel Tower. An experienced camp worker reached up to take it. Seemingly with no provocation, the elephant tilted his great skull and crushed the man into the ground, dumping the uzi off his head in the process.

The crowd erupted around the horrible scene. Williams and all the riders ran in to help subdue the tusker. But it was too late; the force of the animal's head was enough to pulverize and compress the man's body. Those who have observed such attacks say the victim is rendered unrecognizable—not just as an individual, but as a human being. This was the sight Williams and the other men took in. They quickly put a cloth over the flattened body and moved him away.

But it was not quick enough to hide the incident from the crowds. It caused near panic among the refugees. One teenage British evacuee recording the event in her diary said that in the aftermath, parties of English travelers found that low-wage coolies were not eager to work for them. Simply carrying suitcases for the British now seemed impossibly risky.

When Susan arrived with the rest of the group, she could see how devastated Jim was. And yet, the focus had to be on pragmatism. Williams convened his party and explained that the allowable luggage per person would now be greatly reduced—just sixty pounds per head. Everyone who had managed to carry some treasured articles beyond their necessities had to give them up. It was a piece of silver here, a fancy green Morocco leather dressing case there. It wasn't just luxuries that went. Even tents and camp beds were relinquished. "After this," Susan wrote, "we felt more like the bunch of evacuees which, in fact, we were."

The Williamses had no valuables to give up, but there was a more wrenching departure for them. Joseph, their cook, had left a wife and children behind, and Aung Net still had some family in Burma. War had a way of slamming borders shut for years. If they continued on to India, they might not be able to return. Faced with this very real prospect, Williams had, in agony, decided they would be safest at home. To take them any farther would just be selfish, he believed. "The time has come," Jim said to Susan, "to tell them they must return."

Jim walked over to them. Susan watched. "It was a hard moment for all three," she wrote. There would never be any way to reward either man for the service and companionship each had brought to Jim for decades. Gathering as much money as he could from his own pockets and those of everyone he knew, he scraped together a year's wages for each. Aung Net had rarely been out of Jim's sight for the last twenty-two years; from first thing in the morning till late at night, they were together. And now they were parting under the worst circumstances possible, with no prospect of keeping in touch. All Williams could do was warn this simple and trusting person, who had meant more to him than nearly anyone else in all of Burma, to tell no one about the money he carried. By the time they all said their last good-byes none of them could even speak.

Williams watched Aung Net as he trailed after Joseph into the forest "without a backward look." He would never see or hear of him again.

TWO DAYS LATER, THE Williams-Bostock party set out, Williams scouting ahead, women and children next, elephants behind. They were heading into the high country of Manipur, where they would be hiking for more than a week. The rocky, narrow path pointed upward, and day after day, they trudged forward single file with thousands of others. Indian travelers passed by with all their worldly goods crammed into boxes atop their heads.

Conditions worsened. Cholera became an increasing problem. Dead bodies, bloated and covered in maggots, were left lying in the track. Sometimes masses of butterflies hovered above them. With no time for burials, Williams would try to heave the corpses over the steep embankments before the children caught up. Still, the "tell-tale stench" of decay would rise up, swamping the path, and the mothers would hurry their children past.

It was getting colder as they ascended to higher elevations. At night they scratched out a little area to sleep in with a thin blanket.

Some of the tea companies in India had dispatched men to build shelters along the route, but most had not been finished, and few were without piles of excrement from the throngs of earlier travelers. The rations were meager, and the hiking became more and more difficult. Everyone lost weight. Their one diversion might have been the wireless, but when they could get a clear signal, the news they heard was terrible.

On March 8, 1942, Rangoon fell to the Japanese. Looters prowled the fancy neighborhoods of the capital, racehorses roamed the streets, and fires—many set by Westerners as they left in an effort to leave nothing of value to the Japanese—burned out of control. It was not only a crushing psychological defeat; there also were dire consequences to losing the only real port in Burma. Now, Allied supplies would have to come overland from India. Given the terrain and the lack of roads and infrastructure, this would be an enormous problem.

War correspondents who had descended on the country painted a bleak picture. Without Rangoon, all of Burma was overwhelmed, and India was threatened. Thousands of refugees poured out of the city, heading northwest for India. Their numbers grew as they were joined by people from all corners of the country all headed in the same direction, clogging the few poor roads available.

With Burma behind them, the Williamses and their fellow refugees were dealing with mountains. At five thousand feet, the water situation worsened. The elephants were often denied a decent drink for more than a day, something Williams thought unconscionable. Little Treve was walking on his own now. It had become an exhausting trek for the skinny four-year-old. No matter the age, everyone was hungry and tired.

The group trudged on. Every turn in the road simply led to another turn. Finally, cornering a bend, they saw a vista open up: miles of flat plains below. They were leaving the mountains. Before them was a single road stretching out for miles and choked with other travelers kicking up plumes of red dust as they scuffed along.

All told, about six hundred thousand desperate refugees headed for India, most heading west, but some taking the inhospitable northern route through the Hukawng Valley. It was the largest migration of people in history up to that point. Only about fifty thousand were British; most were Indian. Eighty thousand may have died in the effort.

As excited as he was about emerging from the mountains, Williams saw that the very end of the trek was going to be tricky. Several ravines lay ahead, all of them bridged by spindly structures that could not hold the weight of an elephant. At each crossing, the uzis would have to steer the animals around the span—down steep banks and then up the opposite one. The uzis were warned that even if a bridge appeared substantial, they were not to attempt it. Ultimately, one did. The bridge gave out under the elephant's feet, and though she was able to cling to the bank, her rider was pitched forward. The noise and surprise sent the female charging backward in a panic. Williams saw the elephant—no rider, no pack—racing toward him. He tried to stop her by brandishing a walking stick fitted with a spearhead. It did not sway her. He had to leap out of her way as she barreled past him. She turned around then and headed in the same direction as traffic, blowing by him again. Amazingly, he saw her clear the ravine in a motion that science has said is nearly impossible—she appeared to jump it. All was well, though. The elephant, not wanting to be separated from her mates, got back in line with them.

The upside was that, at least momentarily, she had swept the path of the crowds of people. Susan and Jim tried to joke about it with Treve, but, the little boy, who had hiked a hundred miles, "just hung his head—utterly weary, and too done in to be diverted."

By the time they reached their destination, the town of Palel, over the border of Burma, in the Indian state of Manipur, the group was spent. Susan, despite her pregnancy, looked gaunt. She had lost about fifteen pounds. The elephants, too, were in poor condition, but now could be set free to bathe and eat. The animals and uzis remained in Palel while Williams and Bostock accompanied the women on British Army trucks the next 160 miles to the railway at Dimapur. Williams was grateful that the uzis would have a rest. The men "had sacrificed everything to save British women and children and to get them over the filthiest tracks that evacuees had ever passed."

Once the families were on their way, it didn't matter that the road was bumpy or that the lorries had no decent suspension; everyone was grateful to be sitting. They stopped for two nights in a large refugee camp in Imphal. Set up by the tea plantations, massive airplane hangar–like sheds made of bamboo housed hundreds of evacuees. Each family got its own eight-foot-square platform and the chance to take a bath and have a proper meal. Short messages could be cabled home.

For Susan and Jim, however, the relief of the moment was ruined by terrible news. They were forced to endure another separation.

This time officials told them that no "Burmans" would be allowed to cross into India. Jim pulled every string he had, and an exception was made for Treve's nanny. But no amount of pleading would make a difference for poor San Pyu, who would be allowed no farther. Jim promised San Pyu that after the women were safely on their way, he would come back for him. Susan observed, "He looked forlorn and lost, standing there next morning, as with heavy hearts we waved good-bye."

From Imphal, it was a 130-mile army truck trip to Dimapur. They arrived at 7:30 p.m. with the rain and were fed the kind of staples they had not seen in some time—tea, toast, and jam. At eleven thirty that night, at the warning of the whistle blasts, they boarded the train. A derailing at the first launch delayed them a day, but then the women were finally safely aboard a moving train. Susan looked out the window at Jim standing in the heat on the platform, waving good-bye. He was dressed in his usual field gear—crisply pressed after their recent laundering opportunity—but the man inside the clothes looked worn out. It pained her. He caught the change in her expression. "Don't worry!" Jim cried out to her over the sound of the train. He shouted that he was happy she and Treve were safe now. "We'll meet up again sometime soon!" he promised. The steady rhythmic whoosh of the engine drowned everything out, the train lurched forward, and they waved frantically until they could no longer see each other.

CHAPTER 22

NO. 1 WAR ELEPHANT

—————

AFTER MEETING UP WITH JIM'S TWO BROTHERS IN CALCUTTA, Susan and Treve settled in Shillong, the pleasant and mild capital of Assam, where Nick, the eldest of three Williams men, owned a bungalow called "East Knoll." Nick did not live there, but the house would be shared with another woman, Mrs. Robertson, and her two small sons. The city, with its posh British club, movie theaters, and Western restaurants, provided a surprisingly comfortable life. Their house had a nice landscaped yard and a commanding view of the snowy Kanchenjunga mountain, which is part of the Himalayas. The household even included a cook and a butler.

Knowing that his pregnant wife was being looked after and that his son was safe, Jim could focus on helping refugees. All the way back to Burma, he made good use of his elephants, this time transporting supplies and building a camp for the refugees who continued to flee west. He and Bostock even spent a few weeks running the camp before moving on. Once back on Burmese soil, they helped with road building. But so complete was the Japanese drive that in April even people squeezed up against the far western border, like Williams, were forced to evacuate. The British Army soldiers had been ordered to retreat, and the final rearguard troops were expected to go through within weeks, just before the monsoon rains broke.

Orders or no orders, Williams searched for San Pyu and Aung Net, but could not find any trace of either one. He had sent them back into Burma thinking it was the safest place for them, but by war's end perhaps a million Burmese would be dead—killed by soldiers, worked to death, or simply starved by the chaos of war.

He had another search to conduct, too, this time for Bandoola. He found the tusker safe for the time being with Po Toke, just outside Tamu. It was good to get his hands on the bull, to speak to him, and give him whatever sorry excuse for a treat he could come up with—probably a bit of his own lunch. Po Toke seemed bewildered, beaten even. He felt betrayed. He was sixty years old, and as the British fled and Bombine collapsed, he realized that he would never see the pension promised him.

What could Williams say? He understood. He turned back to the elephant. Bandoola himself was magnificent. Now in his peak years, the tusker was unequaled by any elephant, wild or working. Standing there, even with war roaring right up to him, the bull was serene.

Williams felt sure that the elephants would be vital to the Japanese and the British. It galled him to think of the animals falling into enemy hands. So he had planned to march at least two hundred out with him. But with the roads still packed with refugees, it would be impossible. He could only trust that the riders and their elephants could hold out till the British returned. The Japanese, said to be supreme jungle guerillas, were no match for the uzis, Williams figured. His men could vanish into the forests with their elephants and never be found.

Williams wanted Po Toke to do just that. And he had come prepared to help, having gathered all the cash he could. Handing the money over to Po Toke, he told him to "hide if you can." He vowed to return. Po Toke, though skeptical of Williams's promise, took the offering.

The master mahout ordered the tusker to sit. *"Hmit!"* Bandoola slowly lowered himself to the ground and the old man scrambled atop him. Williams said his good-byes and watched the elephant amble into the forest, headed in the direction of Po Toke's village in the Kabaw Valley, just east of the Chin Hills. Williams counted on

Po Toke's knowledge of secret trails and impenetrable parts of the forest to stay safe and unseen. He was thankful that the jungle could swallow up even an elephant.

Williams hiked back to Tamu. The only good news was that by this point General William Slim had taken over operational command of the British forces in Burma. The man was smart, unpretentious, and a soldier's soldier. He would become one of the most respected and beloved officers of the war. The demoralized troops needed someone they could believe in, and Slim more than fit the bill.

The organization of the defense of Burma, initially under the Far East Command in India, would never be straightforward. Slim had a lot to do, but when he took control of the Burma Corps in March 1942, he had few resources. The Japanese were committing more to the area than he could. The ratio of Japanese to Allied planes had always been lopsided, but now the gap widened to perhaps 900 Japanese aircraft against 140 Allied. The Royal Air Force was withdrawn at the end of March. British and Chinese troops continued to retreat from each stand. Mandalay was bombed, killing more than two thousand people.

The surge of refugees, which Williams was now joining, was desperate. Some people had managed to ride in cars or trucks for part of the journey, but after Tamu, real roads ended. The track toward India through the mountains was not fit for most vehicles, with the exception of Jeeps, though even those had a tough time making it. Anyone who had driven to Tamu now had to get out and walk.

Williams headed to India on foot, with just a simple kit on his back and a friend's black Labrador retriever, Cobber, by his side. Walking among a human torrent of thousands, he saw misery and sickness everywhere: families torn apart, having to make terrible decisions, perhaps leaving one dying child behind in order to save another. Relatives were separated and frantic to be reunited. Newspapers in India were full of agonizing personal ads taken out by those who had become separated from their families on the trek. Everywhere there was starvation and illness. Extreme heat, lack of food, arduous walking, and exposure to disease picked off even the youngest and most robust. One group of Bombay Burmah families had set off for India from the other side of Burma, in Siam. Out of the twenty children who had begun the journey, only one survived. Those who had traveled the longest learned several survival tricks, among them, obtaining salt by scraping and eating the dried sweat on their own skin, and when thirsty, stealing water from the radiators of abandoned cars.

As Williams followed the path on the ascent to the Manipur hills, he found two sobbing Indian children. The brother and sister were tiny and wretched. Their mother, not much more than a teenager, had collapsed against an embankment in the scorching sun. She was crumpled in the dust of the road, sick, starving, and dehydrated, as thousands trudged by her. Williams knelt by her side, cradling her. Despite the danger of communicable disease, he brought his canteen to her lips and she drank. She could not speak, but the man who had spent a lifetime with animals almost understood her better without words.

"In her eyes," he wrote, he saw gratitude, a "blessing." But also terror for her children. He felt she was wordlessly asking him: What will become of them? They looked at each other and then silently she died in his arms. "The change came suddenly, and a moment later I realised that I was left alone with the responsibility of these two children." He could not carry them for the long trek ahead. He stood frozen, gathering his senses, and then for no reason he could even articulate, he turned back with them for a short distance. A Jeep, something very rare on that road, jounced toward him, and behind the wheel was a staff captain he recognized from Tamu. Williams stepped in his path to block him. The captain immediately waved him off. "Can't be done, old chap," he was saying. Williams asked that the children be hidden under a tarp in the back, and then he threatened to throw the captain and his jaunty vehicle "down the khudside" (mountainside), if he refused. The captain agreed to take them to a camp in Imphal. "Great was the lump in my throat," Williams wrote, when the two were loaded safely into the Jeep. Later, when Williams had made it to Imphal himself, he checked in and found the siblings alive, in good health, and being tended to in the orphan section.

The monsoon season arrived in May. The deluge was as relentless as the Japanese: thunderstorms, drenching rain, and torrents running down hillsides "baring the ribs of the earth," as one American correspondent described it.

Mandalay fell to enemy forces, which continued to drive up from the southern part of the country and spread out to the rest.

On May 5, 1942, American general Joseph "Vinegar Joe" Stilwell, who had arrived in Burma just as it was collapsing, sized up the Japanese threat. He headed to India, on foot, like the other refugees, leading his staff to safety. Retreating British forces, exhausted and ragged, headed that way, too. British casualties and losses were high, and the Japanese, with their superior numbers, air support, and training, sustained few. The outcome was demoralizing. At the end of his trek, Stilwell said, "We got a hell of a beating. We got run out of Burma and it's humiliating as hell." It wasn't much solace, but at least there was news that the Japanese were experiencing a few defeats in the Pacific and on land in New Guinea.

On the home front, in Shillong, Susan gave birth in safety to their daughter, Lamorna, on September 10, 1942. Jim was with her, as he had been ordered to stay put for several months to help with timber surveys. Seeing that his family was comfortable, well fed, and safe, he carried a "gnawing ache to get back to those left behind" in Burma. Knowing that his elephants could be of real use to the war effort, he spoiled to see how many he could round up. Finally, in October 1942, as the Fourteenth Division slowly made a return from India into the border area of Burma in the south, Williams was summoned by Noel Mackintosh Stuart Irwin, general officer commanding the Eastern Army. The high-ranking general had a newly minted commission to offer him: that of elephant adviser. It was an odd position since there were no elephants to advise. At least not yet.

By the beginning of November, Williams was posted as a lieutenant colonel to the Fourth Corps Headquarters in Jorhat, Assam, which was a straight shot 273 miles north of Tamu. Eventually he would be part of the famous Fourteenth Army, which by 1944 would be a million men strong, the largest Commonwealth army in the war, whose field of operation was about one hundred thousand square miles. It was for the most part an Indian army; but with an international cast of fellow soldiers including Englishmen, New Zealanders, Canadians, South Africans, East Africans, and Chinese; and from Burma, Burmans, Kachins, and Karens, among many others. Fighting with them would be the Americans of Merrill's Marauders, as well as the pilots of the Flying Tigers.

Williams's post would come under the jurisdiction of two of the most famous officers of the war: Slim, and Vice Admiral Lord Louis Mountbatten, the supreme Allied commander of South East Asia Command, or SEAC. (Americans, not surprisingly, weren't gung-ho about fighting to help regain British colonial territories. One joke had it that the acronym *SEAC* stood for "Save England's Asian Colonies.") Of the two leaders, Williams's philosophy was best matched to that of Slim. Slim had verbalized it to some of the officers under him: "I tell you, therefore, as officers, that you will neither eat, nor drink, nor sleep, nor smoke, nor even sit down until you have personally seen that your men have done those things. If you will do this for them, they will follow you to the end of the world. And, if you do not, I will break you."

The intelligence service soon realized what a resource Williams was. He spoke Burmese and retained a mental map of every road, creek, railway track, and hidden jungle path in north-central Burma. They couldn't get enough of him. Officers peppered him with constant questions. Still, because he felt he could be doing even more for the cause if he were in Burma with his elephants, he went straight to the top. One day, during a work break, he defied protocol by walking over to Irwin's office and poking his head in to ask for a word. Speaking directly with the GOC could be dicey, especially given Irwin's reputation as a rude, even belligerent, commander with a superior sense of his own abilities.

Waved in, he got right to the point: He wanted a Jeep and his freedom. The Japanese had not penetrated as far as Tamu, and Williams wanted to get back there "to find out if there are any elephants not yet in the hands of the Japs." He had no idea how many of his old teams were still free, nor did he know how those who had been conscripted by the Japanese were being employed. His hunch was that plenty of the resourceful riders had kept their animals hidden, and that even those who had been captured were being used solely for transport—a waste of elephant talent. Only a teak man understood the scope of their ability. Building anything could be a snap since they could act as cranes where no crane could be transported, deftly lifting logs into place at a height of nine or ten feet. They could tow vehicles bogged down in mud, or haul timber for boat construction at the major rivers. Most of all, the elephants could move the army farther and faster across undeveloped terrain by building bridges and enlarging tracks. Tanks and Jeeps wouldn't be thwarted by wide rivers and deep jungle. Additionally, "elephant bridges" could be constructed with materials at hand, saving the precious modular, lightweight components of a new kind of bridge called a "Bailey bridge" for crucial hot spots. In short, elephants could help win the war.

Williams knew Burma so well that he could sketch scenes of villages from memory. Note the insignia of the 14th Army at the top.

The commander agreed.

In order to operate where he wanted, however, Williams was assigned to the Special Operations Executive, the British dirty tricks department, a much different branch than the more straitlaced Secret Intelligence Service. From that point on, he was part of the elite Force 136: soldiers who functioned behind enemy lines in Burma, didn't play by the rules, sabotaged the Japanese at every chance, and lived by their wits.

Assigned to the elite Force 136, Williams intended to go behind enemy lines in order to reclaim his elephants.

Jim, who had been writing to Susan daily, dashed off a note telling her that he was not sure how frequently she would hear from him. He would keep writing, but mail service, even by military courier, would not be reliable.

Driving his own Jeep, with Cobber the black Lab riding shotgun, and speeding south toward Burma during the most beautiful time of year, Jim Williams was himself again. Out from under army red tape and given the license to rejoin his elephants, he felt that he could finally do some good. But the wave of euphoria was short-lived.

Near the familiar village of Tamu, a potent and stomach-churning stench overtook him, enveloping his open-air Jeep. The scent was not new to him, but the magnitude was of another order. Swinging the Jeep toward it, covering his mouth and nose, he drove onto what looked like the set of a horror movie, a place one visiting journalist would dub "the city of the dead."

Here, as Williams remembered from his own departure, were hundreds of cars and trucks piled up and abandoned. When Williams last saw them six months before they were empty. Now, they were full.

He looked at the occupants, and from every vehicle they stared back at him with empty eye sockets. They smiled in horror, each mouth a toothy grinning rictus. There were skeletons sitting upright at the steering wheels, and rotting corpses leaning against passenger side windows. Every windshield framed a macabre portrait of the damned.

What had occurred was obvious to him. These were the people who had arrived too late, when the rains had started. Desperate, starving refugees had made it this far, but could go no farther as the wall of water and deep mud trapped them. Before them, the mountains were impassible, behind them, the Japanese firmly held the rest of the country. Having no other shelter, they ducked out of the pounding rain into cars, buses, and even ambulances. Without food, they slowly died there.

Williams zigzagged the Jeep around the still traffic and geared down to a stop, the vehicle shuddering as it was turned off. He stepped out. He might have wanted to run from the putrid smell, but he felt drawn in. As he walked through the silent town, he found dead bodies everywhere, all fixed in place performing the most mundane tasks—sitting upright, hunched over moldy tables, holding a telephone receiver in the telegraph office, or reclining on beds that then collapsed beneath the weight of their rotting bodies. There was nothing he could do for any of them now. He got back in the Jeep and drove away. The scene, he wrote later, told him "a gruesome story."

Setting up camp in the nearby village of Moreh, Williams quickly formed the idea to create his own irregular army. A very small one. It would be made up of a few others like him who had spent their lives in Burma: men who had been tested by years in the forest, who lived through loneliness and illness, who spoke Burmese, and understood that uzis were human beings who deserved respect. With them, he suspected he could penetrate enemy lines and sneak elephants right out from under the noses of the Japanese.

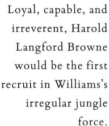

Loyal, capable, and irreverent, Harold Langford Browne would be the first recruit in Williams's irregular jungle force.

The first "hire" was Harold Langford Browne, his old buddy now with the Indian Twenty-Third Infantry Division of the British Indian Army. Browne was irregular, all right. "South African by birth and a man of magnificent physique," Williams said, "with broad shoulders and narrow hips, Scandinavian blue eyes, and hairy all over, like a gorilla." Most important were his loyalty as a friend and his affection for the uzis. He would not tolerate any colonial posturing toward them. "Harold was more loved by the Burmans than anyone I ever knew," Williams noted. "And he knew plenty about elephants."

Browne's decency and decisiveness came through in one of his first tasks—torching the city of the dead. He took the quick ride up to Tamu, poured gasoline over all the cars and corpses, and struck a match. It was a funeral pyre that was respectful of the dead, but also provided a hygienic scorching vital to the health of those who would now be working in the town.

Williams and Browne, were next joined by Stanley "Chindwin" White. The short, burly, energetic man had an essential quality that was compulsory when joining Williams's team: "Of all the round pegs in Army square holes—he was one," Williams wrote. An odd-ball. White, as his nickname implied, was acquainted with every inch of the Chindwin as a river captain. Conversant in Burmese and Hindustani, he was a crack shot, a comedian, and a bit of a jungle polymath.

"Harold Browne and Chindwin White made a grand team," Williams wrote. "Their intimate knowledge of all Burmans was extraordinarily useful." Their first objective would be to regain their elephants. Not an easy task: The Japanese, who now occupied the whole of Burma, had issued a directive ordering all uzis to report for the war effort. Noncompliance was punishable by death. And while it was true that Tamu, which was experiencing an unusual break in the monsoons, seemed to be an island for the British, enemy patrols could nevertheless be near.

Williams felt certain there were men still loyal to him who would take a risk to come back. The best strategy would be simply to put the word out that he was looking for riders and elephants. Of course, the elephant Williams most wanted to draft was Bandoola. Browne, who had spent the last several months playing cat and mouse with the enemy in the nearby forests, left Tamu for Po Toke's village of Witok on a mission to find the tusker. He had no idea what he would discover.

At the start of the occupation, Po Toke had tethered Bandoola in a remote area and spent months moving him around to avoid detection. Because Bandoola couldn't forage, Po Toke had had to hand-feed him. The elephant master had stretched the allowance Williams had given him for six months. And he had exhausted himself gathering the hundreds of pounds of food Bandoola required.

Broke and despairing, he still couldn't capitulate. He would never comply with the Japanese call for elephants. He had decided it was better to lose his beloved elephant to the forest than to the Japanese. So in an exquisite bit of bad timing, just days before Browne's arrival, Po Toke had followed his secret path deep in the jungle to Bandoola. Removing the tusker's leg chains, he told him, "Keep clear of wild tuskers and don't fight." Then he set Bandoola free.

When Browne appeared, everyone in Witok, especially Po Toke, was touched that he had risked his life to reach them. He wasted no time in outlining for Po Toke what he and Williams wanted to do. The haggard elephant man was game. He just needed to find Bandoola.

Browne also conscripted another old colleague, an "Anglo-Burman" named MacVittie, and the three men hiked back to Tamu. Williams was shocked by Po Toke's haggard appearance, but the old elephant man wanted only to strategize about finding Bandoola and safely marching him to Tamu. As eager as Williams was to secure the tusker, he insisted on fattening Po Toke up with combat rations before allowing him to go on the mission. Po Toke agreed to spend two days eating and resting. Then he and MacVittie, just the two of them in order to avoid attention, set off.

Three days later, Williams, in his hut, heard a commotion outside.

It was, as he had hoped, Bandoola. The tusker was huge and healthy, and he walked forward with Po Toke and MacVittie sitting on his neck. It was an arresting sight. "I have never seen even a wild elephant in such magnificent condition," Williams wrote. Here was his friend of twenty-two years. Courage and strength in the flesh. His gray bulk firm and sure, his step silent. There was the familiar scraping sound of skin as the elephant flapped his freckled ears to cool himself. How confident, even cocky, Bandoola looked with his jaunty curved tusks.

Williams walked forward to greet them, addressing the elephant in Burmese and reaching out to pat him. Bandoola's presence offered instant serenity. First, there was always the current of energy that seemed to pass from his skin into Williams's palm. Then the rumbled greeting that was more felt than heard. There was something more, too: Just having Bandoola on their side seemed to portend victory.

There couldn't be a more auspicious start for Williams's new work. Like the great tusker of Kipling's "Toomai of the Elephants," Bandoola would become "the best-loved and the best-looked-after elephant in the service of the Government."

Williams framed it as a historic moment. "Bandoola was presented to me to be enrolled as No. 1 War Elephant," he wrote, "the first of the elephants to fight for the freedom of Burma from the Japanese, and worthy of his glorious name."

CHAPTER 23

THE MAKING OF
ELEPHANT BILL

———

ELEPHANT COMPANY CONSISTED OF EXACTLY ONE ELEPHANT. THAT had to change. Fortunately, Williams and Browne heard that a group of uzis and their more than three dozen elephants, drafted by the Japanese, were gathering about forty miles to the east. They were poised to depart south for Mawlaik, Williams's old headquarters, now held by the enemy.

There was no time to lose in intercepting them. Williams sent runners with word that he was in Tamu waiting for them if they could make it. It was a dangerous request, but as Williams always said, it was easier to skulk by the Japanese with elephants than with Jeeps. The elephants, with their bells silenced, as they would be throughout the war, could be moved undetected at night with no headlights to give them away.

The uzis got the message and immediately headed out after dark to join Williams, entering a forested area where Japanese patrols were frequent. There were more elephants than riders, but the uzis' wives, who were accustomed to traveling with them, pitched in as substitutes.

The next day, Williams excitedly watched forty elephants stroll into camp: twenty-five good, mature working elephants, plus fifteen extras—young (under twenty), pregnant, with calves, or thin and out of condition. He walked out to greet them, patting trunks, slapping flanks, and speaking to them in Burmese. They formed the nucleus of No. 1 Elephant Company, Royal Indian Engineers. Bandoola's comrades-in-arms. From that moment on, Williams knew for sure that his uzis, wherever they were, would risk their lives to rejoin him.

He and Browne pitched camp on the northern outskirts of Tamu, in the village of Moreh, to establish their elephant camp headquarters. It was the start of a campaign to attract greater numbers of uzis and elephants to their side. Gathering them was perilous work, but that was expected of anyone in Force 136, those authorized to penetrate enemy lines. Williams made his way through danger zones with the help of his network of informants—the villagers who were the eyes and ears of the forest. He received astonishingly accurate and swift intelligence on the movement of the enemy.

Again and again, he went out himself to escort uzis and elephants "safely through the lines after dark, with bells, if any, muffled." Later, air travel helped him cover more ground. Aboard a two-seater observation plane, he penetrated enemy lines, swooping down low over villages to drop personal invitations.

One day he and the pilot ventured eighty miles into Japanese-held jungle. Williams first tossed out "a chit to announce myself" from the air. A few minutes later the pilot landed them safely in the middle of a paddy field. People came running out of huts, fields, and forests, shouting his name and expressing joy that he was still alive. "They informed me that there were Japs all around, that the Japs were very angry because I had been taking their elephants away, and that there was a price on my head."

He stayed only fifteen minutes. But a few days later, these very villagers had managed to smuggle forty more elephants to him. He was building his army.

General Slim himself was amazed by the loyalty shown to Williams. After all, his men and their families were civilians and not subject to military law or discipline. They could do as they pleased. Slim said, "That they stayed, in spite of hardship, danger and separation from their homes—with at one time what seemed like small prospect of ever returning to them—was the measure of Elephant Bill's leadership and of their trust in him." Elephant Bill: Williams had earned a new nickname among the soldiers. No one was sure who started it, but it caught on fast. Word of his exploits was spreading quickly, too.

Jim hoped Susan wouldn't hear of them. In his letters to her, he played down the hazards, telling her instead about the antics of Browne and White, and the joy of reuniting with his elephants. Susan's letters, in return, sustained him. The baby Lamorna was healthy, and Treve was growing in haste. The little boy was full of mischief—he had mastered the art of chewing betel nut, spitting the red juice as the Indians did. Susan was shocked to report, too, that she had caught the little girl next door showing her "fanny" to Treve.

Jim's unit had cobbled together harnesses and dragging equipment for two dozen elephants just as the first request for work came in. The commanding officer of the Royal Engineers of the forward division wondered if the animals might help haul some logs for a bridge. The sappers, or soldier engineers, were delayed, and he thought Elephant Company could prepare for their arrival. This was when Williams heard the true calling for his charges: not just as draft animals or as cargo bearers (which army brass always seemed to be pushing for) but as master bridge builders.

He asked what sort of bridge was to be built. "Blue prints, pink prints, and even white prints were produced from a pig skin portfolio," Williams wrote. Architecturally, it was grand. But to simply cross a shallow two-hundred-foot-wide waterway in the middle of the jungle? Williams realized he had to speak plainly: He thought of the structures he was taught to build so long ago and had been using and making ever since. "Picking up a pencil and paper, I drew an 'Elephant Bridge' with a rough calculation as to the number of logs it would require, number of elephants available, and said, 'That will take 15 days to complete, and we want no sappers—it will carry anything on wheels or tracks.'" The heaviest load it would have to bear was ten tons, and Williams assured the officer that his homely little jungle span could withstand twenty. The chief engineer had wanted a wide bridge, configured for two-way traffic, but Williams told him two simple bridges, the kind the elephant men and elephants were accustomed to building, set side by side, would do the trick.

The elephants could drag practically anything, including broken-down vehicles, but Williams knew their true calling in the war would be as master bridge builders.

They shook hands, and the officer said he'd come back with word from the higher ups. Williams didn't bother waiting. The harness equipment was sorted for twenty-five elephants, and the uzis were given their marching orders for the sizes of the logs required. A nod from a passing brigadier was all he needed. They started work on December 2, 1942, and were finished ahead of schedule, on the fifteenth, precisely when a whole brigade and their trucks passed over it.

ON JANUARY 3, 1943, Elephant Bill was summoned to a meeting with the famed colonel Orde Wingate, who would be leading an elite guerilla unit called the "Chindits" (a derivative of the mythical Burmese lion called the "chinthe") behind enemy lines in Burma the following month. Wingate, whom *Life* magazine called "a big-headed Scot who reads Plato for fun," planned to operate deep in enemy territory in Burma using a radio to coordinate supply drops by plane. Wingate was known for his eccentric, imperious behavior, which won him few friends. He was so unorthodox—he might tie a raw onion around his neck as a snack or greet visitors naked—that his sanity was often questioned. Just the year before, while depressed, ill, and taking a powerful antimalarial drug, he had tried to commit suicide by stabbing himself in the neck. But Wingate was a brilliant and fearless tactician, and Williams recognized his remarkable intelligence as the colonel grilled him about the terrain on an illuminated map of Burma in the commander's war room. Wingate hoped to blow up enemy-held bridges and railways.

Orders poured in for Elephant Company to build more bridges all around the Moreh-Tamu area, where the Twenty-Third Division was now headquartered. Williams was raring to go. But he always needed more elephants. And so did the Japanese. "This battle for elephants," the *Daily Mail* of London said, "has constituted an impor-

One of the many articles written about "Elephant Bill" during the war.

INDIAN INFORMATION   Regd. No. L-5060

An unusual prisoner of war—the first Japanese army elephant to be captured in the advance down the Tiddim road.

"ELEPHANT BILL" IS BACK ON THE JOB

"ELEPHANT BILL"—he knows 600 elephants in Burma by name and can recognise each one on sight—is back on the job again in the Tamu area "re-enlisting" elephants the Japs have been using.

"Elephant Bill" is Lt.-Col. J. H. Williams. His official designation is "Elephant Adviser to the 14th Army."

He will long be remembered in Burma for the remarkable feat he accomplished when, arriving in Tamu during the 1942 evacuation, he managed to get away, by elephants to Imphal, all the women and children belonging to employees of his firm, the Bombay-Burma Company.

This meant sending the elephants with their human cargo up the telegraph track which climbs straight up and down the sheer mountain sides. The Tamu road was still to be built.

Later Lt.-Col. Williams organised the elephants for the first Wingate expedition.

"Elephant Bill"—he first arrived in Burma in 1920—certainly has a way with elephants, writes an Indian Army Observer. They allow him to operate on them without a murmur.

Recently when the Japs were cleared from the West Bank of the Chindwin, and an elephant was brought in, he recognised it as one he had worked with as a forest manager before the war.

When it is all over, "Elephant Bill" hopes to sit back for a while and write a book about elephants. It ought to be good.

RED CROSS RELIEF WORK

Red Cross has so far received over Rs. 28 lakhs in cash contributions for its famine relief work but taking into consideration milk supplies received as gifts as well as those paid for by Provincial and State Governments, the value of the milk the Society is distributing is estimated to be nearly Rs. one crore.

Issued fortnightly by J. Natarajan, Principal Information Officer, Government of India. Printed in India by E. G. Tilt (Manager) at The Civil & Military Gazette, Ltd., Lahore : Communications for the Editor should be addressed to the Bureau of Public Information, Government of India, Lahore, and not to the Printers.

tant part of the general war out here." On the ground, both sides maneuvered and fought to acquire them; from the air, elephants were legitimate targets. One foreign correspondent described what happened when American Volunteer Group air units spotted Japanese soldiers moving supplies on elephantback: They "machine-gunned the elephants, and when that failed to drop or even halt the beasts, the flyers dumped fire bombs, hoping to start stampedes." Another report from the *Daily Mail* said that as the Japanese captured the elephants and used them to haul supplies, "We had no alternative but to attack the elephants wherever we could find them. More than 50 were killed by RAF bombers."

The fact that securing the elephants was a matter of dangerous warfare became apparent immediately. A group of uzis from the Karen minority got word to Williams that their group of forty-nine riders had twenty-nine elephants hidden in the jungles along the Chindwin. They wanted to join Williams, but the fifty miles that separated them was daunting. Here there were not only elephant camps that had gone to the Japanese, there were also plenty of enemy troops who were on the trail of Wingate's Chindits.

Knowing what they were up against, Williams requested the party of men and elephants be escorted by two platoons. But the guards never materialized. Instead Chindwin White and some Indian soldiers (so nervous, Williams said, they had "the jitterbugs") tried to make do. By sticking to dense jungle, they safely marched forward, mile after mile. By the time they reached the Chindwin it was sunset—not the best hour for a crossing, but they would try. Unfortunately, the elephants weren't game. As Williams well knew, the timing of river crossings was an elephant prerogative, involving that complicated psychological process of determining whom to follow. That night, no one stepped forward to swim in the darkness. The men knew better than to attempt any bullying. The crossing would have to wait till morning. The fettered elephants were left on the east bank, and the uzis were ferried over to the safer west bank for the night.

Within hours, Japanese soldiers had quietly infiltrated the area. When they stumbled upon the elephants, they hid near them, waiting to ambush their returning riders.

In the morning, oblivious to the presence of the enemy, White gathered eight boatloads of uzis and paddled back toward the elephants. As they neared the bank, a Japanese officer jumped out from behind a tree shouting "Banzai!"—a cry that often panicked Allied troops. The water around the boats exploded with gun and mortar fire. All the boats capsized, three Indian soldiers and one uzi were killed, two uzis were wounded, and the elephants were lost to the Japanese. The rest of the men swam back to the west bank. They would never know what became of the animals, but years later Williams heard that several had been shot out of a misguided belief that as the working animals of Karen rather than Burmese uzis they would be unmanageable.

The work of recruiting more elephants went on. During the hot weather of 1943, seventeen new animals were drafted. It wasn't enough. There were requests for bridge building throughout the slice of land that sat between the border of Manipur and the Chindwin River, but mainly they were working in the Kabaw Valley, a place that had earned the name "the Valley of Death" among military men during the exodus in May 1942 when refugees died in the hundreds of malaria, smallpox, dysentery, dehydration, and plain exhaustion. The Japanese were also becoming more aggressive just to the south, and there were constant clashes between the British on patrol and infiltrating Japanese soldiers in the area Elephant Company worked.

It was only getting worse. In a position directly south of Williams's, in the coastal area of Arakan, a large, months-long British offensive had gone badly. Everything from problematic command structure to equipment failure to weary soldiers was to blame. The toll of those killed and severely injured was three thousand—more than twice what the Japanese had sustained.

It was time for regrouping, retraining, and reorganizing.

IN MAY 1943, WILLIAMS was called back over the border to Jorhat HQ in Assam and asked hypothetically what would happen to Elephant Company if all of the British soldiers in the Kabaw Valley were ordered to retreat to India once more before the monsoon broke in June.

As much as he missed Susan and the children, he didn't like the idea at all. This was a pivotal moment in time. Despite the British losses, the average soldier believed that the tide was turning—or at least he could imagine the tide turning. That was because of Wingate and the behind-enemy-lines Chindits. They had done some damage to the Japanese, whom average soldiers had considered invincible. Even Slim had said with equal contempt and admiration that the Japanese soldier was "the most formidable fighting insect in history." But the Chindits had traveled as lightly as possible, skirting the enemy and blowing up bridges and railways. There were finally some successes everyone could celebrate.

British Army soldiers could conceive of beating the Japanese. The Chindits might have become a crack fighting force, but they hadn't started that way. Many of them were just regular guys. "A regiment of the United Kingdom's city-bred tinkers, tilers and bookkeepers matched their wits against the Japanese and the jungle and won—not decisively, but won," the Associated Press reported. "They had proved Brigadier Wingate's contention that quick training could make Allied troops equal to the jungle and the Japanese."

Wingate lost a third of his men in the effort. And hundreds who did return were so debilitated they could no longer serve. Slim would call the mission "an expensive failure." Nonetheless, the whole endeavor made great propaganda: The courage and determination of his effort boosted British morale. Because of the Chindits, they began to feel that they were as fit for jungle fighting as the Japanese.

So Williams was angry that just when it seemed possible that the British could retake Burma from the enemy, HQ was thinking of pulling back for a retreat during the monsoon. It would dismantle everything he had been working toward. And, worse than that, it would mean that once again his riders and all the local people who had provided help and support would see the British turn tail. He couldn't bear it.

There was nothing he could do but try to keep his elephants in Burma. And the only way to accomplish that was to stay put. He argued to be allowed sit out the monsoon in country with Browne. Army brass might have thought that was an impossible thing to do, but Williams had spent nearly twenty-five years in monsoon-lashed jungles. He got his way.

He returned to Tamu, only to find that the local villagers had planned a *pwai,* or celebration, for the army. How ironic. Here the Burmese were planning to honor the very men who were abandoning them once again. Williams decided to keep the news of the retreat quiet.

On June 12, 1943, Williams received a letter of gratitude from HQ. Lieutenant General Reginald Savory wrote:

My dear Williams,

I came round to see you yesterday to say goodbye but unfortunately you were out. This note is to bid you farewell and to thank you for the great assistance you have always given me. My job would have been very different and much more difficult had we not had your elephants to haul timber and make bridges, and it is a comfort to me now to know that your Elephant Camps are so situated that they can help in the maintenance of our forces in the Valley if necessary throughout the monsoon.

I also have to thank you for the help you have given me in passing on information of the country based on your deep local knowledge.

On the rainy evening of June 17, 1943, Williams watched in the fading light as the last army trucks rumbled over a low causeway the elephants had built. "What the riders thought I don't know. All I could tell them was that Browne and I were remaining with them."

CHAPTER 24

ELEPHANT COMPANY
HITS ITS STRIDE

———

WILLIAMS AND BROWNE, ALONG WITH COBBER, THE LABRADOR, hunkered down through the summer monsoon season. "Those really were, I think, the bloodiest rains that two Europeans ever weathered in Burma," Williams wrote. It was a long slog, and, in addition to the discomforts of ceaseless rain, Williams began to feel a recurrent burning pain in his abdomen, which he decided to ignore. He was still able to get mail from Susan. Ringworm had plagued the community in Shillong, and Treve, though he never contracted it, was forced to wear a hat as part of a campaign to stop its spread. By now, Williams's niece and nephew Diana and Michael were living with them again, too. And Susan's letters were full of stories of high jinks—Michael sometimes picked chilies from a bush in the yard and bit them, even though the burn would send him scurrying up the driveway crying every time. Diana and Treve often climbed out their second-story windows onto the thatched roof and dove into each other's rooms. Susan loved having them all together again—four little faces looking up and listening each evening as she read from a translation of scary German fairy tales.

In the early stages of Williams's monsoon stay, Gurkha soldiers— Nepalese recruits—universally respected and loved by the British, came to Moreh, many sick with fever. By this time the Japanese had cut off supplies of quinine from the Dutch East Indies, causing a shortage. Williams managed to acquire a ration of the drug, which he administered, but it was too late for some. "I had to make fourteen crosses by the end of those rains," Williams wrote.

Elephant camp soon became a hub of activity and information. The military men who were deciding where, when, and how the troops could return from their retreat were constantly dropping in. The strategy to recover Burma was under debate for months on end, and specialists of all stripes and branches landed at Moreh to study the situation. Elephant camp turned into a hostel. A visiting reporter counted a major general and four colonels among one day's tally.

Their journey was an easy commute from Imphal to the north since the two areas had been connected by what was a novelty throughout the region—an all-weather road. Imphal, despite its status as capital of Manipur, the eastern province of India, had been a provincial complex of villages inside a six-hundred-square-mile teardrop-shaped plain. But under Lieutenant General Geoffrey Scoones, Fourth Corps (part of Slim's Fourteenth Army), it grew into a vital logistical base, complete with a communications center, an airfield, ordnance depots, cottage hospitals, and ample supply dumps.

On Tuesday, November 23, 1943, four war correspondents made their way to Moreh to visit elephant camp and the increasingly fabled Elephant Bill. It was a matter of military security that they not reveal their location. So the dateline on Philip Wynter's dispatch read SOMEWHERE IN BURMA. Here, the reporters found a small, comfortable compound of a few huts surrounded by barbed wire and guarded by Gurkha soldiers. By midnight, the group had settled in at Williams's bamboo home and were knocking back Indian-made rum, smoking cigarettes, and trading stories. This even though the enemy was so close, one wrote, that lookouts could see "the smoke of Japanese cooking fires." Nonetheless, it was a party.

The newspapermen wanted to know everything about the elephants, and Williams was happy to oblige with story after story of his life with them. Despite their fun, the men were there to write the dangerous ever-shifting story of the war in Burma. "Our troops occupy Burmese villages one day, and the Japanese are there the next," Wynter observed.

> A form of guerilla warfare is in progress on the central section of the Burma front. The front line is a pattern of outposts and patrols scattered along the mountains and jungles of the frontier.
>
> British troops, tough Indians, and Burmese guerillas are operating in and behind the Japanese front line. Their weapons range from tommy-guns to bows and arrows, and their transport from jeeps to elephants.

He reported on how dirt tracks were being converted to real roads thanks to No. 1 Elephant Company. "They use elephants for laying teak logs in making bridges and culverts."

Williams was popular with the press not only because of his personality and the unique work he was doing; he also provided some relief to the unrelenting stories of the misery of the soldiers. Jungle life was killing them.

All the things Williams had become acclimated to—the heat, the threat of disease, the terrain—were daunting and deadly to the new soldiers. They might hike across hot dry plains one day and then be mired in mud with fifteen inches of rain falling the next. Roads turned into rivers. Tracks became quagmires. After the rains came smothering heat and humidity that made their skin bloom with fungus and rot, and caused corpses to bloat and blacken.

The men were tormented by blackflies, mosquitoes, ticks, and leeches. They suffered from dysentery, cholera, dengue fever, scabies, trench foot, and the infection of skin, bones, and joints called "yaws." And most of all malaria.

During a particularly bad spell, while 10 soldiers a day were evacuated because of wounds, 120 were left suffering from malaria. Eighty percent of American forces contracted dysentery in another siege, but they kept fighting. Some had to go into combat with the backsides of their pants cut away.

There was also the simple, hard-to-describe strain of jungle life—

pitch-black nights, vegetation so dense that it made them claustrophobic, no water at all, or water rendered bitter with purifying tablets, encounters with deadly snakes. The stress of battle could drive soldiers to nervous breakdown, or what they called going "jungle happy." And their plight would be a protracted ordeal—the fighting in Burma would be the longest campaign of World War II. As one military man said, "No other army fought for so long. No other army met such a ferocious enemy. No other army had to cope with such atrocious conditions."

As bad as it was, eventually the tide began shifting, and the British finally held the advantage. A number of factors were involved.

After some questionable leadership at the beginning of the engagement, the troops now had a savior in Bill Slim—the most capable commander imaginable. The number of Allied soldiers at last was superior. The supplies were better. They had bigger, finer tanks. And, crucially, with the addition of American airpower, they owned the skies, which meant soldiers on the ground could dig in and claim turf knowing that they would be continually resupplied.

Something else changed, too. The Japanese began to struggle. They had overstretched themselves, fighting too many enemies on too many fronts. The soldiers in Burma were not supported. And they hated the land, calling Burma *jigoku,* or "hell." The packaging of their food supplies rusted, and the contents rotted, while the American K ration stood up to tropical humidity. Among the Japanese generals, there was a saying: "I've upset Tojo. I'll probably end up in Burma."

Slim's Fourteenth Army, better trained and better equipped, eighty thousand to one hundred thousand strong, was geared to retake Southeast Asia. With the end of the monsoons, troops stormed back into Burma.

There was a new burst of activity in and around Williams's camp, and the work of the elephants increased. The engineers had gone from skeptical to astonished by the elephants' finesse. In fact, Williams wrote, "The demands for the elephants here, there and everywhere were more than I could cope with." The animals had become so sought-after Williams had to tackle a couple of issues.

One was an ongoing argument about which branch they belonged to: the Royal Indian Army Service Corps or the Royal Engineers? Williams always considered the elephants bridge builders and not pack animals. This point was obvious, he said, but still "the problem was far too difficult for General Headquarters to decide." All in all, he found it reprehensible that this kind of paperwork and red tape sometimes got in the way of their mission. He was a victim of it personally, too. His rate of pay was up for debate for a year among the army clerks who couldn't calculate an elephant adviser's precise grade. (He was furious once when he learned that little Diana, Treve, and Michael had begged for money from soldiers in Shillong after hearing him talk about his financial woes.) The pay scale war went on until Slim himself intervened on Williams's behalf.

The other issue was the elephants' proper care. Elephant Company was dispersed among many different troops. The animals, in various-sized groupings, were sent off with their uzis to help where they were needed. Williams couldn't be with all the elephants all the time, so they were left in the hands of soldiers who didn't understand the sensitive creatures at all, and didn't listen to the uzis. The Gurkhas would all pile onto the elephants' backs and use their ears to sling their rifles on. British troopers would order the uzis to tie the elephants up at night when the animals needed to go find fodder. When they did follow the basics of elephant care—freeing the animals after a day's work, for example—disaster sometimes struck. One Gurkha sentry covering the late shift saw a loose elephant nearby. Either unnerved by the approach or lusting for ivory, he shot at the elephant's head. Williams raced to the scene and happily found that the tusker survived. The bullet had entered just under the eye, traveled down through the cheek, and then ricocheted into the chest. The cheek wound was the size of a "five-shilling piece." That was easy enough to treat, but the bullet itself, which had lodged in the chest, had to be removed surgically. Still, the tough bull recovered enough to be back on the job in three weeks.

Throughout the war, Williams would treat elephants who had sustained gaping wounds in bombing raids. Others recaptured from the Japanese had blistered, weeping burns where acid from the batteries they had carried had leaked onto their backs. These were "some of the most appalling wounds" he saw on the conscripted elephants. It was not unusual in these cases to encounter wells in their flesh half an inch deep. If the animals were lucky enough to reach Williams, the first thing he did was relieve them of any pack duty. Then he treated them with a dusting of M&B powder, or M&B 693, a fairly new sulfonamide antibacterial, which, in fact, was trusted enough to have been used to cure Winston Churchill's pneumonia in 1942.

One of the best elephants in Williams's care—Okethapyah, or Pagoda Stone—was killed by a land mine. The officer in charge was so distraught by his death that he drove twenty miles over a rough, dangerous track to tell Williams.

Occasionally, Elephant Bill would get calls in the middle of the night on the field phone about tuskers nosing around camp seeking salt bags or other rations. If the camp was close enough, he would drive over to shoo the animals away.

Williams issued notes on elephant management, but still there were problems. Finally he refused to supply his animals to any troops who consistently treated them improperly.

All of the injuries and illnesses prompted Williams to create a sick camp, or elephant hospital, on the bank of the river Uyu, a tributary to the Chindwin. It grieved him to see his animals suffering. His career had been spent trying to make the lives of working elephants better. Now he saw creatures who had no understanding of war being sacrificed to it. "To inspect the wounded and sick elephant casualties in that sick elephant Camp, pained me as much as a first field dressing station filled with the wounded men," he wrote.

The area in and around elephant camp was still chaotic. The war was intensifying, and there were enough elephants to form a few brigades. While some of them were kept in smaller bands, Bandoola was part of an elite group of forty-six elephants working eight miles north of Tamu. Williams placed him there not only because he deserved to be among elephants of highest rank, but also in order for the tusker to stay close to headquarters in Moreh. Bandoola's group did the most complicated and toughest road and bridge building. They were the ones shown off to reporters, which meant that just as Williams gained fame, so did Bandoola.

Time magazine wrote, "The most famous elephant assisting the Indian Army is Bandula, named after a famous Burmese general." The story promoted an exaggerated legend about him: "Bandula's mahout receives 'danger pay,'" the magazine said, "because the elephant has already killed two keepers." An Australian newspaper claimed the count was up to five.

Life magazine's reporter described the actual work of bridge building in detail. He watched as an elephant placed a log next to several others. "The elephant kneels down and nudges the log gently with his head, then stands back and has a look at his work. If it isn't right yet, more shouts and kicks come from the uzi. The elephant kneels down once again and gives another nudge, headwise. The job is right this time so the uzi and the elephant go to get another log."

That was the basic work of the elephants, and it went on, almost always with the sound of gunfire in the background. Bandoola remained fit and healthy, yet the war affected the animals. With their freedom so often curtailed, they became restless and agitated. As a result, during this time, Bandoola challenged and killed two other tuskers, who had to be replaced from other groups. In a logging camp, Williams would have separated such big, cocky tuskers.

It was a terrible loss in every way, but, Williams wrote, "One forgave Bandoola anything." Despite some deaths and the occasional lost animal, Elephant Bill was building up his herd. Throughout the war, it would be a numbers game—gaining 3 elephants here, 50 there, until at one point he had accumulated 1,652.

ELEPHANT COMPANY WAS HITTING its stride. And, as usual, the animals were showing Williams how smart they were. For one thing, they became accustomed to the roar of engines far faster than he had predicted. And, for another, they figured out how to get what they needed. They weren't receiving their peacetime rations of fifteen pounds of salt a month, but they discovered where they could find

Even during the war, time with the family in Shillong meant children, dogs, and mischief.

the mineral themselves. They kept track of drop zones, and at night snuck over looking for bags of salt that had broken open on impact or that lay nearby undetected.

Williams was completely immersed in his world of elephants, but two days before Christmas 1943 there was a miracle: He was given

During leave, Williams could drive his Jeep to Shillong to be with his family. Here, he is shown with Susan, Treve, and niece Diana.

seven days' leave to visit his family in Shillong. Treve had just turned six, and Lamorna, whom Williams hardly even knew, was a little over a year. Williams drove four hundred rough miles west in his Jeep, which now sported a red elephant insignia on the side, arriving on the family's doorstep on Christmas Eve. Despite the gut pain continuing to plague him, Jim reveled in the happy, if short, reunion. He taught the children how to climb trees—hoisting himself up to demonstrate—and warned them to always keep "three bits" of themselves attached while moving only one limb at a time. He made "telephones" for them out of matchboxes and string. And he nursed an injured carrier pigeon he had found, convinced it was vital to the war effort. Treve was especially proud to show the neighborhood children his father's Jeep.

Susan and the cook prepared the best meals they could from their stocks. Jim's favorite was kidney pie and mashed potatoes. They had evening cocktails again like in the old days. He slept soundly. And he could open presents with all the children laughing and playing around him.

At four o'clock on the chilly dark morning of January 1, 1944, Jim was back behind the wheel, heading east with an Indian assistant. The headlights illuminated the dark tunnel of the roadway—walled in on both sides by thick jungle. He was lost in thought as he swung around a corner and his headlights flashed on what at first glance looked to him like a calf. As he came to a stop, he realized that there "in the middle of the tarred macadam road," was a lordly male Bengal tiger in his "finest full winter striped coat." The five-hundred-pound cat sat up and blinked into the headlights, his warm breath forming small cloudbursts in the cold air. Startled perhaps, yet lazily confident. His size was astonishing, and as he slowly unfolded himself to stand up, his great head came level with the windshield. With every inch he gained as he stood up, the Jeep seemed to lose an equal amount, shrinking to the size of a toy. And Williams said, "I felt myself shrinking into a toy driver." Reflexively, he honked the horn.

The tiger turned his back to saunter down the road. Williams noted his furry testicles swaying as he disappeared around the bend.

Behind the wheel, Williams lit a cigarette and gave the animal time to clear the road.

As he sat there, he considered what had happened. He could have taken the opportunity to bag a trophy. But he found himself identifying with the cat, who was as reluctant to leave the warmth of the road as he himself had been to leave his family. And, besides, Williams had gotten over the urge to kill wild things long ago. As it would turn out, he would have to confront the animal twice more that early morning. Each time, the tiger refused to enter the forest, only running to beat the Jeep to the next bend. Ultimately, when the cat did vanish for good, Williams popped the vehicle into high gear, with "mixed memories of Christmas-trees and tigers" floating in a reverie.

On his return to Moreh, there was finally news he had hoped for. The army was getting serious about returning in force. All elephants were called upon to work on improving the main road from Tamu eighty miles south to Kalemyo. Rumors were swirling that the Japanese planned to march right up the Kabaw Valley, exactly where the road building was going on. He saw more men and more activity. With the movement of British forces and equipment into the area, and Allied planes streaking overhead, Williams was certain they planned to take a stand.

Imphal, not actually even in Burma, would be the center of the action—the place both sides had fixed as a turning point in their campaigns.

The Japanese were plotting a massive assault on this important Allied military complex (as well as Kohima, a supply pipeline city to the north). Its strategic location and rich stockpile dumps would enhance their control of Burma and enable them to stage their next move—an invasion into the heart of India. General Mutaguchi Renya ordered only light supplies for his troops, believing that victory would be swift and that his men could live off the land in the meantime.

The Allies, on the other hand, were certain that the Japanese had overestimated their hand. Slim had accomplished the seemingly impossible—he had moved tanks into the jungle-clad terrain. He also possessed better airpower for fighting and resupply. The Allied strategists planned to dig in, luring the enemy so far west they would overextend themselves. While the stocks of the British soldiers would be replenished by plane, their adversaries would starve. All of this planning was top secret; Williams knew nothing for certain of the long-range view, but his deduction was right.

A preview of what was about to happen in the fight for Burma played out on a smaller scale in February 1944 in the south, in the area known as the Arakan. The Japanese still had the advantage of speed and surprise, but they were beaten because they were outnumbered and, crucially, the British now had planes on their side.

The Arakan brought the first solid victory in Burma. But emblematic of all the fighting in the country, the victory was bloody and savage, and had come with an enormous toll. There were horrors large-scale and small. During the clash, the Japanese captured and murdered thirty-five patients and medical staff at a field hospital. In fact, the winning Allies lost more men than the retreating Japanese: eight thousand casualties for British and Indian forces; five thousand for the Japanese.

In early March, Williams received a call on the field phone from the divisional commander that seemed to contradict his theory about a British resurgence. The officer sounded dour and invited Williams to lunch with General Geoffrey Scoones and Major General Douglas Gracey at Imphal the next day. It was unsettling.

Williams immediately walked over to Browne's hut to tell him. Browne, seated at his table, folded up the crossword puzzle he was working on, and brought out the rum. They tried to hash out what might be in store. It was no good. They were mystified, and no amount of intelligent guessing would get them anywhere. They were in such a funk that they couldn't even muster their usual cocktail-hour banter. They ate an early supper and retired.

At headquarters the next day, Williams was led into a tent that served as the divisional commander's office. The information he was about to receive was considered confidential. He was asked how long it would take him to march all of Elephant Company out of Burma. It sounded to Williams an awful lot like another retreat.

"My heart missed a couple of beats, in bitter disappointment," Williams wrote. Still, he walked over to a large map on the desk. "Knowing the exact position of every elephant in the Valley," he said, "I estimated it would take five days to assemble all animals." He said there would have to be two rendezvous sites: one at Kanchaung, eight miles north of Tamu, and one at Mintha, another twelve miles north of that.

He was told to keep all information under wraps, but received permission to divulge the details to Browne. A secret code for the last-minute exodus was established, one that Williams would receive on the military phone at elephant camp.

Williams drove off in his Jeep. He stopped at the satellite elephant camp near Mintha to tell them, as cheerfully as he could feign, to pack up. Then in the blackness of the jungle night, he drove back down to elephant camp. It was a morose nightcap with Browne as he laid out the situation. The two men went off to their bunks, trying to sleep for a few hours despite the sound of heavy gunfire in the jungle.

What Williams could not know was that the elephants were being evacuated to keep them safe during the hell that was about to erupt. The orders from HQ heralded the largest offensive against the Japanese to date in the effort to reclaim Burma. This would be the decisive campaign, the turning point in what until then had been a demoralizing arena for the Allied forces. Now there was air superiority, organizational streamlining, and better training and morale. In addition, the British had managed to transport tanks to Imphal, something the Japanese thought impossible considering the jungle-covered mountains that enclosed the plain. If everything went according to plan, Elephant Company would return to bridge building in a matter of months.

CHAPTER 25

A CRAZY IDEA

─────

For the next four days, Williams and Browne set about organizing the elephants. Reserve rations were dumped at the rendezvous sites, and the uzis' wives and children were transported by truck to safety. C. W. Hann, who had temporarily replaced Stanley "Chindwin" White, would be in charge of Bandoola's elite group of forty-six elephants in Kanchaung, eight miles away. Browne would go up to Mintha to lead the ragtag group of thirty-three there to Imphal. The ethnic Karen uzis, who had lost their elephants during the ambush at the Chindwin, gathered at the elephant camp compound with Williams. They would be divided into two groups to assist the elephant teams.

On the morning of March 16, 1944, as the Japanese were hitting Tamu hard, everything seemed set for the elephant evacuation, and at noon, the camp phone rang. The voice on the other end uttered the secret code to withdraw. Word also came that the Japanese had crossed the Chindwin just to the north and were gaining ground quickly. The enemy would play into Allied hands, but not on the Allied timetable. Slim had anticipated their movement, though the Japanese were risking everything, coming earlier than expected and in greater strength.

The first phase was going to be rough. The enemy, with their own strategy for victory in Imphal, plotted a three-pronged advance—from the south, east, and north. Williams could not know any of that, but he sensed from the increase in battle noise that enemy troops were marching his way. He jumped into his Jeep and raced up to Kanchaung to tell Hann and Browne they must start at dawn the next day. Williams unfolded a map and drew out the route for Hann to follow to Imphal. Hann seemed stunned by the enormity of what was being asked of him and the very real risk of being discovered by a Japanese patrol. If you can't do it, Williams said, the only alternative is to shoot the elephants here and now. That appeared to stiffen Hann's resolve. When Williams left, he told Hann: "Au revoir, and the best of luck. You can make it. You must. Don't worry if you lose any animals en route, but push on with your main body."

From Hann's camp, Browne went on to Mintha to tell the men what the plan was. He then traveled back to elephant camp to help Williams close it down, figuring he would run up to Mintha again at dawn. He went to bed while Williams kept working. They could hear the sound of traffic as the army moved men and equipment all night. At midnight on March 17, 1944, the field phone rang: The Japanese had crossed the Chindwin to the north in strength. They were invading via two main roadways. The good news was that British soldiers were headed north beyond Mintha, where Browne needed to go.

Hann departed nearby Kanchaung on schedule, headed for Imphal. Browne left elephant camp at first light to meet up with the second group of elephants. When he reached Mintha, he would send word back. Williams had a bad feeling about the Mintha group, though he didn't know why. In camp, he waited. It was nerve-racking. Hour after hour dragged on. He called HQ, reporting that the Kanchaung elephants were on their way, but the movement of the Mintha team remained a mystery. He was ordered to abandon elephant camp immediately and head for Imphal to prepare for the arriving elephants.

Before Williams could begin burning sensitive maps and materials, Browne returned "all bandages and lots of blood." His truck had been cruising along at 40 mph when it "took a tree square in the nose, and a hell of a mess was the result." The truck was totaled. He had never made it to Mintha. A passing medic had fixed him up on the spot, and warned him that no traffic would be allowed through now as "scrapping" with the enemy was expected within two hours. He had rushed back to elephant camp hoping to catch Williams. The two men called on higher-ups to allow them to drive to the waiting elephants at Mintha. Their request was repeatedly denied. The Japanese offensive made travel on that route impossible. They could not reach the elephants. Though the chance of it was remote, they hoped to connect with the group in the hills as they headed to Imphal.

Hours later, with the sounds of war raging all around them, they drove out, worried about the elephants and what the evacuation as a whole meant. "The Japs were back," Williams wrote. "I was again on the run, and had lost touch with thirty-three elephants." After spending the night at the midway point of Palel, they reached Imphal on March 18, 1944. The good news was the continued Allied air superiority: "Make no mistake, we control the skies in Burma," crowed the *Daily Express*. But for Williams, there was only chaos and concern. He learned that the Mintha elephants had never even started their march, but had been dispersed into the jungle where they at least stood a better chance of evading the enemy.

There was no word at all from Hann and Bandoola's party. It was beginning to look as though Elephant Company was finished, lost in the very hills the Japanese were infiltrating.

Defying orders, Williams and Browne refused to just sit and wait at Imphal. In the chaos, no one would know where they were, so they put miles on the Jeep, covering every road not yet in Japanese hands. Each time they bumped into British troops headed north, Williams would ask, "Have you seen any elephants?" As anxious as they were, this always struck the fighting men as comical.

Williams checked in at brigade headquarters and learned how close the Japanese were. On March 20, 1944, there was a titanic clash between Allied and enemy tank divisions near Tamu in which all the lighter Japanese tanks were destroyed. It was an auspicious bulletin, but not the information Williams was looking for. A brigade major manning the field phone finally hung up and turned to Williams:

"Sorry, Sabu. Your elephants were mistaken for Jap elephant transport in the high bamboo, and were shot up coming down the slope from Sibong." Williams felt sick, but it soon became clear that this was a small group of unknown elephants, and not Hann's band. Still, time was running out. Senior officers began to think all was lost and that Williams and Browne should just evacuate. So the two men again dodged their superiors and continued their search, heading back into unsecured zones in their Jeep.

Finally, with no time to spare, Williams located Hann. He was within two days' march of the Imphal Plain. He had been through hell, getting so close to the enemy that he had had to travel at night to evade them. But he made it, losing only one animal. Bandoola and the others were safe. Williams made sure they were on track and then drove back to Browne with the good news. At HQ, he received orders to head north and west of the Imphal Plain with the remaining forty-five elephants once they arrived.

By now Williams understood his evacuation was temporary. His elephants were prized animals. In fact, army officials estimated the value of this group in what today would be hundreds of thousands of dollars. High command wanted them far from the raging fighting. There would be no bridge building in this heated battle, but the hope was that afterward there would be much work for the elephants once again.

Getting out of the Burma-India borderland would not be easy. Between Imphal and the safety of British-held Assam were a series of five mountain ranges, five to six thousand feet high. It was wild country, rugged, dangerous, and not mapped in any detail. It was terrain Williams was unfamiliar with, and the elephants weren't equipped for. Furthermore, there were no highways, and the few existing tracks were likely held by the enemy.

Even under ideal conditions the journey would have been nearly impossible. Williams had to plot their escape route and order supplies. Physically, he was not well. A tooth had begun to throb, and the pain in his gut that he had told no one about persisted. He needed to find transportation for the uzis' families who could not possibly join them on this trek.

He contacted a friend doing refugee work in the area and booked safe passage for the women and children of the riders, and then advanced Browne and Hann on a five-day northwest course to get them to the outer edge of the Imphal Plain. He would meet them for the start of the real trek. In the meantime, he and Chindwin White, who had now returned to the fold, set off in the Jeep to scout out the best exit point. Williams suspected that following the Barak River from where it began as just streams in Manipur would make sense. It drained into the Surma Valley in Assam, providing water and good greens for the elephants the whole way.

At three in the afternoon, Williams and White arrived at the bridge that crossed the Barak on the Imphal–Dimapur Road. They stopped at milepost 102 and were pleased with what they found. Even if it meant dealing with waterfalls and gorges, the Barak had a lot to offer, especially since the most logical route—the Silchar-Bishenpur Track—was now unsafe for travel.

By the time they got back to camp, however, news had come in that the Japanese had just swarmed the Imphal–Dimapur Road exactly at milepost 102, where Williams had stood less than three hours before. Their planned route was now off-limits. What they had available to them was merely a foot track.

Williams then went to the corps commander. Blueprinting the escape route was a waste of time. It was best, Williams argued, if they simply packed up and left. Instead of filing his flight plan, he wanted to be free of red tape so he could head out, improvising as necessary. Permission was granted, providing that at the very least, Williams would stop in the village of Tamenglong to signal he had made it that far.

For Williams, it looked like he finally had everything necessary for a departure. But, again, the picture shifted. The Seventeenth Division, an exemplary force with Gurkha battalions, had returned to headquarters through the enemy line, bringing with them sixty-nine women and children—mainly families of Gurkha soldiers who had been in Japanese hands in the Chin Hills. These refugees also needed to get to Assam. With hot spots igniting all around, no one in the military had time to deal with them, and so they were left in the middle of a war zone. They would either have to hunker down somehow, or make their own way out, perhaps with the aid of an inexperienced soldier. The odds were against them either way.

Williams volunteered to take them, knowing full well that the addition of the fragile refugees would hamstring his effort. It was going to be difficult enough to thread a group of jungle-hardened riders, soldiers, and elephants through the unmapped, hostile, and mountainous terrain. The sick women and children would slow them down, making them more vulnerable to the swift-moving Japanese soldiers. The chances were great that they would stumble into a swarm of enemy soldiers who were notorious for their barbaric methods of killing captives. The 1942 exodus was fresh in Williams's mind. The families had barely escaped that time; now the conditions were exponentially worse. There were fewer supplies to last them on a longer, more arduous, and unknown route. It was all too likely that in these higher elevation mountains the elephants would lose their footing, panic, and be pitched down the side of a cliff. And the half-starved human travelers would be susceptible to any jungle ailment.

Still, Williams said if five members of the group—the pregnant women and elderly, were evacuated by plane, he would escort the rest. His offer was happily accepted, and the development recast a dangerous quest into one now deemed suicidal.

The pessimism of all those around Elephant Company was summed up by the chief field doctor. He said that despite the brutal fighting breaking out all around them, if he were given the chance to leave the war zone with Williams, he'd refuse. "I'd rather stay here and starve, Bill," he said. Even Slim wondered how Elephant Bill might avoid capture in his "trek across pathless mountains" as "the Japanese made their great bid for victory."

Williams had faith, though, and it wasn't centered on other people. "The more I saw of men . . . the better I liked my elephants," he wrote.

He soldiered on. The elephants—including Bandoola—the sixty-four refugees, and the uzis were moved to a starting site at the farthest northwest corner of the Imphal Plain, called "one of the most forsaken spots in the world." The whole plateau was locked away from the rest of the world by dense, jungle-covered mountain ranges.

Williams slipped back to Imphal proper in order to have his bothersome tooth extracted. He would take no chances, having suffered terribly from the bacterial infection known as trench mouth in World War I. From his commanders, he received a red parachute which he was told to spread on the ground every day so their journey could be followed by air—"someone else's idea!" he said with well-placed skepticism. He had a massive undertaking ahead of him. But he possessed the finest elephants in the world, the most loyal riders, fifteen days' rations, and a case of rum from an old friend, Steve Sutherland, who had told him, "Say nothing, Bill, but if there is nothing else you will need on this Hannibal trek, I am sure you will need that." He also had twenty-five years of experience surviving the surprises of the jungle.

He was grateful that Susan was safe in India with the children. He dashed off a quick note to her, which stood a good chance of being delivered. He told her he "was commencing a trek" and said that she "should not expect to hear" from him for some time. Everything he could do to prepare was done. He left Imphal to join what was left of Elephant Company at the base of the mountains at the edge of the plain.

"I was alone again, for a short run in my Jeep to camp with my old Labrador dog Cobber," Williams wrote. "He seemed to realise the whole situation and leaning over gave me one slobbering lick, and a cheering tail wag; he was looking ahead through the windscreen, tongue hanging out with a broad grin, as if to say 'Next stop, Surma Valley.'"

Williams, Browne, White, and Hann huddled to talk through their plans. It was agreed. At dawn the next day, April 5, 1944, they would begin their journey through the mountainous, mysterious, and inhospitable borderland.

The elephants would be loaded up with the rations, the few essentials they would need to cook and sleep, and the frailest of the refugees who could not walk. The Karen camp workers were outfit-

ted with Stens—British submachine guns—and rifles. And the officers were given their instructions.

Po Toke approached Williams with bad news about Bandoola. He
was on musth, chained some distance from the rest. From the temples of the tusker's great head came a small trickle of liquid, which
was just forming dark streaks running down toward his mouth. Po
Toke and his rider would stand guard holding a spear. It was a horrible stroke of luck. "Tell him he can stay there and starve unless he
wants to behave himself," Williams said. Bandoola had an edge to
him but was not acting out. When Po Toke looked at his boss, Williams said, smiling, "I'll risk him on musth." He pointed to the range
of blue mountains to the west, and said the climb "will soon knock
the musth out of him." Williams knew the hard travel would extin-
guish the tusker's raging hormones; he just hoped that in the meantime, Bandoola wouldn't "upset the biggest apple cart I have ever
had to push."

Williams woke the next morning to familiar sounds. All around
him in the predawn cool of subtropical India came the hushed stirring of people and animals. Workers were striking tents, stoking
breakfast fires, and softly clanking buckets as the animals were watered and fed. Despite the foreboding of the morning, Williams was,
as always, charmed by the muted poetry of an elephant camp coming
to life, the way that in the morning mist, still under the dark sky, the
animals loomed huge and ethereal. Just like the little elephant boy in
one of Kipling's stories, he could look up at one of his tuskers "and
watch the curve of his big back against half the stars in heaven." Per-
meating everything was the scent he loved: the earthy, oaty essence
of the elephants.

The animals were now illuminated in the amber light of the rising sun—forty-five full-grown adults; eight babies. They were all
lined up together except, of course, for Bandoola. Williams walked
over to his friend and saw that "his musth glands were discharging
freely down his cheek but I ignored them, for this was no time for
meeting troubles half way."

At the treeless foothills west of Imphal, with the two main roads
out having been blocked by the enemy, the peculiar group began

their ascent over the only passage left them—a graded mule track. Williams drew a straight line west on his map from Imphal over the uncharted range of mountains to the safety of the Balladhun tea plantation in Silchar: 120 miles, and he knew every one of them would be hell.

The unit was large in every way possible: fifty-three elephants, forty armed ethnic Karen soldiers, ninety uzis and elephant attendants, sixty-four refugee women and children, and four officers: "an extraordinary collection," Williams noted. "What was ahead no one knew, nor did anyone discuss it."

Williams might have been disheartened except that he was amazed by "the cheerfulness of the Burmans" and the strength of the spirited refugees. Many, if not most, were unfit for a long march, but because the elephants were loaded with supplies, only the sickest could ride. "Pity," Williams wrote, "was a luxury we could ill afford."

They walked all day, the last of the stragglers catching up to the main group at dusk. Williams chose a campsite by a clean, rushing river to spend the night. There was water and plentiful forage for the elephants. The animals were unloaded and walked to the river's edge. It was easy to spot Bandoola and to see that he was placid again. "As I had hopefully predicted," Williams wrote, "that first day's march knocked all the thoughts of springtime or whatever musth might be described out of even Bandoola's head and brawn."

The next morning, they were up and out early once again, as they would be day after day. It was torture for the refugees who had begun the expedition in poor physical condition, yet they never complained. Williams was touched by their stoicism. Each morning even the lame would insist on walking. Only about seven of the sickest would mount elephants from the start. As each mile passed, the number of those riding elephants would increase so that by the end of the day, about a dozen refugees would ride into camp. But again the next morning, tired and sick women and children would gamely walk for as long as they could. For their part, the riders were so attentive to the children that they were given extra cigarette rations in compensation.

After a couple of days, Williams and White split off. Fulfilling the one promise to HQ, the men were diverting to Tamenglong to send off a signal. The two would then rejoin the main group, which was heading due west to an area Williams had identified as Haochin.

In the village, Williams and White found chaos and fear. The outpost had only thirty armed soldiers, one Indian officer, and an inexperienced civil servant. And the movement of the enemy was unknown. The men were waiting for Thomas Arthur "Tim" Sharpe, a member of the Indian Civil Service who had not arrived when expected.

Williams sent his message relaying his intended route, and he requested an airdrop of supplies for the men stranded in the area. He and White decamped as quickly as possible, unknowingly passing right under the noses of a "strong" Japanese patrol of fifty men. Williams and White made it back to the elephants, but just behind them, Sharpe, who had, apparently, been following in their tracks, was captured and, they heard, bayoneted repeatedly before being shot by the enemy.

The group climbed higher and higher, starting every day at sunup and not stopping until just before sundown. Even then there was little comfort. Nights were lashed by chilling rains. Illnesses got worse, healthy travelers became sick, hungry, and sore; everyone was dropping weight. "The cold, at the altitude we now were, brought on attacks of malaria amongst the women, and we soon had a number of fever patients to look after," Williams wrote. "There were cases of sore feet, dysentery, pneumonia and abscesses of the breast."

"Some of the elephants were in need of first aid as well," he wrote. "But we could not let our invalids rest and recuperate; we had to push on. Every day we marched from dawn until after five o'clock in the afternoon, always in fear of a Japanese ambush."

Then it got worse. The game trails petered out and vanished completely in the thick vegetation. Every step the elephants would take had to be cleared by track-cutting and digging parties. The women who felt able-bodied insisted on lending a hand—using jungle knives to slash at undergrowth and bamboos. Williams noted that the more treacherous and hard-won the travel became, the more beautiful the scenery: lush greenery, stunning vistas, mist rising up from the valleys.

They kept going. He figured they had now reached five thousand feet. "The great beasts were painfully slow in climbing," Williams wrote, "and Browne had difficulty, owing to some of the older animals nearly collapsing." Somehow, as always, Bandoola thrived. He was "the pride of the forest," Williams wrote.

The map continued to fool them. Villages marked on it had long evaporated. People shifted their home base often. But graves and other clues to recent habitation allowed Williams to roughly follow the indications sketched out.

On the ninth day, Williams was scouting ahead when he came to an area "far, far off the beaten track," where the map seemed to register an escarpment running north to south, parallel to a creek. Sure enough, he found the creek and good fodder for the elephants. The group could stop early and have a chance to rest up—something they had been campaigning for—in the comfortable, lush spot.

Since everyone else was a long way behind him, Williams indulged his curiosity. He crossed the creek and continued toward a point in the ridge that from the looks of the map seemed the most manageable spot to scramble out of the next day. He thought he might as well check it out while he had the time.

Plunging into the thick vegetation, he found it was slow going. The climb was quite steep and the bamboo dense. Unpleasant for him, it would be punishing for the elephants—but not impossible. For two miles of the reconnaissance run, he thought the route would be the way out, as onerous as it was.

Suddenly, however, he came to a withering sight: an insurmountable wall, "a sheer rock face escarpment," 270 feet high. Williams wrote, "My heart sank." It was taller than some of the pyramids he had seen in Egypt. Just looking up at the summit was dizzying.

The wall had to end somewhere. He turned to his left and painstakingly traced the base of the cliff heading south. After a mile there was no change, "not a single place," he said, "where I could have possibly climbed it myself. There was no question of an elephant climbing a perpendicular cliff."

Experienced jungle salt that he was, Williams did detect an area where the thick vegetation had been slashed probably a year before. Near it was a scree—an area of tumbled rock, providing a few footholds. He surmised that this may have been a natural exit for some agile nomad in the area. Still, while an athletic forest dweller could maneuver his way up, it simply wasn't a place most of his party, never mind an elephant, could climb. They would have to search for a way around the impenetrable wall of stone, no matter how arduous the going.

Nonetheless, he marked the spot, slicing a large blaze on a tree with his knife, in the unlikely event they could find no better outlet. Exhausted now, he slashed his way back to the creek. Waiting for the elephants, Williams focused on their predicament—it would take at least two days to sort out their strategy, and this would be as good a place as any to rest the animals and allow them to feed and bathe.

The elephant bells were still silenced since the threat of the enemy remained, so just a faint rustling announced the arrival of the large group. The elephants appeared in single file, each with a rider, some carrying children. Slowly, quietly, methodically, the grand procession of gray gathered by the water, and the air began to hum as the elephants grew excited in anticipation of being freed from their loads. Their foreheads plumped and vibrated as they rumbled, their faces pinching into what looked like tiny, sweet grins as they squeaked.

Williams spoke to the men and the refugees, explaining the problem. His audience was initially somber, but when he announced that this would require a two-day standstill, the women cheered. Williams couldn't help being amused by their delight, but he did explain, "that there was hard work and serious trouble ahead, not because there was no path, there had not been for days, but that it was impossible to get on until we had found an ascent and then dug a path up the escarpment."

While the riders unpacked the loads from the elephants' backs and brought the animals to the creek for bathing, the women gathered their clothes, even stripping off most of what they had on, to do laundry.

Before sunset, cook fires were burning, freshly scrubbed clothes were strung up, and little makeshift beds had been set out for the children. Williams, Browne, Hann, and White ate their meager rations and agreed that three parties would set off in the morning to survey the area. That night everyone slept well knowing they would stay put for a while.

At dawn the next day, the British officers, each with a band of men, were off to the escarpment—Hann would travel its base north, White south, and Browne would assess the climbing at the landslip. Williams stayed in camp, tossing a grenade in the water, providing the grateful refugees a bonanza of fresh fish.

Browne, the blue-eyed "gorilla"—so called because he was tall, strong, and athletic—slashed his way quickly to the tree Williams had marked the day before. He stood with his team at the bottom of the cliff and looked up, studying potential foot- and handholds. There wasn't much, but he figured he'd give it a try. Scrabbling, sweating, and continually calculating his next move, he grabbed at any protruding rock and hefted himself upward. Skin scraped, knees banged, he managed to get himself to the very top of the ridge. Once up, he hiked out a way and discovered two things: a small trail that led south to the larger Silchar-Bishenpur Track and on into Assam; and a lively village of Chin people—a large ethnic minority with many different tribes and clans spread throughout the border area of India and Burma. They spoke a Tibeto-Burman language that Browne could not understand, but still, there was no better man from the elephant party to make contact with the locals. Williams always said that Browne was the Westerner beloved above all others by the people in that part of the world. He had a natural rapport. And so it was that he spoke with the villagers about the landscape and best way to travel. When it was time to find his way back down the escarpment, two men hefted their spears and volunteered to accompany him.

Back at camp, the South African recounted to Williams what he had found: It was possible to reach the top, but just barely. He worried about Williams's vertigo—he had a horrible fear of flying in planes—and if it acted up, they'd have to blindfold him. His new friends told him that the route was, in fact, the most accessible portion of the whole escarpment. He mentioned that at the top of the ridge, they would be close enough to reach the Silchar-Bishenpur Track, the jagged but well-worn route through the mountains that connected the Imphal Plain to the town where they were headed. But both men agreed that would not be an option. In fact, "That was the one place we wished to avoid," Williams said, "as until we had crossed over the track to the west, I could not feel that we were clear of a likely chance of meeting with a Jap patrol, and my orders were to avoid trouble, not look for it."

Ultimately, Browne's judgment squared with Williams's—if White and Hann returned empty-handed, they were out of luck. Most of the humans in their party could not make it up the escarpment, never mind the elephants.

They had a long wait. The travel was such rough going, even without climbing any rock, that neither White nor Hann returned until dark. Hour after hour, mile after mile, they had spent the entire day looking for a way out. They never found one.

Apparently, the escarpment spread limitlessly, north to south, with no letup, as though the earth simply vaulted dizzyingly to a new height right there. It was no surprise that the local men were right: The slight landslip that Browne had summited was the sole accessible point. The only alternative was to turn south or go back the way they came, and both would have meant marching directly toward enemy lines. Williams didn't know how they would make their way around the obstacle, but he knew they couldn't retreat.

The thought of landing in the hands of the Japanese was horrifying to any soldier serving in Burma. Williams knew that even the women and children would not escape their cruelty. In Hong Kong and elsewhere, the Japanese had bound and bayoneted captured soldiers and nurses alike.

As the war went on, troops witnessed evidence of sadistic treatment of other soldiers at the hands of the Japanese. One frontline fighter in Burma said, "It's strange: after the initial few days I wasn't worried about being killed, but I was really concerned about being wounded and captured because they had a habit of tying our wounded to a tree, leaving them overnight, and then using them for bayonet practice the next day. On another occasion a couple of our chaps had their private parts cut away when they were captured and I can only imagine the horrors and the pain that went with bleeding to death under those circumstances."

When they saw how "the Japs butchered all our wounded," many soldiers would reciprocate in kind. "We were not merciful to them for the rest of the war. We didn't take any prisoner," one said. Another recalled finding a dozen captured Gurkha soldiers tied to trees. "They'd been slit right down the middle by the Japanese. They were cut in two and that really infuriated us. We thought, 'Right, if we see a Jap again, there's no mercy.'"

Women, just like the men, were disemboweled, too, but often raped first.

Being taken prisoner could be worse. The fate of POWs in Japanese hands was a ghastly one. In Burma, men were routinely starved, beaten, and worked to death in camps overrun with disease. By war's end, the tallies showed that of the British soldiers captured by Germans, about 5 percent died. Of the Britons taken by the Japanese, the death toll was an astonishing 25 percent.

Years later, historians would try to explain the complicated reasons for such behavior. In part, they would conclude, it was a cocktail of harsh discipline, national fervor, religion, childhood education, a cultural embrace of obedience over individuality, and a demand for utter allegiance and bravery that was enforced with physical punishment. But to an Allied soldier in the field, it didn't matter why. They simply never wanted to find themselves at the mercy of the Japanese.

That night, Williams could make only a couple of decisions with confidence—rations would be cut starting immediately. However they intended to get out of this mess, he knew it would add days to the anticipated travel time, and food would run out unless measures were taken preemptively. The near-starvation regimen was doing nothing for the mysterious and searing pain in his midsection that nearly doubled him over at times. But it had to be done.

He also decided that ditching the elephants wasn't an option. It was a consideration so unfathomable to him that he never even seriously considered it. He had seen elephants that had once been in enemy hands, and he was furious about their treatment: They had been kept in poor condition and even had their tusks sawn off, right to the sensitive root, for the ivory. "The way in which the Jap had elephants 'tipped' was criminal," Williams said. It would not happen to Bandoola and the other creatures he had spent his life with.

THE NEXT MORNING, THEY spread the red parachute out by the creek, as instructed by army superiors. Williams had no expectation that a passing Allied plane would spot them. Then he led the scouting party out—Hann, Browne, White, Po Toke, another senior elephant man, and the two guides from the Chin village. The group fought their way once again through the jungle to the landslip. At its base, everyone stood sweating in the heavy daytime heat, swatting bugs against their skin, and staring, heads tilted back, at the sheer rise. There was one very narrow ledge around the face of the cliff high up, and a few outcrops of rock just below it. Was it enough to do them any good?

All of them had to test the wall that day—Williams included. "I was not blindfolded," he wrote, "but I did many crawls on all fours!" Somehow, he made it all the way up and then managed the even scarier descent.

Maybe it was desperation or an aftereffect of the adrenaline released during the climb. But back on solid ground, an idea began to surface—a preposterous solution that they didn't even believe themselves: They would cut steps into the rock linking the natural ledges to create an elephant stairway. And they would complete it in two days' time.

No, it was impossible.

Or was it? The cliff was composed of porous sandstone. Cutting into it was feasible.

Existing ledges weren't ample enough for the elephants' footing. And, yet, there was a fix for that, too. The brush sprouting from the inner wall could be hacked away, gaining make-or-break inches of width for the stairway.

An elephant stairway. In a kind of communal madness, as they talked, they began to persuade themselves it could work. They refined the plan, hashing out the details. Tentatively, they began to accept the idea, brainstorming over the calculations.

Eventually, they had to grapple with the literal elephants in the room: What would the huge, ungainly animals do? Even with the maximum amount of engineering they could render to the escarpment, would it be enough to accommodate them?

Williams had seen elephants do some amazing things, but nothing like this.

CHAPTER 26

THE ELEPHANT STAIRWAY

———

WILLIAMS KNEW AT THE OUTSET THAT THERE WOULD BE SEV-eral places where the elephants would essentially have to stand on their hind legs to reach the next step, as if negotiating a ladder—and all the while, the animals would be able to see the astonishing drop to the jungle floor below. That's if they could be persuaded to even initiate the ascent in the first place.

What if the uzis got them started, and halfway up one of the elephants began to balk or even tried to turn around? It was too grisly to imagine. The falling animal would crush everyone and everything below. The frenzy would be contagious.

But what about the corollary: If panic can spread across a group of elephants, how about confidence? This was the lesson Williams had gleaned from the river crossings, and it was the insight that the entire operation hinged on.

So, could an elephant leader take this on? And who? They knew when presented with a wide waterway that they were expected to swim. But brought to a steep stone ladder, they might not know to climb. This time, the elephant riders would have to divine the answer—somehow absorb what the elephants knew. If Williams were to attempt it at all, he knew men would have to set the order of the lineup. Through the entire discussion, Po Toke had kept silent.

Po Toke's opinion was important, but Williams knew he would speak only when he was ready.

While the others began the long hike back to camp, White went up and over the escarpment with the two locals. They would check in at the village to hire as many men as possible for the work of clearing and cutting.

Elephant Bill had a lot to think about. And the farther he got from the escarpment the more doubt entered his mind. No one had ever even heard of such a thing happening. Hannibal, crossing the Pyrenees and Alps with his war elephants, perhaps. But had they encountered a hazard like this? There had always been scholarly disagreement about Hannibal's exact route. Williams knew this would be a totally novel task for his elephants, who had been living a strained life ever since the war started and whose condition had suffered on the current march.

The whole way, Po Toke kept to himself. The old man wasn't letting on. Finally, when they made camp, Po Toke, like a jungle oracle, spoke. "All will be well, Thakin," he said, addressing Williams with the traditional address of "Master." "Bandoola will lead."

He gave his benediction. Still, Williams wondered if Po Toke could really believe it himself. He so wanted it to be true that he dared not press him. In Williams's quarter century in Burma, Bandoola had never disappointed. Now the knowing, agile, self-assured elephant might just pull off a miracle.

The plan was on, and as often magically happens in thick forest, people materialized to help. White had gathered about twelve men with good jungle knives, and that very afternoon, instead of returning to camp, he brought the party to the landslip. They began their work from their vantage point above the cliff, working their way down.

White joined the others in camp by evening, with everyone determined to get a good night's sleep.

Better fed and rested than they had been in days, "every fit man and woman in the camp was on that road next morning at dawn," Williams wrote. They assigned four teams to different sections of the cliff face. All agreed that Williams should be nearest the base, he said, "in case I got giddy and fell over!"

The entire crew worked as hard as they could—sawing steps into the stone or clearing jungle growth from the inner wall where there already was footing. Williams was struck by their good humor.

Just before sundown, the workers stopped and looked at the continuous, rough staircase zigzagging up the cliff face. There was no better test subject than Williams himself, so, tired but game, he headed up. He had to crawl on all fours occasionally, but not as often as before. And he appreciated that wherever possible, brush was piled on the outer edges to obscure the terrifying view of the drop to the floor below. He made notes and calculations about necessary adjustments.

He scrabbled down. No doubt it was better. But was it good enough? He couldn't say for sure. "One thing we knew," he wrote. "There was no turning back."

At camp that night, they focused on food and rest. And in the morning, they returned to the work site for one more full day of building the elephant staircase. Hours of backbreaking work continued, and before sunset, they all stood assessing the remarkable sight before them.

There was no denying that there were still two hellish points where the track was squeezed and precarious. At one, a series of steps no wider than an elephant's foot had been carved out. At the second, it was questionable whether a narrow rim would have the structural strength to withstand the weight of the elephants.

But after forty-eight hours of grueling work, it was done. Both Po Toke and another senior elephant man felt the rock had been modified to the full extent possible and they agreed, as Williams put it, that "if we could not do it now we never would." Williams was anxious—all these lives were in his hands. Over the years, his colleagues had teased him about how much he believed in the elephants. Maybe this time he had overestimated them.

He could only head back to their Spartan little camp and pray that everyone rested, that sleep would come to the minds racing with anticipation. Final instructions were solidified: Williams would head up first, then Po Toke would walk just ahead of Bandoola with his rider; the big bull would lead, and then the other elephants would start. The animals would carry their normal packs, as well as their riders to guide them, but no refugees. The women and children would go next; those who could not climb would be carried by the men. There was to be no talking.

That night the group ate by the campfire. The elephants, who could not wander freely in this salad bowl of vegetation, were tethered nearby and served large piles of forage gathered by their riders. The animals were always a little restless when confined, but they had plenty to eat and seemed content.

Everyone bedded down, the fire dwindled, and the sounds of the night descended. There were small noises from the big elephants—the sandpaper scrape of an ear, the snaps of stems as they fed, and the soft, moist grate of their chewing. There were rumbles, also—to those who loved the elephants, they were as soothing as a cat's purr. From the humans came snores, murmurings, and restless shifts in position. Even extravagant dreams could not match what might happen the next day.

Dawn came quickly.

Camp was broken quietly and solemnly. Williams wore the same jungle uniform he had for years—khaki shorts and shirt, canvas high-tops—and made a solitary walk through the wet green forest to the escarpment while everyone was still in camp. He had intentionally isolated himself, perhaps because he didn't want his own anxiety to affect the elephants. Confidence, or the lack of it, he always said, was something they picked up on with acute sensitivity. This was one of his ten commandments of elephant life.

When Williams reached the landslip, there was just enough light brimming on the horizon for him to begin his climb. Dizzy, he crawled upward on all fours. He made it over the worst patch—the stairway—climbed another two hundred yards, then forced himself to crouch down to wait. High above the jungle, he sat stone still, listening. There was the sound of rushing water from the creek below, and, as if to reinforce how much was riding on this risky endeavor, the "distant thuds of gunfire" from the Silchar-Bishenpur Track to the south. The fighting was catching up to them; Williams could hear that. What he couldn't know was that the Japanese were taking a hammering.

He would have two hours alone. "Many were my thoughts," he wrote. Among other worries, he thought about Susan. By now she would be hearing about the great battlefield Imphal had become, and she'd be sick with concern. It was enough to set off the pain in his stomach, which had grown only more acute during the trip.

With Williams sitting midway up the elephant stairs, lost in thought, the uzis broke camp, took their positions, and led the elephants single file to the cliff face. Elephant Bill felt their arrival more than he heard it. But given his problem with heights, he couldn't peer over the edge to watch. What he didn't see was Bandoola, rider atop his head, and Po Toke behind him, striding right up to the base of the escarpment. When he got there, Po Toke commanded with quiet confidence: *"Thwar."* "Climb." It was an order Bandoola understood from negotiating piles of teak logs.

The elephant placed his two front feet on the first narrow step. Then, with incalculable strength and balance, he drew his hindquarters up and stood with all four feet on the tiny ledge.

He stayed motionless for a minute, then two, then three. For nine full minutes, the elephant seemed to ponder his next move. And then he decided. It was exactly like those moments at river crossings, when a young female became the leader with a resolved plunge. And it came just when those watching thought he was going to tumble backward. Bandoola drew up his front feet—again, slowly and carefully—and placed them on the next step. And so it went. Silent, deliberate, precise. Upward.

About an hour later, Williams, waiting anxiously and still unable to even glance downward, was startled. Bandoola's great head and tusks materialized before him like a god's, filling the sky. Man and elephant were eye to eye. Williams peered into that big, dark eye fringed with enormous lashes that he knew so well. There was confidence.

Far from precarious, Bandoola seemed as secure as the mountain itself. The elephant was standing nearly erect, like a person, and in slow motion he heaved himself entirely to the next step. The uzi atop his head kept peering down as Bandoola expertly, delicately, precisely stepped into position, his cushioned feet nearly swallowing up each stone rundle.

Williams's depiction of one of the most incredible moments of his life: Bandoola climbing the elephant stairway.

Williams moved upward and, daring to look down, he could see through the elephant's legs. And then there appeared a figure: Po Toke was following closely behind.

Williams turned, without uttering a sound, and clambered the rest of the way up. Success was far from certain, but he "prayed for good luck."

He would wait at the top two more hours to see Bandoola again, knowing there were no rest breaks for the animal; each step was a test of strength, balance, and trust.

Altogether, it would take the elephant more than three hours from base to summit, where Williams now waited. When Bandoola appeared at the crest, Williams noted, "My relief and excitement cannot be expressed in words." The eleven-thousand-pound animal had done what was asked of him, and it took him to the very limit of his endurance. It was plain to see the toll the extraordinary climb had taken—for an hour after Bandoola reached the top, his legs continued to quiver with involuntary contractions.

What a relief it was to be able to place a palm against the animal's side and know he was safe. Williams could feel the familiar bristle brush sensation of the elephant's hide that always left his hand tingling. He might not have wanted Bandoola to discern his trepidation at the beginning of the mountain climb, but he surely wanted Bandoola to read his emotion now. A silent knowledge passed between them. To Williams, Po Toke, though outwardly solemn, seemed to be suppressing a giddy sense of accomplishment as well.

One by one then, all fifty-two of the other animals completed the ascent. Not one fell or refused to climb. Williams, the man who thought elephants were capable of anything, was humbled by their achievement. It was a wonder.

"I learned more in that one day about what elephants could be got to do than I had in twenty-four years," he would write. "It was a moment of greatness, a heroic moment in which Po Toke had his full share."

The British adventurer who had spent his life in the company of elephants felt, high up on the mountainside, that he had witnessed the ultimate in the bond of trust: "the climax of animal-man relationship." Everything he had learned from elephants and about elephants was put to use in one stroke: All those lessons about trust, confidence, the meaning of leadership. The way they had always intuited his intentions. The fact that they could assess situations. That they were loyal. That their courage surpassed even their physical strength. That they knew, just as Ma Chaw had, that Billy Williams was their good friend. Here was nothing less, he wrote, than the validation of his "life's work."

Years later, General Slim, speaking of this climb, would say, "This is the story of how a man, over the years, by character, patience, sympathy and courage, gained the confidence of men and animals, so when the time of testing came that mutual trust held."

Elephant Bill felt the enormity of it.

After the animals had ascended, the refugees materialized, the last of them arriving at dusk. "No day ever seemed longer," Williams wrote. Everyone had summited, but they were not yet safe. The top of the ridge was an uncomfortably vulnerable berth to sleep—after all, they had been listening for hours to close gunfire. But with sundown, they had no choice. There could be no more movement in the dark. Williams hoped his luck would hold out one more night, for in the morning, they would cross into territory that was beyond the reach of the Japanese. It was the last time they had to post sentries.

Staying on the ridge was better for the elephants, anyway—all of them had experienced even greater trembling in their legs than Bandoola. Everyone rested.

The next morning, they began their descent down to the Barak River, a waterway that eventually becomes part of the Ganges Delta at the Bay of Bengal. The slope was steep and punishing in its own way, but the footing was good and there was no sheer rock.

Once they reached the water, Williams decreed an extra day of rest and recovery for the elephants. There would be the luxury of a good scrub down for them, including time to soak and to drink as much of their bathwater as they could take in. Good forage along the banks of the river provided hours of relaxed eating. And without threat of Japanese patrols, they could be given a little more freedom. What a relief to know that any loud sound—a cry from a child, a trumpet from an elephant—wouldn't reveal their position to the enemy.

Of course, even without assassins at their backs, there was still a week of arduous travel ahead. And by now, some of the children had come down with fever. The group would follow the river, which was a sure route to Silchar, but one marked by quicksand, mud, swamp, and stands of bamboo and cane so dense they were nearly impenetrable. It was a wonder the gear wasn't stripped off the elephants' backs as they squeezed through.

They were nearly two weeks out and fast approaching the end of the rations, which had been calculated to last them fifteen days. The map was not always reliable, but Williams figured that all told, they might have to march more than twenty days before reaching help. The only consolation was that the last portion would be through easier country.

Every day, they hiked nearly to the breaking point and always on empty stomachs—in the final stretch, rations for the officers were down to half a cigarette tin of rice a day each, supplemented by whatever the jungle could provide for the pot. There were still enough supplies for the women to make chapatis, the traditional flatbread that the men had with jam.

Fortunately, they came to a village where they purchased a pig for roasting. After an escape by the animal and an argument with the seller, two free-roaming pigs (the villagers always let them out to forage) were shot and cooked. When someone else in the village tried to extort money from Williams over damaged banana trees, he felt it was a sure sign they were reentering civilization.

Yet they still had much wild ground to cover.

Out of the mountains, they struggled through swamp. At one point, they hiked for eight miles in a riverbed with knee-deep water and a bottom so muddy it pulled like quicksand, Williams wrote. Adding to the misery, the jungle crept not only right down into the water, but sometimes the bamboos grew straight across, so the travelers couldn't even hug the banks. Slashing at stands of bamboo protruding through the surface of the water often left sharp stems that could cut the feet of those following. The children and some of the women hopped aboard the slow-moving elephants. Others who walked on their own found their clothes to be an impediment and stripped them off. "It was no time or place for modesty," Williams noted, and "they were quite beyond caring."

It took them twelve hours—from 5 a.m. to 5 p.m.—to cover only ten miles that day. At night, when everyone was "just dead beat," they were grateful to find one "open patch" of land. Williams, wet, exhausted, and nearly skeletal, sat down and spread the map out once more. Unless the vague cartography was misleading him, it looked as though they had just one more march before they reached the tea plantation.

In the morning, everyone geared up. But it was decided that, as they drew near to the location where they expected to find the plantation, only Williams, nine elephants, and the sickest of the refugee children would proceed. Since they would be arriving unannounced, a small party would be the gentlest introduction. The remaining group would simply wait and rest up till word was sent back.

At the front, Williams led Bandoola—the only elephant who, throughout the ordeal, had remained in good condition. On the big elephant's back was a pannier loaded with eight Gurkha children, all in such high fever that their little heads drooped over the edge. "I don't think there was ever an elephant so powerful but with such a fragile cargo," Williams recalled.

As usual, when Williams acted as scout, he traveled a good distance ahead of the elephants. Alone in the forest, he advanced through the dark shade till the world opened up to sun.

"I had the astonishing experience," Williams wrote, "of walking right out of the wall of dense jungle into the open plain of the tea estate—an ocean of green tea, as far as the eye could see. I had come out exactly where I had planned on the map. There were doves cooing. I felt a lump in my throat, and could hardly believe my eyes."

About a mile away, he could see "a large bungalow typical of so many planter's bungalows in Assam." He said a private prayer of thanks that the children burning with sickness were not far behind him and would soon reach a hospital. It was April 26, 1944—three weeks after his caravan had left the Imphal Plain with supplies for only fifteen days.

The house was built upon a *tillah*, as they called it in the area, a small hill just forty or fifty feet higher than the sea of green tea planted for miles around it. "As I approached," Williams would recall, "I could see a figure in a white shirt on the verandah. . . . A man hailed me in a Scotch tongue": "Faur are ye comin' fae an' faur are ye gaun ti? [Where are you coming from and where are you going to?] You'd better come in for a dram!"

Williams said there was nothing he'd love more. When he stepped onto the porch, he saw a lovely table set for breakfast. The planter, James Sinclair, a middle-aged bachelor, introduced himself and offered hot coffee and new-laid eggs. As Williams tucked into the meal, he explained the plight of the refugees. Sinclair had heard a rumor about the journey, but he had thought that it was the Japanese leading elephants in his direction.

When White appeared with the children atop Bandoola, Williams rushed out to tell them that Sinclair had already arranged for the estate's doctor to attend to them. They were whisked away to receive food and immediate care.

At last, Williams could get to a telephone and call in to Silchar proper, still twenty miles away, to alert the civil authorities. He arranged for the refugees to be taken into a well-run camp. Knowing the women and children were safe, Williams said, "would be my greatest relief." Before sundown, all the Gurkhas were settled in the city.

That night Williams and his men relaxed in luxury. He and White enjoyed the indoor plumbing, proper dinner, and clean sheets that Sinclair offered. Somehow, two bottles of rum remained from the case handed to Williams in Imphal. They opened one now and shared it with their host. Browne and Hann, with the other bottle in their possession, camped out with the elephants and the uzis. The air was crisp and the surroundings beautiful. Overhead, the sky was crowded with stars. To the elephants, too, tea country was a dream: a buffet of greens and plentiful water for drinking and bathing.

The next morning, with Sinclair's help, the men established the elephants and uzis in a camp nearby. Williams planned for them to stay for a while.

To start fulfilling his administrative duties, and despite his fear of flying, Williams grabbed a military plane and traveled southeast to the city of Comilla to check in with his superiors. They were shocked he was alive. None of the RAF planes had ever spotted the red parachute.

Williams also tracked down the location of the Karen uzis' families. They were living in a refugee camp in another part of Assam, and he sent Browne and White with two senior elephant men to visit them and bring back news to their husbands. Arrangements were made for the families to be reunited later.

Within two weeks, Williams made his way over to check on the Gurkha refugees. They had been transformed. Well-fed and scrubbed up, they were healthier looking than Williams had ever seen them and anticipating the next phase, in which they would rejoin their fathers and husbands.

When this was all taken care of, Williams made his way to Shillong to find his own family. "He looked as thin as a scarecrow," Susan wrote. To her, Jim's journey had been nothing more than hearsay. Now, seeing him in her own home, she could at last believe it. He wasn't in her arms long. Almost immediately he was admitted to the hospital, the horrible burning in his abdomen diagnosed as a duodenal ulcer. The frequent pain would persist for the rest of his life, as the simple cure of using antibiotics for the condition was a long way off. After six weeks' recuperation—in the hospital, and with Susan at East Knoll—Williams returned to his elephants.

He secured long-term accommodations for what was left of No. 1 Elephant Company. The elephants, he said, needed a long rest after what they had been through. So they would stay for about four months in one of the greenest, ripest, most beautiful corners of the world, only a quick two-mile hike down the road from the bungalow where he was staying.

Williams battled the administration, which attempted to transfer the animals to Delhi as part of the Indian Army, and he withstood the wrath of the tea planters who didn't want to lose their crops to the hungry herd. He secured months of peace in the green Eden of Assam for the elephants. It meant rest and plentiful food for Po Toke and the other elephant men he had worked with so long. Eventually, their bridge-building services would beckon once again, and Williams would move his group back to Burma, where their work would change the course of history. In part due to the 270 bridges they built from local materials, lightweight prefabricated sections were available to construct the largest known Bailey bridge, which was built across the Chindwin at Kalewa in December 1944. It was a decisive logistical coup. Without that bridge ensuring the flow

Kalewa Bailey Pontoon Bridge
December 1944.

Williams sketched this Bailey bridge, which was built across the
Chindwin at Kalewa in December of 1944. Historians say the
elephants made this logistical coup possible.

of men and supplies, the winter campaign might have ended in nothing more than a standoff instead of a victory.

But that would come later. At the moment, the animals needed relief, as their lives depended on it. And by the summer of 1944, the Japanese were on the run. For now, Bandoola and the other fifty-two elephants would be "in safety from the horrors of war."

Williams visited the tusker in his green refuge and, as usual, brought him sweet tamarind balls. In the shade of some trees, he had Bandoola lower himself to the ground. He stood close to the elephant and fed him, watching the animal's eyes halfway close in satisfaction as he noisily ate each treat.

For the elephant wallah, who had always experienced melancholy during great transitions, this was an especially tough one. His life with elephants was coming to an end. He couldn't see all the details of what was ahead, but of this he was certain: He would return to

Burma, the Allied forces would continue their victory there, and when the fighting was over, he would leave. The world he loved was not just disappearing; it was already gone. The British Empire would shrink away from its borders. Williams had lost the Burmese members of his family, and the elephants were next. The effect of the separation would be momentous. The bond he had forged with the animals was something so large and deep he could frame it only in spiritual terms, saying they were his "religion."

Toward the end of the war, Williams grew nostalgic
for the peaceful days with his elephants. This is one of his
watercolors from that time.

Seeing this prospect, he began to stoke what would become a favorite fantasy: that many surviving war elephants would become free, wild elephants. He even enumerated to himself, like a catechism, all the reasons the scenario was plausible: He knew hundreds of elephants had vanished in Burma during the fighting. Yes, he conceded, many must have died. But a good portion of them had to have simply run off, and another set must have been injured. Of those injured, many would have been able to heal themselves with elephant remedies, such as sealing wounds with mud. In fact, he was sure the escaped elephants must have "greatly outnumbered those that lost their lives."

In small but meaningful scenes throughout the remotest parts of the jungle, one by one, he imagined these hero elephants meeting up with their wild cousins, just as they had night after night in their logging days. But this time there were no teak bells around their necks, no uzis calling them in the morning darkness. "Herds of wild elephants show no resentment when domesticated animals join them," Williams wrote. "This tolerance is just one of the things about elephants which makes one realise they are big in more ways than one." Though he had always thought logging elephants had a good life, he found himself now pining for them to have something better. The war sometimes made men harder and softer at the same time.

Even with this reassuring vision of the future, he stood next to Bandoola and cherished every second of the present. Here, in this oasis of tea, as he passed his hands over the barrel of the tusker's body, he had the chance to hold on to something fleeting, and let time stand still for just a moment. *"Htah!"* he called to Bandoola. And the great tusker rose up.

EPILOGUE

────────

James Howard Williams was mentioned in dispatches twice for gallantry in facing the enemy, and awarded the Order of the British Empire in 1945. The Japanese had been defeated, and though Bombine struggled to continue operations, remote pockets of Burma were not welcoming places for the families of forest men.

On a wintry day in February 1946, Jim Williams and his family returned home to England. They settled in Jim's birthplace in Cornwall, though his mother and father were long dead. Like many who had spent their entire adult lives in the far-flung corners of the empire, they found the homecoming unsettling. Initially, Treve absolutely hated England, which was not his home, and he would always remember the unhappiness of "the cold and chilblains and food coupons." He missed his beloved nanny Naw Lah terribly. For Jim it was an unbearable uprooting. Characteristically, he did not speak of his distress. To a certain extent, he had already experienced this same inner conflict during his extended leaves. "However much I swore that I wanted to be home, when I was home I found myself yearning to get back to the everyday difference of the jungle," he wrote. Now, as fond as he was of his boyhood world, a sense of exile again crept in. Many men who had spent their working lives in the East were terrified of going home to England and living on a pension. Gone were the spacious home, the servants, the ponies, the cars, and the memberships in every club. But for Williams it went much deeper than that. He had found the best of himself in Burma. Back in England, the man who was so exquisitely tuned in to elephants and so adept at jungle survival could only search for a new purpose. He had always joked that his life with elephants provided him with the skills to do only one thing in retirement: "to follow performing elephants in the sawdust ring, dressed as a clown, carrying a bucket and spade." He purchased meadowland and a nearby water mill to grow daffodils for the London market, and for a time was an executive for a pesticide company. Nothing seemed quite right—nothing except the rugged beauty of Cornwall and his beloved family.

Treve was more than a bit like him—smart, full of energy, and fascinated by animals. Lamorna was bighearted and curious about the natural world. In school she struggled in part with what would now likely be diagnosed as dyslexia, and she had difficulty being accepted by the other children. Jim and Susan took her out of school and allowed her to learn in her own way. She would never fit into a "normal" role in society, but she was loved. Always fond of misfits, Jim treated her with a rare understanding and acceptance.

In Cornwall, Jim reveled in some of his old pastimes, once again roaming the moors and indulging in his favorite childhood treats, including kidney pie and Cornish pasties. In no time, he began to lose his lean jungle frame.

In November 1948, after Williams made a trip to America, *The New Yorker* published a long profile of him by E. J. Kahn, Jr. The subsequent attention led to a contract for Williams's memoir, originally titled "Elephants in Peace and War," which he had started writing during his hospital stay in wartime. Published as *Elephant Bill* in 1950, it was a bestseller, opening a new world to Williams in which he could travel widely and lecture on the creatures he missed so much.

But he still longed to be with them in the flesh. In the early fall of 1951 an invitation came. Dick Chipperfield of the famous Chipperfield's Circus phoned to ask "Elephant Bill" to visit his twenty-seven female Asian elephants while they were performing in Exeter, 120 miles away. It stirred something long suppressed. "Having said goodbye to my elephants, I felt they could never again occur in my life," Williams had written. But here the animals were, once more coming to his rescue. "I accepted with alacrity," he wrote.

Williams sketched out two different covers for his memoir.

En route his mind was full of the majestic jungle elephants he had known: Bandoola, Ma Shwe, Mahoo Nee, little Guide Man, even crazy Taw Sin Ma. Every one had been so important to him that before he left Burma he had gone on an arduous pilgrimage, visiting the 417 elephants he could reach, just to say good-bye.

Unfortunately, by then, he had already seen the last of his beloved elephant Bandoola. The great tusker had been killed before war's end, in circumstances that would haunt Williams for the rest of his life. It was, he would always maintain, nothing short of murder. After the long vacation at the tea estate, Bandoola and the rest of Elephant Company had returned to Burma. As the Japanese were driven out of the country, more and more animals joined the Allied elephants' ranks. In the unfolding victory their services were in even higher demand for bridge construction, hauling teak to sawmills for boat-building, and ferrying supplies. The elephants had never been pushed harder. "Bandoola carried the brunt of the heavy work," Williams wrote. "He even worked by moonlight." But Williams checked in constantly and found the tusker in robust condition.

Then on one of Williams's visits to Po Toke's work camp, Bandoola was absent from the inspection line. When Williams inquired, Po Toke said that Bandoola had been missing a couple of days. In fact, the tusker had not been seen for several. Despite the war effort's urgent need for timber, Williams bucked orders and shut down the camp's operation, sending every man available out to scour the forest for Bandoola. There was no sign of him. Williams sensed something was wrong, but just then, he was called away by his superiors. Five days later, he rushed back to Po Toke's camp and learned that Bandoola had still not returned. When Williams unleashed his fury on Po Toke, the old mahout, sobbing, admitted that Bandoola was dead. He claimed he did not know what had happened.

Two riders led Williams to the body. "There lay Bandoola," Williams would write. He stared in disbelief at the rotting corpse, not quite ready to comprehend that his hero was gone. Bandoola's right tusk had been hacked off, and the left remained plowed into the earth where his head had fallen. A single bullet fired directly into his skull had killed him. Williams shook with grief and anger. Storming back to camp, he assigned sentries armed with Sten guns to guard the body round the clock. If the executioners returned to fetch the remaining tusk he knew his Karen soldiers would shoot to kill. He wanted revenge.

Williams began a scorching investigation, interrogating soldiers and searching the huts of a local Chin village. The bullet that killed Bandoola was a .303, a standard military cartridge. Its identification did nothing to narrow down a likely culprit. He fired Po Toke, who had lied to him for more than a week, and confiscated all local weapons, but his inquiry produced no leads.

Heartsick, he had Bandoola's left tusk removed. It was a talisman he kept with him for the rest of his life, one that was meant to remind him of the life of Bandoola, but instead always filled him with sorrow for the tusker's senseless death. He came to believe with increasing certainty that Po Toke had killed him out of a deranged attachment to the great animal. Po Toke, Williams was convinced, was unwilling for anyone else to take over the tusker's care. As Po Toke faced the end of his own working days, the fear of a new handler for Bandoola had become "a haunting worry." Releasing him to the wild in this area must not have seemed feasible to Po Toke, but if it had, Williams wrote, he would have happily been an accomplice, helping to give the tusker his freedom. Such was the complicated and often paradoxical relationship between the two men that in the agonizing days after the discovery, Williams was filled with a bitter kind of love for Po Toke. Here was the man who had taught him everything and shared with him this astonishing creature. Without Po Toke there would have been no Bandoola. But he had also destroyed that elephant in the glory of his prime. Williams was filled with fury against Po Toke the murderer. Yet, while Williams saved Bandoola's left tusk, he prayed it was Po Toke who possessed the right. After all, these tusks were sacred to only two people in the world. And Bandoola was their bond.

Williams grieved Bandoola as he would a brother, and he buried him as a war hero. Somewhere on the border of Burma and India is a monument. Carved on a giant teak tree, "preserved for humanity," are the words BANDOOLA BORN 1897, KILLED IN ACTION 1944. Williams never saw Po Toke again. Harold Browne later heard Po Toke had become leader of a gang of dacoits, and in 1954, an American working out of the embassy in Rangoon sent word to Williams that Po Toke was alive and making his home in a village just a few miles outside of Witok, near Moreh.

Back in England, the circus elephants gave Williams a chance to reconnect with his old life. He was led to them as they stood "munching meadow hay." The great swaying, chirping, ear-flapping beasts were eager to know him. They met his eyes, and their dancing trunks stretched to close the gap between him and them. He walked forward and his hands instinctively reached for them. He read them by touch, the way he used to in his old life. He clasped their trunks, and passed his knowing palms along the barrel of their bodies. They made him laugh and maybe even cry: The look and feel of them. The sounds they made. The clean way they smelled. It felt like a homecoming.

He was shown a young calf with a small, infected hole in her ear that wouldn't heal. Chipperfield assumed it was a bullet hole from her capture in the wild. Williams examined the sore, explaining it was a piercing that a string would have been tied to during her training. The old elephant wallah cleaned the area and lanced the small boil, briefing the circus men about how to care for it in the coming days. He was Elephant Bill again, if only for a few moments.

When it was time to go, he surprised even himself. He started to walk away, but wheeled back around, suddenly casting off his overcoat to rub its lining against the hides of the elephants, "determined," he said, "to take the scent of them home with me."

Williams would go on to write several other memoirs: *Bandoola* (1953); *The Spotted Deer* (1957), published in the United States as *The Scent of Fear;* and *Big Charlie* (1959) and *In Quest of a Mermaid* (1960), both published posthumously.

J. H. Williams found a new career writing about his elephants, though he resisted the celebrity status that came along with it.

His books provided much-needed income and much-resisted celebrity. There were movie options over the years involving Gary Cooper, Ernest Borgnine, and even Sophia Loren, though no films were ever made. Williams tried his hand at screenwriting and got as close to Burma as Ceylon (Sri Lanka) and Siam (Thailand) in the process. He was flown east to scout out film locations and, best of all, to conduct elephant casting calls. Back home, he was involved in purchasing five elephants to ship to Borneo to become teak haulers, and he had another adventure, transporting a huge circus elephant cross-country.

In the spring of 1957, Treve left for Australia where he would go to veterinary school, fulfilling a shared dream for both father and son. As he stood waving to Treve at the docks of Southampton, Jim's eyes filled with tears, and he whispered to Susan that he would not live to see the boy again.

He was right. On July 30, 1958, at the age of sixty, James Howard Williams died during an emergency appendectomy. So accustomed to the burning ache of his ulcer, he mistook the new, sharper agony as more of the same. The man who never spoke of his woes stoically bore the pain of a burst appendix until it was too late.

ACKNOWLEDGMENTS

———

My first companion in pursuit of the J. H. Williams story was Robin Perkins Ugurlu, who came with me to Tasmania in the spring of 2010. Robin had provided me with a remarkable cache of letters from her family archive for my book *The Lady and the Panda,* and in the decade since, she had become a close friend and international travel partner. She's such a charmer that wherever we go, doors and hearts open to us. As we set out to meet Williams's son Treve, I thought that talent might prove useful.

I already had the six memoirs (one written by Williams's wife, Susan) that make up the substantial published record of the life of Elephant Bill. What I needed were the traces that were unpublished, unknown, private. I had been in touch with Treve, a well-known racehorse veterinarian, for several months, yet I still did not have a clear impression of how much archival matter he possessed. As is often the case with research, I just had to go and find out.

The moment of truth came at Treve's lovely house in a picturesque town in northern Tasmania, where he had set out, on the polished table in his dining room, a small overnight suitcase of letters and clippings—a little anticlimactic, but I was grateful to examine whatever material existed. Robin and I began to sift through the yellowed papers while Treve worked upstairs in his study examining X-rays of a Thoroughbred's legs. The three of us broke for lunch that day in the village pub, and later, after more reading, there was supper, Scotch, and conspiratorial laughter. Before bedtime, we were a tight-knit trio.

The next morning Robin and I again arrived at Treve's to discover that he had lugged down a massive chest filled with archival treasures: unpublished manuscripts, autobiographical screenplays and movie treatments, typed speeches, diary fragments, handwritten notes and essays—it was the El Dorado of Elephant Bill files. Apparently, though we hadn't even known we were on probation, Robin and I had passed muster. I was ecstatic. It was clear that from this immense cache would emerge the heart of this book: the truer, funnier, earthier, and more emotional James Howard Williams.

There is no way to adequately thank Treve for his contribution. This book was made possible by his generosity, insight, and drive. Besides providing an enormous repository of materials, he was unstinting in sharing memories and helping pin down dates that his father had left vague. By knowing Treve, I could know, to some extent, James Howard Williams in the flesh—witnessing through the son the father's rangy physique, his great zest, his humor, his stamina, and, above all else, his kindness. Jim Williams still has a voice every time his son speaks. All of these things were a blessing for a biographer, but beyond that, I've once again made a beloved friend. As Treve put it once during a passing disagreement, "We're mates, that's for life, nothing will change that." Thank you, dear Treve, for everything.

I am also indebted to Denis Segal for uncovering J. H. Williams's government, employment, shipping, and military records in London. I was told that Denis could discover in ten minutes files that would take other scholars ten years to track down. It turned out to be true. And Denis has contributed much more. His own experience in the British military in India during World War II provided many insights. His supercomputer of an intellect was always humming, waiting to field any question. And even though the research is done, our email correspondence has sustained the exquisite pleasure of knowing him.

Thanks also to Dr. Kevin Greenbank, archivist and administrator, Centre of South Asian Studies, University of Cambridge. Kevin provided me with invaluable materials on Burma, including footage of tea planter and World War II refugee rescuer Gyles Mackrell, and introduced me to Denis Segal. Kevin is a modest man but an incredible polymath. I thank him for allowing me a glimpse of his astonishing "other" lives—musician, heroic activist, and writer. His accomplishments might have intimidated me, but Kevin's wicked sense of humor kept our communication down to earth.

Much love and many thanks to Diana Clarke. Di is the little girl in this story who broke my heart. When she arrived with her brother, Michael, at Jim and Susan's front door in 1940, she was only three years old, motherless, and quite ill. She immediately became a beloved member of the family, one whom Treve still refers to as his sister. In helping me, she recollected details about Jim and Susan that only a daughter could. She is, today, as brave and kind and generous as she was then. Late in the project, she offered an example of British decorum. I was on the phone with Treve and Di the day they had a reunion in London. They had not seen each other in decades and I asked Di if they wept. "Oh, no!" she objected. But then she paused, and whispered, "We just blinked a lot." I am honored to consider her a friend.

As always, thanks to Jan Freeman, a friend and editor without equal (she'll roll her eyes at such a superlative). I hardly write a personal letter without requesting Jan's red pencil. A colleague once asked how I had the nerve to show Jan my "raw copy." It's actually easy, because along with being an exacting reader, Jan is the tenderest of friends.

John Bostock, son of Geoff Bostock of the Bombay Burmah Trading Corporation, generously provided me with his family's private correspondence, which recorded the exodus from Burma they shared with the Williamses in 1942. Among his father's papers was the "Evacuation Scheme," a detailed seventeen-page outline of the supplies and logistics necessary for the trek and the names of all the evacuees. Everything was calculated with precision down to the last bedroll, tin bath, and fork. His mother's letters home, full of detail as well as emotion, provided an invaluable glimpse of the journey.

To David Air and his posse of retired tea planters, many thanks for providing insight and information on the details of Elephant Bill's stay in Silchar.

I am grateful to Felicity Goodall, author of *Exodus Burma,* who was unstintingly generous in sharing her research, and to Harvard scholar Kyi Thant, who kindly edited the Burmese phrases used in these pages.

And then there are the elephants. They are the reason Billy Williams traveled to Burma and the inspiration for this book. They, and Williams's love for them, are what first attracted me to this story and sustained me throughout. I knew I could not understand the man if I did not understand his elephants. The journey toward that end has been one of the greatest gifts of my life. And the biggest part of the education was provided by two remarkable elephant matriarchs— Ruth and Emily.

In 2010, Dr. Bill Langbauer, the head of the Buttonwood Park Zoo in New Bedford, Massachusetts, invited video artist Christen Goguen and me to come down and meet "the girls." Emily had lived much of her life alone in the zoo, when it was run-down and sad. Ruth had arrived in the 1980s after being abandoned by a private owner in a dump in Massachusetts. Known as a striker—one who lashes out with her trunk—and a dangerous elephant, Ruth was rehabilitated by a curmudgeon with a heart of gold—a keeper named Bill Sampson. Bill was patient and dependable, and he turned Ruth into a lap elephant—a trustworthy animal who thrives on love and attention.

Christen and I visited the girls every other week for nearly two years, learning about life, love, and all things elephant from Emily and Ruth. They taught us to close our eyes when reaching up to rub them (sand rains down from their hide), where they liked to be scratched (often along the tire-tread "elbow" of their trunks), and how easy it is for elephants to open a coconut (the girls would just place a foot on the hard shell, close their eyes in anticipation of the pop, and press). Of course, they had bigger lessons to provide, too. I didn't need to be convinced of what J. H. Williams wrote about elephant emotions, but the girls validated all of it—they have courage, kindness, intelligence, humor, and loyalty. I hope these deserving animals receive the expansion and renovation of their living space that some of my friends have fought so hard for.

The elephants didn't come with an instruction manual, but I have been fortunate to have five remarkable guides: Bill Langbauer, Jenny Theuman, Kay Santos, John Lehnhardt, and Katy Payne.

"Dr. Bill," a renowned elephant researcher, opened his mind, his home, and, as the head of Buttonwood at the time, his zoo to me, giving me full immersion into the hearts and minds of these incredible creatures. Dr. Bill is a scientist, a skeptic, and a man of integrity and joy, and like his elephants, he inspires one to be a bigger person in his presence.

Jenny and Kay, sensitive and insightful elephant keepers, let me tag along, sharing their observations on elephant life. Jenny is smart and talkative, Kay quiet and intuitive; both are masterly elephant whisperers.

John Lehnhardt was my elephant guru on my very first book, *The Modern Ark,* and has remained a friend and adviser on all things elephant ever since. He was a curator at the National Zoo then, and now he is beginning a remarkable endeavor—making a sanctuary for elephants in Florida.

Finally, Katy Payne is a gift from Ganesha. I had read and reviewed her book *Silent Thunder* and for years had admired her work on elephant behavior and vocal communication. I had hoped to introduce myself someday. Then, in 2009, as I headed to Truro for my annual visit with filmmaker Cynthia Moses, I found out that Katy would be joining us for the week. I hadn't even realized that Cynthia, most generous and plugged-in of friends, knew Katy. I had long talks with Katy that week, and many strolls with her on the beach, but my favorite memory is sitting on her bed one windy afternoon as she read my book proposal and I reread *Silent Thunder,* taking turns quoting favorite passages from each other's work.

If we were elephants, my dearest friends would be my *twai sins,* sister matriarchs with whom I share fierce loyalty but no DNA: Amy Macdonald, Mary Savoca Crowley, Ellen Maggio, Jan Freeman, and Louise Kennedy. I thank them all for their unstinting support.

Thanks also to Jane von Mehren at Random House, for believing in this story, and to Jonathan Jao for his vision and the strength and delicacy of his editing. To his assistant Molly Turpin, too, my gratitude for a fine and astute reading.

I continue to be indebted to my literary agent, Laura Blake Peterson, at Curtis Brown, Ltd. Laura deserves credit for the good fortune I have enjoyed in the world of books. Magical opportunities seem to just fall into my lap because of her. I never see the effort, just the wonderful result. She is so breathtakingly good at what she does, and so smart, funny, kind, and courageously protective, that I benefit every day from being associated with her.

NOTES

————

Among the archives of J. H. Williams, kept by his son Treve Williams in Tasmania, were many documents, writing fragments, private letters, Susan Williams's handwritten timeline of her married life, screenplays, movie treatments, and original manuscripts as they were written before being edited. (The original manuscript for *Elephant Bill* was titled "Elephants in Peace, Love, and War.") I coded this material sequentially as Document 1, Document 2, Document S1, and so forth. J. H. Williams wrote five memoirs and his wife, Susan, one.

ABBREVIATIONS

EB	J. H. Williams, *Elephant Bill*
SOF	J. H. Williams, *Scent of Fear*
FOEB	Susan Williams, *The Footprints of Elephant Bill*
FOEB MS	Original manuscript for *The Footprints of Elephant Bill*
EB MS	Original manuscript for *Elephant Bill*

INTRODUCTION

xi **with a dash of mysticism** J. H. Williams, " 'Elephant Bill,' " *The Times* (London), July 31, 1958.

xi **who could talk to elephants** Kenneth Joachim, "Elephant Bill Is No More," *The Herald* (Melbourne), August 4, 1958.

xi **Williams had evolved into** J. H. Williams, " 'Elephant Bill.' "

xi **"than any other white man"** James Bartlett, "Never Say 'Lah-Lah' to a Wild Elephant," *Daily Express* (United Kingdom), May 8, 1953.

xi **the lives of countless refugees** J. H. Williams, " 'Elephant Bill.' "

xi **wild mountainous terrain** Philip Wynter, "*Life*'s Reports: Elephants at War / In Burma, Big Beasts Work for Allied Army," *Life* magazine, April 10, 1944.

xii **"a holy war"** Marshall Pugh, "Let Animals Teach You to Live," *Daily Mirror* (London), Wednesday, April 1952.

xii **The *Daily Mail*'s headline** "Elephant Bill Won His War," *Daily Mail* (London), no date. From the archives of Treve Williams.

xii **how much he owed Williams** Sir William Slim, "Uncommon Adventure," *Broadsheet, The Bulletin of "World Books,"* published by the Reprint Society, LTD., London, no date. From the archives of Treve Williams.

xii **It was the elephants** Pugh, "Let Animals Teach You to Live."

xii **"I've learned more about life"** Ibid.

xii **"Not a bad way to learn"** Ibid.

xiii **Courage defined them** Ibid.

xiii **how to be content with** "I Speak for Myself," radio broadcast transcript of "Elephant Bill" (Col. J. H. Williams, OBE), Disc No. DBU 52898, September 18, 1950, 1220 GMT. See also the original essay typed by Williams for the broadcast, which is slightly different, pp. 1–2.

xiii **"the most lovable"** J. H. Williams, *Elephant Bill* (Long Riders' Guild Press, 1950), p. 320. Hereinafter cited as *EB*.

xiii **"God's own"** Ibid., p. 166.

xiv **"The relationship"** J. H. Williams, *Big Charlie* (London: Rupert Hart-Davis, 1959), p. 37.

xiv **"I am convinced"** *EB*, p. 64; Susan Williams, *The Footprints of Elephant Bill* (Leicester: Ulverscroft, 1975), p. 119. First published 1962 by William Kimber. Hereinafter cited as *FOEB*.

xiv **had become his religion** Document Fragment 14, p. 4. Handwritten notes on the relationship between man and animals by J. H. Williams.

CHAPTER 1: THE SHOULDERS OF A GIANT

3 **the raging Yu River** J. H. Williams, *Bandoola* (London: Rupert Hart-Davis, 1955), p. 153.

3 **a sound like thunder** A. W. Smith, "Working Teak in the Burma Forests: The Sagacious Elephant Is Man's Ablest Ally in the Logging Industry of the Far East," *National Geographic,* August 1930, p. 246.

4 **chocolate-colored torrent** J. H. Williams, *Bandoola*, p. 153.

4 **a thousand elephants by name** Frank McLynn, *The Burma Campaign: Disaster into Triumph* (London: Vintage Books, 2011), p. 10. First published in 2010 by The Bodley Head. McLynn estimates that there were twenty thousand working elephants in Burma. And A. C. Pointon, *The Bombay Burmah Trading Corporation Limited: 1863–1963* (Southampton, UK: Millbrook Press, 1964), p. 45. Pointon says there were 3,028 BBTC elephants in Burma, the Salween, and Siam.

5 **he could keep water** Communication with elephant keeper Jenny Blackburn Theuman, December 19, 2010.

7 **"No one who works"** J. H. Williams, *Bandoola*, p. 144.

7 **Now, seven years later** Conversation with Treve Williams, June 13, 2012.

7 **The others were either** Pointon, *Bombay Burmah Trading Corporation Limited*, p. 59.

7–8 **Then Bandoola would** Document S1, p. 53. Autobiographical screenplay. From the archives of Treve Williams.

8 **maybe a hundred miles to go** J. H. Williams, *Bandoola*, p. 154.

CHAPTER 2: INTO THE JUNGLE

9 **On a crisp November day** J. H. Williams, "Elephants in Peace, Love, and War" (the original, unpublished manuscript that became *Elephant Bill*), pp. 3–8. Hereinafter cited as *EB* MS.

9 **still practiced head-hunting** Charles H. Bartlett, "Untoured Burma," *National Geographic,* July 1913, p. 852.

9 **performed human sacrifices** R. G. Woodthorpe, "Explorations on the Chindwin River, Upper Burma," *Proceedings of the Royal Geographical Society and Monthly Record of Geography,* n.s., 11, no. 4 (April 1889): pp. 197–216, http://www.jstor.org/stable /1801163, accessed October 25, 2013.

9 **into ghost cats** Sir Herbert Thirkell White, *Burma,* Provincial Geographies of India (Cambridge: Cambridge University Press, 1923), p. 33.

9 **remote and little-known corners** F. Kingdon-Ward, *Burma's Icy Mountains* (London: Jonathan Cape, 1949), p. 5.

9 **barbaric tribes** Captain F. Kingdon Ward, *In Farthest Burma: The Record of an Arduous Journey of Exploration and Research Through the Unknown Frontier Territory of Burma and Tibet* (London: J. B. Lippincott, 1921), p. 18.

9 **on January 26, 1920** J. H. Williams's WWI records, National Archives, London.

10 **Billy had led** J. H. Williams's WWI war records, British Library. Ref.: 1OR:L/MIL/14/67886.

10 **turmoil of Lahore** Ibid., under heading "Special Services in Peace or War."

11 **Nearly a million** Wade Davis, *Into the Silence: The Great War, Mallory, and the Conquest of Everest* (New York: Alfred A. Knopf, 2011), p. 15.

11 **he truly thrived** "I Speak for Myself," radio broadcast transcript.

12 **"My way"** *FOEB,* p. 370.

12 **"I developed a longing"** *EB* MS, p. 1.

12 **recruiting frenzy** Pointon, *Bombay Burmah Trading Corporation Limited,* pp. 58–59.

12 **elite schools** Harold Braund, MBE, MC, *Distinctly I Remember: A Personal Story of Burma* (Mount Eliza, Victoria: Wren Publishing, 1972), p. 20.

12 **in 1863** Raymond L. Bryant, *The Political Ecology of Forestry in Burma, 1824–1994* (Honolulu: University of Hawaii Press, 1996), p. 64.

12–13 **athletic over academic skill** Braund, *Distinctly I Remember,* p. 57.

13 **"A robust constitution"** Pointon, *Bombay Burmah Trading Corporation Limited,* p. 16.

13 **These firms required** Smith, "Working Teak in the Burma Forests," p. 239.

13 **stellar personal references** Braund, *Distinctly I Remember,* p. 21.

13 **Just under six feet tall** J. H. Williams's WWI records, National Archives, London. Folio 142, ref: 9/11/106.

13 **picked up Hindustani** J. H. Williams's WWI records, British Library. Ref.: 1OR/L/MIL/14/67886.

13 **"good moral character"** J. H. Williams's WWI records, National Archives, London. Folio 142, ref: 9/11/106.

13 **His official offer** J. H. Williams's original employment contract, London Metropolitan Archives. Ref.: clc/b/207/ms 40603/002, Folio 31.

13 **Every day during the war** Martin Pugh, *We Danced All Night: A Social History of Britain Between the Wars* (London: Bodley Head, 2008), p. 4. And J. H. Williams, "Life Offered Only Adventure: J. H. Williams, Author of 'Elephant Bill,'" no page number.

13 **The elder, Nick** Susan Williams, original manuscript for *Footprints of Elephant Bill,* p. 35. Hereinafter cited as *FOEB* MS. She says the firm was Orr Dignus and Co. From the archives of Treve Williams.

13 **"Go down to Penamel cove"** Document S1, p. 3.

13 **On July 7, 1920** J. H. Williams's original employment contract.

14 **Weeks later** Passenger list of the *Bhamo* from the P. Henderson and Co. steamship

line. The passenger cargo vessel *Bhamo* was built in 1908 and scrapped in 1938. Gross tonnage: 5,239.

14 **It was a mild, hazy Thursday** Weather from the Liverpool Observatory records, National Meteorological Archive, Great Moor House, Bittern Road, Sowton, Exeter, UK.

14 **travel between the two countries** Braund, *Distinctly I Remember,* p. 26.

14 **company's home leave schedule** Felicity Goodall, *Exodus Burma: The British Escape Through the Jungles of Death 1942* (History Press, 2011), no page number.

14 **But he was also thrilling** Writing Fragment 8, p. 6.

14 **well-liked high school student** H. J. Channon, "Elephant Bill of Burma: An Early Adventure at Queen's College." Reminiscences of J. H. Williams by one of his schoolteachers. Unknown publication. From the archives of Treve Williams.

15 **Once on board** J. K. Stanford, *Far Ridges: A Record of Travel in North-Eastern Burma 1938–39* (London: C. & J. Temple, 1946), p. 20.

15 **games such as skittles** Braund, *Distinctly I Remember,* p. 27.

15 **a few weeks later** Shipping information indicates these were generally two- or three-week trips, though J. H. Williams says in Document 10a, p. 1, that it was a five-week trip. Stanford, *Far Ridges,* pp. 17–20, indicates that the England to Burma run was a three-week trip.

15 **lonely journey up-country** Document 10a, p. 1. It appears to be a rough draft of the early chapters for *Elephant Bill,* but contains information not in the published version or *EB* MS.

15 **The five-hour-long approach** Cecilie Leslie, *The Golden Stairs* (Garden City, N.Y.: Doubleday, 1968), p. 32.

15 **The wide street** *FOEB,* p. 15.

15 **Colorful buses** Ibid.

16 **It was noted** *FOEB* MS, p. 15.

16 **Loneliness may have been** Smith, "Working Teak in the Burma Forests," p. 241.

16 **The timber even contains** Bryant, *Political Ecology of Forestry in Burma,* p. 23.

16 **As a *National Geographic*** Smith, "Working Teak in the Burma Forests," p. 239. Raymond L. Bryant, "Romancing Colonial Forestry: The Discourse of 'Forestry as Progress' in British Burma," *The Geographical Journal* 162, July 1996, p. 172, mentions the "low incidence of teak" in Burma.

16 **A two-inch ring** *Burma Pamphlets No. 5: The Forests of Burma* (Calcutta: Longmans, Green, 1944), p. 48.

17 **died and dried out** Bryant, "Romancing Colonial Forestry," p. 169.

17 **"The rivers of Burma"** *Burma Pamphlets No. 5,* p. 2.

17 **Because the country** E. J. Kahn, Jr., "A Reporter at Large: Elephant Bill's Elephants," *The New Yorker,* November 20, 1948, p. 96.

17 **"their contact with primitive things"** Smith, "Working Teak in the Burma Forests," p. 246.

17 **five to twenty years** *Burma Pamphlets No. 5,* p. 52; Pointon, *Bombay Burmah Trading Corporation Limited,* p. 13.

17 **Sitting behind** Document S1, p. 2. Differs from published work and amplifies details.

18 **Packed in a teak box** Smith, "Working Teak in the Burma Forests," p. 239.

18 **Rangoon was full** Emma Larkin, *Finding George Orwell in Burma* (New York: Penguin Books, 2004), p. 120.

19 **"Just crackers"** Document S1, p. 3.

19 **women outnumbering men** Pugh, *We Danced All Night,* p. 3.

20 **Green Imperial pigeons** Bertram E. Smythies, *The Birds of Burma,* rev. ed. (Edinburgh: Oliver and Boyd, 1953), p. 423.

20 **channel buoys** Smith, "Working Teak in the Burma Forests," p. 240.

20 **seven lighthouses** FOEB MS, p. 36. The Williams boys were trusted with firearms, and Jim carried a souvenir from one embedded in his cheek. On a bitterly
cold day, when he was sixteen, his hands numb, he had attempted to gently lean his
shotgun against a wall. But it slipped and went off, the pellets ricocheting into his
face. With all the blood, his brother Tom, terrified, ran into the house, shouting,
"Mams, Mams, come quickly, Jimmy is blinded!" A local doctor was summoned
and, using the kitchen table as his surgical table, removed most of the pellets. Not
one had hit his eye. Even then he was a master of the narrow escape.

20 **"as wild as"** FOEB MS, p 369.

21 **"I never looked for"** FOEB, p. 370.

21 **His formal education** J. H. Williams's WWI records, National Archives, London;
Channon, "Elephant Bill of Burma."

21 **popular friend** Channon, "Elephant Bill of Burma." J. H. Williams distinguished
himself in class, as well as on the cricket pitch, the soccer field, and the debating
team.

21 **in 1915** J. H. Williams WWI records, British Library. Ref: 10R/L/MIL/14/67886.

21 **who had died** Pointon, *Bombay Burmah Trading Corporation Limited*, p. 68.

21 **Copious soap** Griffith H. Evans, *Elephants and Their Diseases* (Elibron Classics Series, 2005), pp. 158, 249. First published in Rangoon in 1910.

22 **They usually weighed** U Toke Gale, *Burmese Timber Elephant* (Rangoon: Trade
Corporation, 1974), pp. 7–9.

22 **African elephants have tusks** Shana Alexander, *The Astonishing Elephant* (New
York: Random House, 2000), p. 42.

22 **shows in their temperaments** Conversation with Dr. William Langbauer.

22 **a sense of smell** Raman Sukumar, *The Living Elephants: Evolutionary Ecology, Behavior, and Conservation* (Oxford: Oxford University Press, 2003), p. 149.

22 **They can cooperate** Katy Payne, *Silent Thunder: In the Presence of Elephants* (New
York: Simon & Schuster, 1998), p. 61. Elephants may harbor the capacity for forgiveness, too. One set of female elephants in Africa, sisters, were observed after
what must have been a tremendous fight between the two. The broken-off tusk of
one was still jammed into the other's flesh when they were spotted, walking peace-
fully along side by side. They had made up. And elephants have displayed what
certainly looks like altruism—one calf, still nursing, shuttled his younger brother
under the mother's belly so that the littler one could nurse in his place.

23 **as great as five miles** Payne, *Silent Thunder*, p. 21. Thunder, earthquakes, and blue
whales produce infrasound, too.

23 **taller than many** Gale, *Burmese Timber Elephant*, pp. 7–9.

23 **grow throughout his life** Raman Sukumar, *Elephant Days and Nights* (New Delhi:
Oxford University Press, 1994), p. 77; Gale, *Burmese Timber Elephant*, p. 7. Sukumar
says they grow until age thirty; other sources say throughout life.

23–24 **"an elephant of good quality"** Gale, *Burmese Timber Elephant*, p. 3

24 **lavender shade of his skin** J. H. Williams, *Bandoola*, p. 14.

24 **When asked to choose** FOEB, p. 270

24 **rumble at his own joke** Document S1, p. 41.

CHAPTER 3: MEETING THE BOSS—AND THE ELEPHANTS

25 **new khaki shorts** Document S1, p. 5.

25 **sitting in the portico** Ibid., p. 3.

25 **no one was looking** Document M1, p. 9.

26 **Drinking, most forest men found** Indranil Banerjie, "Burra Peg: Raj Hangover on Indian Drinking Habits," *The Asian Age,* November 23, 2011, http://archive .asianage.com/ideas/burra-peg-raj-hangover-indian-drinking-habits-887. Accessed November 20, 2013. "In India, the need to drink was augmented by the intense loneliness of the Europeans, who first came as traders holed up in dreary, isolated posts with little hope of seeing their home country in the near future. The East India Company not just encouraged drinking but also provided prodigious quantities of liquor for its employees stationed in India. This led to much intemperate behaviour."

26 **brand-new tent** Document S1, p. 7.

26 **next to Harding's** *EB* MS, p. 34.

26 **"how not to receive"** J. H. Williams, *Scent of Fear* (Garden City, N.Y.: Double- day, 1957), p. 12. Hereinafter cited as *SOF.*

27 **"as silently as"** Rudyard Kipling, "Toomai of the Elephants," in *The Jungle Books,* vol. 2 (Garden City, N.Y.: Doubleday, 1948), p. 161.

27 **aids the circulation** Murray E. Fowler and Susan K. Mikota, *Biology, Medicine, and Surgery of Elephants* (Ames, Iowa: Wiley-Blackwell, 2006), pp. 81–82.

28 **"looked as if she"** *EB* MS, p. 4.

28 **Mrs. Fat Bottom** Ibid., p. 8.

28 **into a kneeling position** G. E. Weissengruber, F. K. Fuss, G. Egger, G. Stanek, K. M. Hittmair, G. Forstenpointner, "The Elephant Knee Joint: Morphological and Biomechanical Considerations," *Journal of Anatomy* 208, no. 1 (January 2006): pp. 59–72. http://www.ncbi.nlm.nih.gov/pmc/articles/PMC2100174. Accessed October 8, 2013.

29 **"regularly examined"** Evans, *Elephants and Their Diseases,* p. 16.

30 **more than sixty thousand muscles** Eric Scigliano, *Love, War, and Circuses: The Age-Old Relationship Between Elephants and Humans* (Boston: Houghton-Mifflin Company, 2002), p. 12.

31 **The farther they were** Sukumar, *Living Elephants,* p. 120

31 **It was supposed to be** Evans, *Elephants and Their Diseases,* p. 14.

31 **They had them** Sukumar, *Elephant Days and Nights,* p. 42; Alexander, *Astonishing Elephant,* p. 41.

31 **"I should only be called"** *EB* MS, p. 4.

CHAPTER 4: INITIATION RIGHTS

33 **No matter where** Smith, "Working Teak in the Burma Forests," p. 241; Docu- ment S1.

33 **"Yes, I think so"** Document S1, p. 8.

34 **As a forest assistant** Kahn, "Elephant Bill's Elephants," p. 96.

34 **"A knowledge of Burmese"** Alan Rabinowitz, *Life in the Valley of Death* (Wash- ington, D.C.: Island Press/Shearwater Books, 2008), p. 40. Even to those who had traveled extensively in Asia, Burmese simply sounded different. It is part of the larger Sino-Tibetan language family, is tonal, and tends to give equal stress to all syllables. The written language, though beautiful graphically, can be dizzying to a Westerner—made up of look-alike rounded, circular letters, which are difficult for newcomers to distinguish. The script was developed this way because palm leaves were used for paper, and the gentle curving lines would not tear through the deli- cate fronds the way straight ones would.

35 **Surrounded by** Smythies, *Birds of Burma,* pp. 370, 376, 382–83. Listen: http:// www.xeno-canto.org/species/Otus-lettia.

35 **thickets of pine** Bryant, *Political Ecology of Forestry in Burma,* p. 226.

35 **An old volume** Richard Lydekker, *The Game Animals of India, Burma, Malaya, and Tibet* (London: Rowland Ward, 1907).

35 **three species of rhino** Edwin Harris Colbert, "Notes on the Lesser One-Horned Rhinoceros *Rhinoceros sondaicus,*" *American Museum Novitates,* no. 1207 (November 12, 1942): p. 2; White, *Burma,* p. 91. So healthy was the tiger population that in the few decades before J. H. Williams's arrival, at least two had been shot right in the urban heart of Rangoon.

36 **It was home** John LeRoy Christian, "Burma: Where India and China Meet," *National Geographic,* October 1943, p. 502.

36 **Burma was an ethnically diverse** Larkin, *Finding George Orwell in Burma,* pp. 45, 213; *Burma Pamphlets No. 9: Burma Facts and Figures* (Calcutta: Longmans, Green, 1944), p. 3.

36 **"where God lives"** "Battle of Asia: Land of Three Rivers," *Time* magazine, May 4, 1942.

36 **said a silent prayer** Skype conversation with Treve Williams, September 4, 2012. J. H. Williams belonged to the Church of England.

36 **Sunup this time** Smith, "Working Teak in the Burma Forests," p. 242.

38 **his own four elephants** *EB* MS, p. 4.

38 **Strangers always inspire curiosity** Payne, *Silent Thunder,* p. 14.

38 **targeting the richly** Sukumar, *Living Elephants,* p. 138.

39 **In fact, there were** Caitlin O'Connell-Rodwell, "Ritualized Bonding in Male Elephants," *The New York Times,* July 21, 2011; Payne, *Silent Thunder,* p. 48.

39 **"I'd like to start off"** *EB* MS, p. 5.

39 **"That remark"** Ibid., p. 19.

40 **It was said of** *FOEB,* p. 82.

40 **"By dawn"** *EB* MS, p. 5. Harding called the jigger a "pau peg."

40 **"Good Lord!"** *EB,* p. 19.

40 **He conveyed** Document S1, p. 10.

41 **botanist Reginald Farrer** Jamie James, *The Snake Charmer* (New York: Hyperion, 2008), p. 118.

41 **Right away** Document S1. This version of events, from J. H. Williams's personal papers, amplifies the story told in "Elephant Bill."

41 **Often the uzis would** It would later be called "allomothering" in science, and "allosuckling" if the friend fed the baby, too. Sukumar, *Living Elephants,* p. 132.

41 **"indeed cruel"** *EB,* p. 67.

42 **Carved from teak** Ibid., p. 58; W. W. Smith, "The Elephant Scorns Our Machine Age: He's Still 'A-Pilin' Teak' with an Intelligence and Power Which Tractors Cannot Supplant," *The New York Times,* July 28, 1929.

42 **enough urine to fill a rain barrel** Fifty-two gallons. Murray E. Fowler and Susan K. Mikota, *Biology, Medicine, and Surgery of Elephants* (Ames, Iowa: Blackwell, 2006), p. 389.

42 **Plus, there were** Fowler and Mikota, *Biology, Medicine, and Surgery of Elephants,* p. 72.

42 **communal bunk** Susan Williams, *Elephant Boy* (London: William Kimber, 1963), p. 72.

42 **"a pretty hard life"** *EB,* p. 57.

42 **"My jungle life"** *EB* MS, p. 6.

43 **Most of his** *FOEB* MS, p. 35.

44 **"I have never studied them"** Thant Myint-U, *The River of Lost Footsteps* (New York: Farrar, Straus, and Giroux, 2006), p. 370.

45 **Over the years,** J. H. Williams, "It Happened to Me: The Elephant Goes to School," notes for a talk to schoolchildren, p. 1.

45 **Because elephants need** Scigliano, *Love, War, and Circuses,* p. 14.

45 **Elephants need a lot of it** Elephant digestive efficiency is maybe as low as 22 percent. Sukumar, *Elephant Days and Nights,* p. 56; George Schaller, *The Last Panda* (Chicago: University of Chicago Press, 1993), p. 103.

45 **Asian elephants consume** Sukumar, *Elephant Days and Nights,* p. 56.

45 **While their uzis slept** J. H. Williams, *In Quest of a Mermaid* (London: Rupert Hart-Davis, 1960), p. 41.

45 **the forest was so thick** Woodthorpe, "Explorations on the Chindwin River, Upper Burma."

46 **"Many young animals develop"** *EB* MS, p. 51

46 **well-executed bank heist** Document S1, p. 13b. The destruction of crops by elephants would be a headache for J. H. Williams, but he would always admire the perpetrators. When shown a mud-stuffed kalouk, Williams thought, what "extraordinarily human animal[s]" they were. This act of anticipation and deceit signaled an intelligence not unlike our own. And when they got caught they seemed both chagrined and gleeful, pleased by their own naughtiness.

46 **two-penny notebook** Document S1, p. 21.

47 **Any forester would** *EB* MS, p. 7. "Fortunately they were all friendly and that they could ever be anything else, never entered my head," J. H. Williams wrote.

49 **"Everything of interest"** *EB* MS, p. 10.

50 **The first cuts released** British TV documentary, *Inside Nature's Giants.*

50 **There was her heart** Alexander, *Astonishing Elephant,* p. 17. A normal Asian elephant female's heart would be about fifty-five pounds, but Pin Wa's was enlarged.

50 **No other mammal breathes** Helen Briggs, "Elephant 'Had Aquatic Ancestor,'" *BBC News,* April 15, 2008, http://news.bbc.co.uk/2/hi/science/nature/7347284 .stm, accessed October 9, 2013. J. H. Williams didn't know why then, and even many decades later it would remain an evolutionary mystery. Perhaps elephant ancestors were marine animals who needed strong muscles around the lungs to fight underwater pressure as they breathed through their trunks. That might also help explain why modern elephants are so at home in the water. Science would, in fact, come to hypothesize that elephants have aquatic ancestors.

51 **A meticulous man** Conversation with Treve Williams, Long Island, New York, June 10, 2011.

52 **Everyone was so** *EB,* p. 144.

52 **tin tub** *SOF,* p. 35.

53 **patterns of tusk sets** Gale, *Burmese Timber Elephant,* p. 15.

53 **Tusk girth** Sukumar, *Living Elephants,* p. 120.

53 **But he deduced** *EB* MS, p. 11.

55 **until Bandoola's forties** Gale, *Burmese Timber Elephant,* p. 76.

55 **in charge of about three hundred** Smith, "Working Teak in the Burma Forests," p. 244.

56 **the families of the riders** *EB,* p. 115. For instance, the camp of U Po See, a camp leader Williams respected, did not allow families, only his own.

57 **More than once** All this village description is from *FOEB,* pp. 133–37.

57 **The monks** Larkin, *Finding George Orwell in Burma,* p. 34; *FOEB,* p. 136.

CHAPTER 5: HOW TO READ AN ELEPHANT

58 **When the group reached their first camp** *EB* MS, p. 11.

58 **During the monsoon** *Burma Pamphlets No. 5,* p. 4.

58 **Plaited together** Document S1, p. 13.

59 **"To hunt is to learn"** *EB,* p. 42. As a popular ditty of the time went: "What is hit is history / And what is missed is mystery." And Stanford, *Far Ridges.*

59 **Forest assistants might** Kahn, "Elephant Bill's Elephants," p. 96.

59 **Tigers were plentiful** *Burma Pamphlets No. 5,* p. 5. He would agree with the rational assessment of an authority on Burma at the time who wrote that the forests were home to "big, and so called dangerous, game, and poisonous snakes. The natural instinct of all wildlife, however, is to leave man well alone unless wounded or taken by surprise."

59 **Williams would fill out paperwork** Smith, "Working Teak in the Burma Forests," p. 243.

59 **In the name of progress** Bryant, "Romancing Colonial Forestry," p. 171.

60 **The industry may have** Bryant, *Political Ecology of Forestry in Burma,* pp. 8, 18–19.

60 **The men, using only axes** *Burma Pamphlets No. 5,* p. 50; Smith, "Working Teak in the Burma Forests," p. 243; Goodall, *Exodus Burma.* "With such 'unpromising' tools," an astonished colleague of J. H. Williams's wrote, "the largest trees are felled with speed and accuracy." Smith, "Working Teak in the Burma Forests," p. 243.

61 **Logs twenty to thirty feet** Document fragment 21, "Thoughts on Elephants," p. 4. Fourteen-page typewritten paper from the archives of Treve Williams.

62 **They showed Williams how** *EB* MS, p. 131.

62 **The fourteen-year-old,** *SOF,* p. 153.

62 **a spaniel had** J. H. Williams did not have a dog yet; this one was borrowed for the hunt. Conversation with Treve Williams, June 10, 2011.

63 **"humor and kindliness"** *FOEB* MS, p. 40.

63 **how Williams liked his tea** Conversation with Treve Williams via Skype, February 25, 2013.

63 **he was exceedingly capable** *SOF,* p. 153; J. H. Williams, *Bandoola,* p. 187. "Aung Net was someone to be thankful for," Williams wrote, "a simple, loyal soul."

63 **it was always Aung** *FOEB,* p. 276.

63 **astonishing delicacies** Angela Levin, "Fortnum and Mason: One's Grocers as Old as Great Britain," *Daily Mail,* November 3, 2007, http://www.dailymail.co.uk /news/article-491568/Fortnum-Mason-Ones-grocers-old-Great-Britain.html, accessed October 25, 2013; Jonathan Glancey, "A Facial at Fortnums? Never!" *The Guardian* (London), November 4, 2007, http://www.guardian.co.uk/lifeandstyle /2007/nov/05/foodanddrink.shopping, accessed October 25, 2013.

63 **The intricate patterns** Shway Yoe [Sir James George Scott], *The Burman: His Life and Notions* (London: MacMillan, 1896), pp. 39–41. The dense art covered so much tender skin that boys were generally administered opium to dull the pain during the tattooing. Few could bear having more than a few figures inked in at a time.

64 **special tree bark** Gale, *Burmese Timber Elephant,* p. 4.

65 **Out of the pool** Email with Jenny Blackburn Theuman, elephant keeper, February 22, 2012.

65 **served as a barrier** Sukumar, *Elephant Days and Nights,* p. 48.

65 **They also might grab** J. H. Williams, "The Gentle Giants," *Leader Magazine,* May 13, 1950, p. 18.

66 ***F* for female** Gale, *Burmese Timber Elephant,* p. xii.

66 ***Haing,* a male** Sukumar, *The Living Elephants,* p. 123. The tuskless males, called *makhnas* in India, tended to be bigger than their tusked brethren. And their trunks seemed more thickset.

67 **The uzi told him** Document S1, p. 13a.

67 **As Kipling** Kipling, "Toomai of the Elephants," p. 152.

67 **"When wild elephants are caught"** *EB* MS, p. 42.

67 **"very essence of brutality"** Document M1, J. H. Williams's detailed autobiographical movie treatment.

67 **steeped in tradition** White, *Burma,* p. 85.

CHAPTER 6: THE FAIREST TUSKER OF THEM ALL

69 **deep-set dark eyes** J. H. Williams, *Bandoola,* p. 30.

70 **A superstitious man** Conversation with Treve Williams via Skype, February 9, 2013.

70 **"There are ways"** J. H. Williams, *In Quest of a Mermaid,* p. 21.

70 **Bandoola had been born** J. H. Williams, *Bandoola,* p. 34. Williams says Bandoola was born under a full moon. Using the NASA eclipse website, one can fix his birthdate as November 3, 1897. Ningyan is cited as Bandoola's home village (p. 112). Ningyan later became known as Pyinmana, according to Hugh Nisbet, *Experiences of a Jungle Wallah* (St. Albans, UK: Fisher, Knight, 1910). p. 9.

71 **Although tigers and elephants** Rabinowitz, *Life in the Valley of Death,* p. 32.

71 **a five-hundred-pound predator** Susie Green, *Tiger* (London: Reaktion Books, 2006), p. 12.

71 **courageous Burmese military hero** Thant Myint-U, *River of Lost Footsteps,* pp. 112–13.

72 **In the wild** Sukumar, *Living Elephants,* p. 134; Cynthia Moss, *Little Big Ears: The Story of Ely* (New York: Simon & Schuster, 1991), p. 19. Babies watch their elders to learn which grasses are edible, wrap their trunks around clumps of it, rip it from its roots, and shake the dirt off. The lesson isn't just visual. The calves reach up into their mother's mouths to pull blades out to taste. In between, the learning curve can be comical. Often a baby will manage to tear grass out only to seem to forget what it was for—placing it on top of his head instead of in his mouth.

72 **could not nurse** Sukumar, *Living Elephants,* pp. 129–38. Calves nurse about three minutes out of every hour, and have physical contact about two dozen times an hour.

72 **The system guaranteed** Document S1, p. 30.

73 **He traveled eighty miles** J. H. Williams, *Bandoola,* p. 34.

73 **White elephants came** Jan McGirk, "Found: A Holy White Elephant," *The Independent* (London), August 21, 2004; Alexander, *Astonishing Elephant,* p. 74; Jeffrey A. McNeely and Paul Spencer Sochaczewski, *Soul of the Tiger* (Honolulu: University of Hawaii Press), pp. 102–3; Larkin, *Finding George Orwell in Burma,* p. 121; Sarah Amato, "The White Elephant in London," *Journal of Social History* 43, no. 1 (September 22, 2009): p. 31; Gale, *Burmese Timber Elephant,* pp. 3, 135–46; Evans, *Elephants and Their Diseases,* p. 11; Rita Ringis, *Elephants of Thailand in Myth, Art, and Reality* (Kuala Lumpur: Oxford University Press, 1996), pp. 94–96; Yoe, *Burman,* p. 481; Douglas H. Chadwick, *The Fate of the Elephant* (San Francisco: Sierra Club Books, 1992), p. 348.

Sacred white elephants were rarely actually white. Over hundreds of years, some white elephants may have been true albinos with little or no pigment. But albinism in many animals, including humans, can be incomplete. Almost always, white elephants did have color. It was not a black-and-white, or even a gray-and-white, issue.

Translating the word simply as "white," as we do in English, is inaccurate, and the translation causes an impossible expectation for Westerners. In 1884, a white elephant that P. T. Barnum had shipped to London was met with inevitable disappointment by the public.

The Burmese said there were twelve separate rankings of white elephant. In assigning these, pale skin, white nails, white tail hairs, or white eyes would count toward the designation. Many of the characteristics that distinguished such an elephant, though, were more nuanced; some of them, such as toenail number and shape, have nothing to do with pigmentation.

"It has been therefore found necessary to determine some infallible test points, which will demonstrate the right of the animal to his title," Yoe wrote. "Determining white elephants is quite a science, and there is a very considerable literature on the subject. The Burmese skilled men fix upon two of these tests as superior to all others. One is that the elephant shall have five toe-nails on his hind feet instead of four. This is a good way of making certain, but occasionally there are indubitably black elephants which have the sacred number of toes. These are white elephants debased by sin, labouring under the evil kan of previous existences, and therefore ineligible for the honours accorded to the real animal. The other test is considered perfectly decisive, no matter what the precise tint of the skin may be. It is this: if you pour water upon a 'white' elephant he turns red, while a black elephant only becomes blacker than ever."

There were worst things than finding out an elephant wasn't sacred. Some physical features even marked an animal as profane, bringing bad luck to the owner—among them black spots or warts, skin that looked like that of a rhinoceros, or exhibiting a loose fold of skin from throat to forelegs that resembled bees settling in a swarm.

Gender was not a factor; females could make the sacred cut, though tuskers always created more excitement.

A strange element of the concept of the white elephant emerged in the West. Because the proper care of a white elephant was so expensive, it was said that to receive one as a gift could be financially disastrous. "White elephant" became an idiom for any gift as burdensome as it is valuable. (Though rulers did not ordinarily part with these sacred creatures.)

The untimely death of a white elephant would signal coming catastrophe or reveal some unworthiness in a country's leaders. And the desire to possess these animals could lead to chaos. In the 1500s, Englishman Ralph Fitch wrote of a Burmese monarch, "The king in his title is called the King of the White Elephants. If any other has one and will not send it to him he will make war with him for it, for he would rather lose a great part of his kingdom than not conquer him."

74 **Williams realized** J. H. Williams, *Bandoola*, p. 102. "Po Toke was my master in the study of elephants," Williams said, "my most trusted assistant in their management."

CHAPTER 7: THE BURNING BOSS

77 **"Don't make a practice"** Document S1, p. 29.

77 **After the first elephant** J. H. Williams, *In Quest of a Mermaid*, p. 47; J. H. Williams, *Elephant Bill*, p. 173; letter published in *The Journal of the Bombay Natural History Society* 28 (1922): p. 1125. In his writing, J. H. Williams contradicts himself on the order of elephants killed, and/or the dates. In two books, he tells very different stories about the last elephant he shot. In *Quest of a Mermaid*, he said he shot an elephant for the last time in August 1921, but in his printed letter in *The Journal of the Bombay Natural History Society*, he says he killed the tusker with the "corrugations on the tusks" in May 1922. It's possible he meant May 1921, but very doubtful. In J. H. Williams, *Elephant Bill*, p. 173, he says that Poo Ban, a great tusker in

musth, was the last elephant he shot. The story of Poo Ban takes place in an area of Burma to which he wasn't assigned till about 1930, and yet he had stopped killing long before that date. "The thought of killing even a wild tusker from then on was most distasteful," he would write, "and to kill a tame elephant was tantamount to murder."

77 **"I allowed"** *EB* MS, p. 94.

77 **in his diary** This diary and all of J. H. Williams's journals would be lost in WWII.

78 **Harding never mentioned** *EB* MS, p. 14.

78 **Harding pulled him aside** Document S1, p. 30.

79 **"I'll back you"** Ibid.

79 **If he could do that** Ibid., p. 39.

79 **"If you saw Bandoola"** Document M1, movie treatment fragment. No page number.

80 **In a single decade** Pointon, *Bombay Burmah Trading Corporation Limited,* p. 68.

80 **And each one cost** Smith, "Working Teak in the Burma Forests," p. 246. Today's dollars in consultation with Paul Solman, financial reporter, PBS, September 1, 2011. And Document fragment 21, p. 6.

80 **"practical and humanitarian"** Document fragment 21, p. 5.

CHAPTER 8: SEX, CRICKET, AND BLUE CHEESE

81 **rendezvoused with Harding** J. H. Williams, *Bandoola,* p. 66. The meeting did not take place at Harding's camp.

81 **green canvas mailbag** J. H. Williams, *In Quest of a Mermaid,* p. 28.

81 **specialty cheeses** Ibid., p. 60. Williams had to admit that his boss "knew how to treat a cheese to perfection." And, truth be told, the pungent wheels were providing more tangible satisfaction to Williams than the pretty letter writers. Harding managed to keep his prized provisions from spoiling, and he had them "dressed in a starched white napkin with all the pomp of a London club." Williams wasn't just amused by Harding's obsession; he felt that "it was one of the clues to the secret of his character, this effort to bring an English luxury into the Upper Burmese jungle. Though he was a real jungle salt, I feel that he had never become fully reconciled to being there, that his longing for his native country was constant and nagging, like an aching tooth."

82 **Bandoola would take** According to Document 1, Bandoola could be as gentle as a female.

84 **named Jabo** *EB,* p. 138; *FOEB* MS, p. 64b. Williams, in fever, had fallen asleep in a canvas folding chair in front of his tent. He felt something icy against his skin and opened his eyes to see the beautiful face of a compact, powerfully built half-feral village dog who had pressed against him. When the dog looked into Williams's eyes, his whole hind-end began wagging and wiggling "in default of a tail," which had apparently been lopped off long before. Sick and dreaming of home and the Cornish cliffs, Williams fell in love with this "friendly, sympathetic creature." Jabo—the name means "piebald"—was known to the villagers and the elephant men as a scrappy camp follower. When the dog returned to Williams's tent later, one of the servants threw boiling water at him, scalding him. As sick as Williams was, he ordered chicken and rice cooked for the dog, which he hand-fed to him. (It would be the menu for all the dogs he owned in Burma.) He continued to offer food, and the dog reappeared nervously each day for the meal. Soon, Jabo was following Williams from camp to camp and flattening his little body up against him for pats and hugs. He would never be a truly domesticated dog—he avoided sleep-

ing in the tent, and wherever they went, the dog would bound away from camp looking for love and excitement—but Williams and Jabo became companions.

84 **for a trip to headquarters** Rangoon was confirmed as the destination in an email from Treve Williams, June 26, 2011.

CHAPTER 9: SCHOOL FOR MEN AND ELEPHANTS

86 **coated in green scum** Smith, "Working Teak in the Burma Forests," p. 244.

87 **The sleeping logs** Ibid., p. 246. One of Williams's colleagues found out the hard way how quickly the terrain could be transformed. He had camped on the banks of a little creek, then crossed it for a day of work on the other side. But the rains started while he was out. When he tried to return to his own camp the stream had become a raging river. He stood at the edge, soaking wet, with water pouring off the brim of his hat, staring at a dry tent and good food on the opposite bank. Close but unreachable. "I could see through the mist of rain my own camp tantalizingly near, on the other side," he wrote. He hunkered down as best he could, but was nonetheless exposed to the elements. It took almost two days for the water to calm enough for him to ford, by which time, he "went straight to bed with a roaring dose of fever."

87 **spell of malaria** J. H. Williams, *Bandoola*, p. 195.

88 **Aung Net would gently** J. H. Williams, *In Quest of a Mermaid*, p. 19.

89 **their animist cosmology** H. N. C Stevenson, *Burma Pamphlets No. 6: The Hill Peoples of Burma* (Calcutta: Longmans, Green, 1944), p. 27. Buddhism "is superimposed upon Animism and has not wholly replaced it," explained a series of pamphlets on Burma published during colonial times.

89 **Most are ghosts** Andrew Sinclair, "Spiritual Land of Prayers and Pagodas," *The New York Times,* June 8, 1986.

89 **specific nats** Melford E. Spiro, *Burmese Supernaturalism* (Englewood Cliffs, N.J.: Prentice-Hall, 1967), p. 108.

89 **fond of coconuts** Denis D. Gray, no headline, dateline Rangoon, Burma, Associated Press, February 27, 1983. Story on the persistence of nats in Burmese culture.

89 **cheroots could be left** James, *Snake Charmer,* p. 187.

90 **two elephant handlers per calf** J. H. Williams, "It Happened to Me: The Elephant Goes to School," p. 2.

91 **just how tolerant** Document fragment 21, p. 8. Williams once saw a big old tusker adopt a little female calf who had lost her mother to anthrax. "It was a pathetic sight to see the baby searching between the forelegs of this big tusker for udders, and finding nothing but dry nipples." The calf was weaned on bamboo shoots successfully, though she continued to suckle at the bull's teats.

91 **only three students enrolled** J. H. Williams, "It Happened to Me: The Elephant Goes to School," p. 2.

91 **A small thatched shrine** *EB* MS, p. 43.

92 **They flirted with them** Ibid., pp. 42–43.

92 **Males would spend** Sukumar, *Living Elephants,* p. 179.

94 **arranging a rendezvous** Document fragment 21, p. 8.

94 **Some Asian elephants** Shermin de Silva, Ashoka D. G. Ranjeewa, and Sergey Kryazhimskiy, "The Dynamics of Social Networks Among Female Asian Elephants," *BMC Ecology* 11, no. 17 (2011), http://www.biomedcentral.com/1472-6785/11/17. Accessed November 20, 2013.

94 **The detailed sorting** Virginia Morell, "Asian Elephants Are Social Networkers," *Science NOW,* July 26, 2011.

94 **could control the young ones** *EB* MS, p. 47. Williams wrote that the bull elephant would act like "a stuffy strict old Nurse in the park," who seemed to say to
his charges, "Don't you dare speak to those children coming toward us."

95 **Gathering logs** Susan Williams, *Elephant Boy*, p. 72.

95 **He worried** J. H. Williams, *Bandoola*, p. 82.

CHAPTER 10: DRUNK ON TESTOSTERONE

96 **On a sweltering** Treve Williams, in a June, 13, 2012, conversation, provided the
year as 1922.

96 **Bandoola was right on schedule** Gale, *Burmese Timber Elephant*, p. 45. Wild Afri-
can elephants start a little later—closer to thirty. See also Cynthia J. Moss, Harvey
Croze, and Phyllis C. Lee, *The Amboseli Elephants: A Long-Term Perspective on a
Long-Lived Animal* (Chicago: University of Chicago Press, 2011), p. 278.

96 **The strength of musth** Sukumar, *Living Elephants*, p. 108.

97 **Musth had been recognized** Ibid., p. 101; Scigliano, *Love, War, and Circuses*, p. 76.

97 **"Excitement, swiftness, odor, love passion"** Franklin Edgerton, trans., *The
Elephant-Lore of the Hindus: The Elephant-Sport (Matanga-Lila) of Nilakantha* (Delhi:
Motilal Banarsidass, 1985), p. 81. First published in New Haven, Conn., by Yale
University Press, 1931.

97 **only in 1981** Sukumar, *Living Elephants*, pp. 101, 155; Sukumar, *Elephant Days and
Nights*, p. 38, 39; Payne, *Silent Thunder*, p. 77. Part of the confusion arose because
African female elephants also secrete fluid from their temporal glands when excitedly greeting one another, though the chemical composition of the fluid is different from that of musth bulls. Even Asian female elephants occasionally dribble
fluid from these glands, but its purpose remains a mystery.

97 **levels of the hormone** Sukumar, *Elephant Days and Nights*, p. 38; Alex Shoumat-
off, "Agony and Ivory," *Vanity Fair*, August 2011, p. 125.

97 **Bigger, stronger males** Sukumar, *Living Elephants*, p.114.

97 **running in the opposite direction** Sukumar, *Elephant Days and Nights*, p. 37.

97 **are attracted to them** Sukumar, *Living Elephants*, p. 113.

97 **recognized four stages** Gale, *Burmese Timber Elephant*, p. 45.

98 **A musth bull is pungent** Sukumar, *Living Elephants*, p.116.

98 **He stands tall** Ibid., p.103.

98 **Depending on the bull's age** Ibid., p. 25.

98 **a thousand pounds** Payne, *Silent Thunder*, p. 25.

98 **impairs their immune systems** Sukumar, *Living Elephants*, p. 118.

98 **like dangerous convicts** Gale, *Burmese Timber Elephant*, pp. 45–46. The animals
were given plenty to drink, but carefully. A large drum of water placed within
their reach would be replenished using a long bamboo trough. Droppings would be
swept away using extended rakes. Any food was simply thrown in the animal's direction. No human limbs were ever to be within trunk-length of the wild-tempered
creatures.

98 **argue confidently** Williams, *Bandoola*, p. 89; Evans, *Elephants and Their Diseases*,
p. 175; Sukumar, *Living Elephants*, p. 101; Smith, "Working Teak in the Burma Forests," p. 255. Many believed that musth had nothing to do with reproduction. Over
time, Williams had heard much about the condition as he sat around the campfires
at night, sipping whiskey and learning from the riders. But there was always such
disagreement about it, even in the literature. Because males in musth secrete copious amounts of fluid from their temporal glands, a pair of modified sweat glands
located on either side of their heads, many people thought of musth almost as a

cold: One text even referred to it as "Congestion of the Temporal Glands." But the idea that musth was a medical problem didn't seem plausible to Williams, even this early in his career. He said he "was convinced that there was nothing abnormal about musth, unless the sexual urge was to be considered abnormal." *National Geographic* magazine concurred with the nonsexual diagnosis: "There is no need to go into the question of *must*," the writer, using an alternate spelling, maintained, "that curious temporary insanity which, at almost regularly stated seasons, attacks males. In my opinion, it is not, as some people believe, a sex state. The cause is hard to determine, but it may be an overcharging of certain glands which have their exits in the face of the animal."

99   **the riders called *pa-ket-hlwe*** Evans, *Elephants and Their Diseases,* p. 12.

99   **nearly touched the ground** Payne, *Silent Thunder,* p. 74; Fowler and Mikota, *Biology, Medicine, and Surgery of Elephants,* pp. 104, 353. The elephant's penis is so large that biologists say it is "theoretically possible for an elephant to step on the penis." In fact, one unfortunate elephant in Africa was observed inadvertently kicking his own penis as he ran—he had been wooing a female when a larger bull started chasing him and he didn't have time to retract it.

100   **refined courtship** Sukumar, *Elephant Days and Nights,* p. 41.

101   **The intercourse lacked** Document 1a, p. 55.

CHAPTER 11: MASTER CLASS IN TRUST AND COURAGE

103   **Within two years** Conversation with Treve Williams, June 13, 2012.

103   **at the same site** J. H. Williams, *Bandoola,* p. 100.

103   **They got pregnant** "The Picture Post," May 1950. Article fragment from the archives of Treve Williams. "When a mating or suspected mating is observed," Williams said, "a note is entered in the inspection-book, and on the twenty-first month following that entry the expectant mother is invariably rested. After the birth of the calf she is usually in harness again within two months."

104   **As Williams got better** J. H. Williams, *In Quest of a Mermaid,* p. 106. A local physician, "Doc Picary," taught him some basics, such as how to sew up a wound. For this, Williams scrubbed in on a leg amputation. Though the sight of the severed foot in a waste bin under the operating table nauseated him, he collected himself, taking the doctor at his word that suturing flesh was "a lot easier than darning socks."

104   **Because purified antibiotics** Pugh, *We Danced All Night,* p. 47; Robert H. Ferrell, *The Twentieth Century: An Almanac* (New York: World Almanac Publications, 1984), p. 158. Penicillin would be discovered in 1928.

105   **It provided antimicrobial** "Sugar Speeds Wound Healing," People's Pharmacy, http://www.peoplespharmacy.com/2007/09/17/sugar-speeds-wo/, accessed October 14, 2013.

105   **sugary swallow** Email from Treve Williams, June 14, 2011.

106   **"sure that she liked me"** Marc Bekoff, *The Emotional Lives of Animals: A Leading Scientist Explores Animal Joy, Sorrow, and Empathy—and They Matter* (Novato, Calif.: New World Library, 2007), p. 13. The modern discipline of ethology had not even begun when Williams had that thought. And yet his conclusion would be echoed decades later by a leader in that field. "My baseline concerning animal emotion and sentience is pretty simple," Marc Bekoff has written. "Animals will always have their secrets, but their emotional experiences are transparent."

107   **a life-and-death struggle** Philip Wynter, "Elephants Go to War in Burma: British Officer's Strange Task," *The Argus* (Melbourne), February 29, 1944.

107 **she lifted the baby** Payne, *Silent Thunder*. Payne describes a scene just like this in Africa.

108 **"the finest call"** *EB* MS, p. 54.

108 **a "phut, phut, phut" sound** Sukumar, *Elephant Days and Nights,* p. 94.

109 **a female in her midthirties** J. H. Williams, *In Quest of a Mermaid,* p. 110. He says she could live another thirty years.

110 **Retired elephants didn't have** Article fragment from the *Picture Post,* no publication date or page number. From the archives of Treve Williams.

CHAPTER 12: THE JUNGLE FAMILY HAS NO WIFE

113 **not a spare ounce** Document S1, p. 31.

113 **on leave once** Conversation with Treve Williams on Long Island, New York, June 10, 2011.

113 **an intense love affair** Email correspondence from Treve Williams, June 29, 2012.

113 **despair wasn't unusual** Bombay Burmah Trading Corporation correspondence, letter to "Wroughton," July 8, 1925, London Metropolitan Archives, MS 40609/003. Among Williams's young colleagues, the lack of love was a pervasive complaint. Men who stayed on the job, enduring malaria, dysentery, and broken bones, were undone by loneliness. Right at the moment Williams was in his doldrums, one of his colleagues with Bombine, P. C. Hill, was abruptly terminating a very promising career. He might have tried to conceal the reasons for his resignation, but his superior knew better. The boss wrote in a letter that Hill's "very urgent private reasons" could only mean he had fallen for a woman. To the company, this kind of lovesickness was a hazard as real as typhus, though a girlfriend, the forest assistants knew only too well, was much harder to contract than some bacterial infection.

114 **would not marry** J. H. Johnstone to Christopherton, August 17, 1928, London Metropolitan Archives, MS 40609/003.

114 **if he could hold out** J. H. Williams, *Bandoola,* pp. 103–7; Pointon, *Bombay Burmah Trading Corporation Limited,* p. 45; Larkin, *Finding George Orwell in Burma,* pp. 209–10. While taking a fishing vacation in a remote forest to forget his troubles, he was invited to a village's rice festival. He seemed so pathetically loveless that he was offered a beautiful half-caste girl, who he believed was a sex slave. When he declined, he felt shaken but grateful to know he wasn't so far gone that he would take advantage of such a creature. For love, what choices did Williams have? "It was a general custom," one historian wrote, "from the earliest days for a liaison usually temporary, on rare occasions permanent, to be formed between Englishmen and the attractive daughters of Burma." This was despite the British government's efforts to discourage civil servants from the "practice of co-habitating with native girls, or accepting them as presents."

114 **The writer George Orwell** Larkin, *Finding George Orwell in Burma,* p. 211.

115 **his personal cook** *FOEB* MS, p. 41. Joseph marched ten miles a day with the rest of the men and then got to work setting up his jungle kitchen. For a stove, he used "a twist of iron resting on two stones" over charcoal. An old kerosene tin was his oven for baking bread. He had canned goods, but he always seemed to produce meals from fresh food—vegetables picked up in little villages, bush meat Williams shot for the pot. And, day in day out, he would produce three- or four-course meals for lunch and supper.

115 **used his "stump"** *SOF,* p. 153. San Pyu's right arm and hand were extraordinarily strong and nimble, Williams said, and he was a master with his machete.

115 **she was gone** J. H. Williams, *Bandoola,* p. 107. "While I was swimming I let her

loose in a pool which was clear as gin," Williams wrote. "She came back to the rocks three or four times and chatter-barked to me. Then I caught sight of three other otters schooling in the pool. The three soon became four, because Taupai joined their game and company. It was the last I saw of her, sporting with them in the clear water. I said good-by to her with a contented heart."

116 **consider resigning** J. H. Williams, *Bandoola,* pp. 107–10. As an escape, he poured his energy into a scheme to extract green opal, even applying for a mining license in the area in which he was shown a promising streak in an outcrop of limestone. He fantasized about becoming rich, but the funny thing was that even with all the money in the world he couldn't imagine leaving his elephants. He dreamed of using his fortune to set up a breeding program for them. When the company said it wasn't interested in his opal scheme, he figured he had better collect himself and make a decision one way or another about his future in Burma. The fact that elephants remained an integral part of even his wildest fantasies was telling. He was hooked. He couldn't go anywhere and leave them behind. But he would write later that in making this decision—to stay in Burma or give it all up—he merely flipped a coin. That was Billy Williams's way of keeping private things private, of glibly narrating a story that was actually painfully close to his heart: spin a playful anecdote out of a wrenching decision. Whether arrived at through a coin toss or an agonizing soul search, it was, of course, the life with elephants that won.

116 **bleeding profusely** J. H. Williams, *Bandoola,* pp. 99–100. The story is told out of order in *Bandoola.* The incident happened two years after the stories it's set with. And then Bandoola recuperated for a full year.

CHAPTER 13: "THE MURDER OF ME"

118 **In 1926** Document 3, p. 2. This version is very different from the one in *SOF.* Williams changed the date and circumstances of the stabbing, which occurred in 1926, to fit the story he tells set in 1931. I've relied on private papers for the true story. *EB,* p. 255, also lists the incident as having taken place in 1926.

118 **attracted to trouble** Document 3, p. 2.

118 **"the New Year's resolution"** *SOF,* p. 32.

119 **to a valley near** Bertram S. Carey and Henry Newman Tuck, *The Chin Hills: A History of the People, Our Dealings with Them, Their Customs and Manners, and a Gazetteer of Their Country,* vol. 1 (Rangoon: Superintendent, Government Printing Burma, 1896), p. 6.

119 **a week later** Document 3, p. 3. Differs from *SOF.* Ten days instead of eight.

121 **he rightly figured** Alcohol is a vasodilator.

122 **never made by foreigners** Kenneth R. H. Mackenzie, *Burmah and the Burmese* (London: George Routledge, 1853), p. 23; Document 2, p.53.

122 **an unceasing hell** Marc Abrahams, "Going to Great Lengths for Swear Words," *The Guardian,* March 31, 2009; Mackenzie, *Burmah and the Burmese,* p. 24. Among the endless curses invoked against a perjurer in the Book of Oath were: "May they be destroyed by elephants, bitten and slain by serpents, killed and devoured by the devils and giants, the tigers, and other ferocious animals of the forest. May whoever asserts a falsehood be swallowed by the earth, may he perish by sudden death, may a thunderbolt from heaven slay him,—the thunderbolt which is one of the arms of the Nat Deva."

123 **already been given** Document 2, p. 56. Aung Gyaw had been filled "with a great feeling of remorse and injury far deeper than what I had suffered physically."

CHAPTER 14: BANDOOLA: HERO OR ROGUE?

126 **"The discharge"** J. H. Williams, *Bandoola,* p. 154.

126 **joined Kayem** Conversation with Treve Williams on Long Island, New York, June 10, 2011.

127 **set to retire** Document S1, p. 40. Harding retired about five years before Williams met Susan.

127 **Harding's head** J. H. Williams, *Bandoola,* p. 168. This story is told out of order in *Bandoola.* It had to have happened before he worked in Pyinmana, while he was still working the Upper Chindwin. He was in Pyinmana in 1930.

128 **nature of leadership** Payne, *Silent Thunder,* p. 66. Years later, prominent elephant researcher Katy Payne would ponder these same indicators, and over time her thinking about elephant leadership would evolve. After witnessing group dynamics among elephants, she began to believe it was less a dictatorship of the matriarch, as was commonly thought, and more a matter of agreement and participation from all the elephants. It is complex.

129 **the trunk knocking on the ground** Conversation with Dr. William Langbauer, September 5, 2012. See also Sukumar, *Elephant Days and Nights,* p. 94.

129 **subtle cooperation** Payne, *Silent Thunder,* p. 25.

129 **"authority without being a bully"** Pugh, "Let Animals Teach You to Live," p. 2.

CHAPTER 15: A MURDER INVESTIGATION

132 **wear a metal bell** Smith, "Working Teak in the Burma Forests," p. 244.

132 **"If the killing"** J. H. Williams, *Bandoola,* p. 173.

133 **appear very remorseful** Ann Belser and Marylynne Pitz, "Elephant Kills Keeper at Pittsburgh Zoo," *Pittsburgh Post-Gazette,* November 19, 2002; Moss, Croze, and Lee, *Amboseli Elephants,* p. 124; conversation with Dr. William Langbauer, September 5, 2012. In an American zoo many years later, a generally docile elephant killed her keeper while on a walk with him and her calf. It was a misunderstanding over a squeal from her calf. When the elephant saw the keeper lying crumpled on the ground, she wrapped her trunk around him and lifted him upright. She appeared to be desperately trying to stand him up on his feet again. Another tusker J. H. Williams knew wouldn't let anyone near the uzi he had just killed, employing a behavior scientists call "body guarding."

CHAPTER 16: REBELS AND REUNIONS

136 **Late in 1928** Conversation with Treve Williams, Long Island, New York, June 13, 2012.

136 **most valuable woodlands** Bryant, *Political Ecology of Forestry in Burma,* p. 227.

136 **A few years earlier** In 1923. Ibid., p. 131.

137 **murder of a forest official** Bryant, *Political Ecology of Forestry in Burma,* pp. 137, 138.

137 **Saya San went further** Ibid., p. 138.

137 **"a small fraction"** Williams, *Bandoola,* p. 111.

138 **three distinct chapters** Thant Myint-U, *River of Lost Footsteps,* pp. 8–13; Larkin, *Finding George Orwell in Burma,* p. 11.

138 **The country's monarch** Amato, "The White Elephant in London," p. 31.

139 **The royal couple** Larkin, *Finding George Orwell in Burma,* p. 43.

139 **Indians were recruited** William Fowler, *We Gave Our Today: Burma 1941–1945* (London: Weidenfeld and Nicholson, 2009), p. 62.

139 **The colonialists considered** The Burmese were "regarded as work-shy" according to Goodall, *Exodus Burma*.

139 **53 percent of the population** Goodall, *Exodus Burma;* census from 1931.

139 **swelling in limbs** Conversation with Treve Williams via Skype, February 4, 2013.

139 **experimental anthrax vaccine** In Williams's first year, Bombine lost thirty-one elephants to anthrax; later he would see tolls of nearly a hundred in one season. Williams had used red ink to track where anthrax deaths had occurred. With the worst outbreaks, his little map had looked as if it were running with blood. *EB* MS, p. 57; Pointon, *Bombay Burmah Trading Corporation Limited*, p. 69. The 1919–20 working season saw thirty-one elephants lost from the Bombay Burmah stables; 1923–24 was brutal with ninety-one deaths; and sixty elephants would die in 1927–28.

141 **bursts of eighteen miles an hour** Sukumar, *Elephant Days and Nights*, p. 99. Holly Williams, "How Fast Can a Human Run?," *The Independent*, May 3, 2010, says the fastest runners were clocked between twenty-three mph and twenty-eight mph.

143 **Even at night in the tent** J. H. Williams, *Bandoola*, p. 117. The dog had a strong work ethic, guarding any item he was told to. When Williams needed to leave him behind one morning, he figured the best method for making Ba Sein stay was to give him a freshly caught fish to guard. Ba Sein did as he was told, threatening any of the camp workers who approached. When Williams returned later, before he could get to his own tent, he was told the dog had gone mad. With the prevalence of rabies, it was a horrifyingly real prospect. Williams cautiously walked forward calling Ba Sein's name, ready to defend himself against a frothing monster. "Then I caught sight of him," Williams wrote. "There he was sitting on guard beside the fish, just as I'd left him. He wagged his twisted tail at me." There was nothing wrong with his loyal dog. He was fine. He had just been doing what he was told to: scaring off anyone who came near the fish. Williams felt a wave of relief, and started joking with the animal. "'Are you mad, Ba Sein?' I asked. 'Mad?' he seemed to answer, 'yes, mad with delight!' and he rushed round my legs. We loved each other dearly." As a reward, the fish was baked for Ba Sein and served to him on a bed of rice.

144 **Activists had discovered** David I. Steinberg, *Burma/Myanmar: What Everyone Needs to Know* (Oxford: Oxford University Press, 2010), pp. 34–35.

144 **fight off the rebellion** Thant Myint-U, *River of Lost Footsteps*, pp. 209–11. Crucial to hunting down Saya San was the help given by members of one of the country's largest minorities, the Karens. Many had converted to Christianity and were loyal to the British.

145 **Palway Creek** In the Pyinmana region, near the current capital.

147 **When he fled** Steinberg, *Burma/Myanmar*, pp. 34–35; Thant Myint-U, *River of Lost Footsteps*, p. 209.

CHAPTER 17: TIGER HOUR

151 **Stephen Hopwood** *FOEB*, p. 3; *SOF*, p. 70. Hopwood is mentioned in many texts about Burma at the time, including Bryant, *Political Ecology of Forestry in Burma*, pp. 81, 108, 140; and in a letter from J. K. Stanford linking Hopwood to Kipling, *The Kipling Journal*, http://www.johnradcliffe.pwp.blueyonder.co.uk/textfiles/KJ172.txt, accessed October 25, 2013.

151 **fishing in a stream** J. H. Williams, *Bandoola*, p. 180. Typical of the "conservators" of his time—he said he had shot one tiger and was hoping to bag another. Hopwood observed jungle etiquette, inviting Williams "to pitch down with him on his camp."

151 **served as a field gunner** *FOEB* MS, p. 3.

151 **He was said to know** U Tun Yin, *Wild Animals of Burma* (Rangoon: Burma Civil Service, 1967), p. 136.

151 **Helen's name** *FOEB* MS, pp. 3, 4.

152 **"slender girl"** J. H. Williams, *Bandoola,* p. 180; *FOEB* MS, p. 31. Susan says she's always been "one of the world's lean kind."

153 **She was twenty-eight** Susan Williams's passport, issued September 2, 1932, in Rangoon, documents her birthdate as September 16, 1903. From the archives of Treve Williams.

153 **her gray eyes** Susan Williams's passport, issued September 2, 1932, in Rangoon.

153 **khaki safari outfit** *FOEB* MS, pp. 6 and 19. Susan talks about the incredible "trousseau" Hopwood paid for.

154 **"was it just my hat?"** J. H. Williams, *Bandoola,* p. 181.

154 **"delighted to see"** *FOEB,* p. 61.

156 **"tiger hour"** *FOEB* MS, p. 22.

156 **troubled global economy** Ferrell, *Twentieth Century,* p. 166. Western nations were suffering high unemployment, bank failures, and governments struggling with debt and the inability to pay war reparations.

157 **possibility of timber extraction** Pointon, *Bombay Burmah Trading Corporation Limited,* p. 74.

159 **he could handle anything** *FOEB,* p. 72. While sitting by the fire, suddenly, Molly became alarmed—the hair of her back standing straight as she leaped up from under Susan's legs. The dog ran to Williams and stood wild-eyed, staring into the darkness, where they then heard the muffled cough of a big cat. Williams said only a tiger or leopard would inspire such terror in the dog. Although bold leopards had sometimes invaded camp, Williams was certain that the fire would keep it at bay. He patted Molly, speaking to her reassuringly. Susan noticed how the dog visibly relaxed some and even wagged her tail, but, still she remained alert, and would not sit down. She and Jim talked for a while longer and then Williams saw that his dog was still anxious. He cupped Molly's face in his hands, looked lovingly at her, and said, "It's all right, old girl—he's gone long ago."

159 **most intelligent dog** J. H. Williams, *Bandoola,* p. 206.

160 **"a lovely dog"** *FOEB* MS, p. 20. Susan genuinely loved dogs. She had been pining for one since reaching Burma, but was forbidden by Hopwood because of the prevalence of rabies. She had taken in a little street dog anyway, and when it showed signs of the disease, Susan had to be treated at the Pasteur Institute in Rangoon with a series of painful injections to her abdomen using a large needle.

161 **most fashionable suburb** "Burma: Yogi v. Commissars," *Time* magazine, October 4, 1948.

162 **He Man replied** *SOF,* p. 73.

164 **The thousand-year-old Buddhist shrine** James, *Snake Charmer,* p. 108.

164 **"floodlights by night"** Christian, "Burma: Where India and China Meet," p. 489.

164 **words of W. Somerset Maugham** W. Somerset Maugham, *The Gentleman in the Parlour* (Garden City: Doubleday, 1930), p. 8.

164 **many lamps** Ibid., p. 11.

164 **song of the cicadas** Ethel Mannin, *Land of the Crested Lion* (London: Jarrolds, 1955), p. 22.

164 **thousands of gold and silver bells** Jamie James, "Glorious Golden Pagoda," *The Wall Street Journal,* February 23, 2008.

164 **"Ghoulies and Pixies"** *EB* MS, p. 1.

164 **He was attracted to the unknown** Email from Treve Williams, April 4, 2012.

164 **"community of all living creatures"** Document fragment 21, p. 4.

164 **"It was not necessary"** *SOF,* p. 81.

CHAPTER 18: THE CANNIBAL ISLANDS

166 **Susan Margaret Rowland** Marriage certificate, All Saints, Evesham Parish, No. 142, September 9, 1932.

166 **consisting of 550 islands** Tony Perrottet, "Babar and Me and the Deep Blue Sea," *Condé Nast Traveler,* January 2010.

167 **Some of the islands** Teresa Levonian Cole, "Would You Andaman Eve It?," *The Guardian,* March 3, 2007.

167 **Ptolemy called them** Ibid.; Marco Polo, *The Travels of Marco Polo,* trans. Henry Yule, book 3, chapter 13.

167 **Williams's Burmese friends** Partial document titled "Andaman Diary," p. 4. From the archives of Treve Williams.

167 **He would have three** Pointon, *Bombay Burmah Trading Corporation Limited,* p. 74.

167 **"I had no briefing"** "Andaman Diary," p. 1.

167 **The only timberwork** Pointon, *Bombay Burmah Trading Corporation Limited,* p. 74.

167 **"a Forest engineer"** "Andaman Diary," p. 1. In *SOF,* his name is spelled Jeff, but in "Andaman Diary" it is Geoff. Williams places the name in quotes signifying, presumably, that it is a pseudonym anyway.

167–68 **He believed now** *SOF,* p. 110.

168 **thousands of varieties** Ibid., p. 136; Teresa Levonian Cole, "Only Halfway to Paradise," *The Sunday Telegraph* (London), March 3, 2007.

168 **saltwater crocodiles** Cole, "Only Halfway to Paradise."

168 **robber crabs** Perrottet, "Babar and Me and the Deep Blue Sea."

168 **Singapore-based** "Andaman Diary," p. 2.

168 **Supermarine Southampton flying boats** In Susan Williams's memoir, and in Williams's original manuscript, these planes are referred to as Sunderland flying boats, but this model plane was not yet in the air at that date. In *SOF,* the planes are identified as Southamptons. Supermarine Southamptons were popular British planes between WWI and WWII, and fit the time frame. It's likely that his editors caught the error and fixed it for the published book.

169 **There was plenty of timber** Pointon, *Bombay Burmah Trading Corporation Limited,* p. 74. This source says there was no teak.

170 **"You're on the wrong ship"** *FOEB* MS, p. 33;

170 **a terrible "heartache"** "Andaman Diary," p. 1.

CHAPTER 19: SUNLIGHT AND SHADOW

174 **"It was a glorious morning"** *FOEB* MS, p. 39.

174 **At 9:30 a.m.** Wedding registry from the archives at Evesham Parish, scan of page provided by Katy Tarplee, parish administrator, Church House, Market Place, Evesham; *FOEB* MS, p. 38.

175 **well-stocked saloon car** *FOEB,* p. 93; John Foster Eraser, S. Edward Lunn, and F. H. Lowe, *Round the World on a Wheel: Being the Narrative of a Bicycle Ride of Nineteen Thousand Two Hundred and Thirty-Seven Miles Through Seventeen Countries and Across Three Continents* (London: Methuen, 1899).

175 **the country's second largest city** Larkin, *Finding George Orwell in Burma,* p. 13.

176 **spectacular orchids** Christian, "Burma: Where India and China Meet," p. 504.

176 **Jim and Susan walked** *FOEB,* p. 103.

176 **grow chili peppers** *FOEB* MS, p. 51.

178 **Installing the "wireless"** Stanford, *Far Ridges,* pp. 101–2.

178 **The connection was so deeply felt** Conversation with Treve Williams via Skype, January 31, 2013.

178 **wool blankets** *FOEB* MS, p. 62. One night, they heard coughing coming from the area where the men slept. Jim shouted out, asking who it was. "Old Joseph appeared," Susan wrote, "his teeth chattering as if he was in a bout of fever." "How many blankets have you got old chap?" Jim asked. "Only this one Sahib," Joseph said, as he lifted a tissue-thin cotton blanket from his shoulders. Jim, as was his tradition, had issued warm wool blankets to each man at the start of the cold season, but they always seemed to disappear, often lost in card games. Joseph, however, had sent the substantial blanket off to his wife and children. Jim looked at Susan and she went off to dig one of their two spares out of a trunk.

179 **a sure death sentence** J. H. Williams, *In Quest of a Mermaid,* p. 107.

179 **field clinics** *FOEB,* pp. 176–77. One of Williams's most amazing cases was a tree feller who had been attacked by a sun bear. These small bears with sleek black hair and distinctive orange-yellow V-shaped necklaces of fur have sickle-shaped claws. Their jaws are strong enough to crack nuts. After tangling with the bear, the man was carried in to Williams. A huge sheet of his scalp had been ripped from his skull and dangled down, covering his face. Williams gently raised the gory mass and held it away from the man's face. He cut the hair off, cleaned everything, folded the flap of skin back over the man's head, and stitched it. The man's eyeball was dangling down his cheek. Williams gently pressed it back into its socket, and then sewed up deep gashes in his lips and jaw, where even the bone had been exposed.

180 **"The wonderful beauty"** *FOEB* MS, p. 53.

182 **And everywhere leeches** Kingdon Ward, *In Farthest Burma,* p. 220. Frank Kingdon-Ward, the fearless English botanist who would survive earthquakes, an impaling, and a perilous spill from a cliff, traveled extensively in Burma and wrote with horror about the leeches. "As for me," he wrote, "leeches entered literally every orifice except my mouth, and I became so accustomed to the little cutting bite, like the caress of a razor, that I scarcely noticed it at the time. On two occasions leeches obtained such strategic positions that I only noticed them just in time to prevent very serious, if not fatal, consequences." Men feared them lodging in the penis or anus. They swarmed the traveler, finding purchase on his scalp, armpits, inside his ears, "in fact everywhere," he said.

182 **Gerry Carol** *FOEB* MS, p. 77. Gerry Carol is called "Tony Stewart" in her published book, p. 139.

183 **trebling the quinine** Writing fragment entitled "Second Story, Second Roll: Hydrophobia, etc.," by J. H. Williams, p. 23. From the archives of Treve Williams.

CHAPTER 20: INTO THE CAULDRON

185 **As a boss** Kahn, "Elephant Bill's Elephants," p. 96, says Williams was promoted to forest manager in 1930.

185 **"punkah-wallahs"** *FOEB,* p. 185.

186 **Kipling had seen** Kipling, "Toomai of the Elephants," p. 152.

187 **Aung Net knelt** J. H. Williams, *Bandoola,* p. 187.

189 **The ripples of the Great Depression** Bryant, *Political Ecology of Forestry in Burma,* p. 140.

189 **By the end of the month** *FOEB* MS, p. 76. The night before the Williamses departed, a wild party was thrown for them in the military policeman's bungalow.

Susan broke away early to go sleep on the boat that would take them across the Chindwin in the morning, and at about two thirty was awakened by Williams and two pals. After more drinking aboard the launch, the three men ran as fast as they could down the wobbly gangway. They all made it, and as the two pals sang "Good-bye, Billy Old Boy," Williams tried to run back aboard, but he fell into the murky river, where he had to be retrieved "drenched and muddy."

189 **He sent the snakeskin** *FOEB,* pp. 218–21. Treve Williams still has this snakeskin in a cupboard in Tasmania.

191 **Bandoola was dismissed** J. H. Williams, *Bandoola,* pp. 137–40. Williams thought back to a situation similar to this one in which Bandoola's athleticism and intellect had shined. It took place in a dark, steep gorge along the Upper Chindwin. The floor of it was strewn with boulders the size of houses. After the monsoon, when the water level dropped to a trickle, thousands of logs, some forty-five feet long and weighing a few tons, were left stranded. They were piled up on one another, jammed against a rock wall, or teetering dangerously on top of boulders.

With an assistant, whom Williams called "Gerry Dawson" in his writing, Williams called for nine elephants (ten was considered an unlucky number by the riders). The elephants arrived and set to work. While the other elephants began simply removing logs one by one, Bandoola chose a very different strategy. He would gingerly walk up on the pile until he came to a wobbly log. That's precisely what he was looking for: the keystone. Backing away to solid ground, he would then reach up to move that one creaking log, and watch the rest of the pile loosen and collapse like a house of cards.

Williams was accustomed to Bandoola's grasp of physics, but Dawson, who had worked with many other elephants, was astounded. As it would turn out, Dawson was not as careful with timber as Bandoola had been. Later, like many foresters, he came to an unfortunate end. His forearm was "flattened to pulp" in an avalanche he had set off with dynamite. He begged his helper to cut off his arm. The reluctant man sawed at the flesh, but failed to amputate. By the time Dawson was taken to a hospital, gangrene had set in and he died. He left behind two Burmese wives who were twin sisters.

192 **using their bodies as supports** This has been seen often and is described by Katy Payne in *Silent Thunder,* p. 75. See also Cynthia Moss, *Elephant Memories* (Chicago: University of Chicago Press, 1988), pp. 72–73; Moss, Croze, and Lee, *Amboseli Elephants,* p. 123.

192 **"Send for Poo Zone"** *EB,* p. 224. While they waited for the elephants to arrive, Williams and the men worked hard to keep Bandoola's thoughts here on Earth, trying to keep his spirit from wandering to another realm. In the amalgam of beliefs in Burma, it was thought that the soul took the form of an invisible butterfly, or *leippya.* In death, or even sometimes just in sleep, the winged spirit could leave the body and return to it or it could be captured and kept away. The men tickled the sick elephant, slapped him, and doused him with water in futile attempts to get him up. All the efforts were more torture than help.

193 **He began to clear away** Scigliano, *Love, War, and Circuses,* pp. 16–17. It might seem comical, but this sort of act could have proved deadly as it would years later for a German zookeeper. The man was trying to help a constipated bull elephant. But the animal expelled an enormous wave of diarrhea just as the keeper was administering an enema. The avalanche of waste knocked the man down, and he was suffocated by the subsequent output.

194 **venom stronger than** James, *Snake Charmer,* pp. 116, 145.

194 **By summer** Although Susan says Jeremy was born in England, Treve says he was

born in Burma, and, in fact, this would square with when she says she was pregnant and when her passport shows her going home to England.

194 **He had not been bitten** J. H. Williams, "Second Story, Second Roll: Hydrophobia, etc.," p. 23.

195 **their nanny, Ma Kin** Conversation with Treve Williams via Skype, July 29, 2013.

195 **at Colombo** Susan Williams's passport, stamped by Harbour Police, Colombo [Sri Lanka], November 12, 1934.

195 **when tragedy struck** Conversation with Treve Williams via Skype, January 28, 2012.

195 **"died quite suddenly"** *FOEB*, p. 228.

195 **He was buried** Conversation with Treve Williams via Skype, January 28, 2012; *FOEB*, p. 236.

195 **It seemed the führer's lesson** David M. Kennedy, *Freedom from Fear: the American People in Depression and War, 1929–1945*, Oxford History of the United States (New York: Oxford University Press, 1999), pp. 383–94.

195 **the couple returned to Burma** T. Donald Carter, "The Mammals of the Vernay-Hopwood Chindwin Expedition, Northern Burma," *Bulletin of the American Museum of Natural History* 82, no 4. Susan corresponded with Uncle Pop, who was still going strong. In fact, he was preparing to lead a large expedition from the American Museum of Natural History on a mammal-collecting trip in the far northern reaches of the country.

195 **the Latin names** To her, geraniums were *Pelargonium x hortorum* and the sunflowers, *Helianthus annuus*. Conversation with Treve Williams via Skype, January 31, 2013.

196 **Over the next year** Ferrell, *Twentieth Century*, p. 187.

196 **In April 1937** Fowler, *We Gave Our Today*, p. 62.

196 **In the fall** *FOEB*, p. 279.

196 **on December 12, 1937** Handwritten notation on Susan Williams's passport: "Treve 12.12.37."

196 **Aung Net taught him** Conversation with Treve Williams via Skype, June 6, 2013.

197 **In the spring of 1938** Ferrell, *Twentieth Century*, pp. 201–2. And Peter Jennings and Todd Brewster, *The Century* (New York: Doubleday, 1998), p. 210.

197 **received home leave** Susan Williams's passport and her handwritten timeline of their life in Burma, from the archives of Treve Williams. See also *EB*, p. 190.

198 **Geoff Bostock lived** The Bostocks' daughter Susan was in school in England during the war. Correspondence between Evelyn Bostock (wife of Bombay Burmah manager Geoff Bostock) and her parents, Mr. and Mrs. G. R. Gaunt, between December 21, 1941, and March 25, 1942, from the family archives of John Bostock. See also Goodall, *Exodus Burma:* "in one of the most palatial private houses in Maymyo—Woodstock."

199 **"Mummy" and "Daddy"** Conversation with Diana Williams Clarke via Skype, May 30, 2013.

199 **Susan refused** Ibid.

200 **The Japanese had also landed** Goodall, *Exodus Burma:* "on a beach in Malaya."

201 **nearly a thousand men** Fowler, *We Gave Our Today*, p. 35.

201 **But before Christmas** Goodall, *Exodus Burma.*

CHAPTER 21: FLEEING BURMA

205 **And on January 20, 1942** Pointon, *Bombay Burmah Trading Corporation Limited,* p. 89.

205 **thought it premature** Goodall, *Exodus Burma:* "before it was too late," "heavily criticised."

205 **The company would allow** Evelyn Bostock to Mr. and Mrs. G. R. Gaunt, February 6, 1942, from the family archives of John Bostock.

205 **Horses and pets** Larkin, *Finding George Orwell in Burma,* p. 22.

205 **buried valuables in their gardens** Goodall, *Exodus Burma:* "glass, silver and even antique furniture."

205 **transferred cash** Ibid.

205 **Jim grabbed a few essentials** *FOEB,* pp. 291–92.

206 **Burma was an objective** Fowler, *We Gave Our Today,* pp. 63–64.

206 **At one point** Tim Harper, "The Second World War: Day 3: Global War: Japan's Gigantic Gamble," *The Guardian,* September 7, 2009.

206 **For the most part** Max Hastings, *Retribution: The Battle for Japan, 1944–45* (New York: Alfred A. Knopf, 2008), p. 59.

207 **"Asia for the Asiatics"** Goodall, *Exodus Burma.*

207 **A large portion of the Karens** Thant Myint-U, *River of Lost Footsteps,* p. 210; Harper, "Second World War."

207 **Some in Burma** Fowler, *We Gave Our Today,* p. 65.

207 **About eighteen thousand** Harper, "Second World War."

207 **some who had hoped** Fowler, *We Gave Our Today,* p. 75.

207 **A report at the time** Hastings, *Retribution,* p. 86.

208 **pregnant again** *FOEB,* p. 291.

208 **If Rangoon** Goodall, *Exodus Burma:* "did not order"; *FOEB,* p. 295; Pointon, *Bombay Burmah Trading Corporation Limited,* p. 91. The evacuees were completely isolated. Mail service was nearly shut down entirely. There was no way to communicate with their families back home in England or with their husbands in country—and they had good reason to worry for them: Two of the company's forest officers would soon be killed in Japanese attacks. Burma was descending into chaos. On February 8, 1942, Governor-General Sir Reginald Dorman-Smith went on the wireless to say he was determined to hold Rangoon, though nonessential workers were advised to seek shelter outside the city. He did not order an evacuation.

208 **would be invaluable** Fowler, *We Gave Our Today,* p. 52.

208 **one high court judge** Mr. Justice Henry Benedict Linthwaite Braund (late of the Allahabad High Court), "The Manipur Road: What Has Been Achieved," publication and date unknown.

208 **Williams's friend and boss** "Evacuation Scheme," fourteen-page report prepared by Geoff Bostock outlining possible routes and transportation and supply requirements for evacuating the wives and children of Bombay Burmah employees in 1942. From the family archives of John Bostock.

208 **It was February 1942** *EB,* p. 194.

209 **Tokyo was relentless** Harper, "Second World War"; *EB* MS.

209 **Williams and Bostock** Evelyn Bostock to Mr. and Mrs. G. R. Gaunt, March 25, 1942, from the family archives of John Bostock; "Trekking from Burma: Women and Children Cross Mountains: Extracts from a Letter Written by the Daughter of a Former Birmingham Manufacturer Describing How She and Other Refugees Escaped from Burma," March 18, 1942. Appears to have been written by Evelyn Bostock; from the family archives of John Bostock.

209 **They left Mawlaik** Ibid.

210 **Behind the families** Ibid.

210 **The food stocks** Ibid.

210 **A pleasant feeling** *EB,* p. 196.

211 **women and children sought safety** Evelyn Bostock to Mr. and Mrs. G. R. Gaunt, March 25, 1942.

211 **On Monday, March 2, 1942** This date is provided by the diary account of an evacuee, Jose Johnson, whose story and diary entries are published by the BBC as part of their series, "WW2 People's War: An Archive of World War Two Memories—Written by the Public, Gathered by the BBC," http://www.bbc.co .uk/ww2peopleswar/stories/04/a3338804.shtml, accessed October 25, 2013.

211 **The large outpost** Goodall, *Exodus Burma.*

212 **not just as an individual** Alexander, *Astonishing Elephant,* p. 36. One man came upon a friend long after the man had been killed by an elephant. He mistook the victim for nothing more than a deer hide. When others began to "unfold" the remains, what seemed like strings turned out to be arms and legs. Three layers down was a face. A perfect image of the man's profile, "but absolutely flat, no eyeball even, and that's the first time we even knew what the thing was."

213 **were not eager to work** The diary account of an evacuee, Jose Johnson, "WW2 People's War."

214 **a little area to sleep in** Goodall, *Exodus Burma.* Many travelers knew by now to scrape a hollow underneath where a hip would rest.

214 **Rangoon fell to the Japanese** "World Battlefronts: Bitter Blow," *Time* magazine, March 9, 1942.

215 **Without Rangoon** "To the Offense!" *The New York Times,* March 8, 1942.

215 **All told, about six hundred thousand** Asad Latif, "Speaking for War's Silent Victims," *The Straits Times* (Singapore), November 7, 2004. In Burma Research Society, *Burma Pamphlets No. 5,* p. 1, the figure for refugees is half a million.

215 **Only about fifty thousand were British** Goodall, *Exodus Burma.*

215 **Eighty thousand may have died** Harper, "Second World War."

216 **"had sacrificed everything"** "Elephant Bill Praises the Fighting Devons," *The Exmouth Journal,* December 14, 1957.

216 **no decent suspension** "WW2 People's War." The March 9, 1942, diary account of evacuee Jose Johnson describes the road as "awful."

216 **two nights** Evelyn Bostock to Mr. and Mrs. G. R. Gaunt, March 25, 1942.

217 **with the rain** Ibid.

CHAPTER 22: NO. 1 WAR ELEPHANT

218 **After meeting up** J. H. Williams's two brothers had met the women in Calcutta and helped them with housing; Evelyn Bostock to Mr. and Mrs. G. R. Gaunt, March 25, 1942.

218 **Mrs. Robertson** Conversation with Diana Williams Clarke via Skype, May 30, 2013; email from Treve Williams, November 7, 2012.

218 **with its posh British club** Janice Pariat, "Why Shillong Flips for WWII Jeeps: The Second World War Years Linger in This Hill Town in Strange Ways, and None More Unusual Than in Its Abiding Fondness for Willys Jeeps," *Open Magazine,* April 16, 2011, http://www.openthemagazine.com/article/arts-letters/why -shillong-flips-for-wwii-jeeps, accessed October 17, 2013.

218 **a cook and a butler** Conversation with Diana Williams Clarke via Skype, May 30, 2013.

218 **running the camp** Evelyn Bostock to Mr. and Mrs. G. R. Gaunt, March 25, 1942; *FOEB,* p. 329. Susan says they ran the camp for six weeks, but this is impossible since J. H. Williams evacuated Burma on April 9, according to *EB,* p. 204.

218 **The British Army soldiers** Goodall, *Exodus Burma;* Christopher Bayly and Tim Harper, *Forgotten Armies: Britain's Asian Empire and the War with Japan* (London: Penguin Books, 2004), pp. 110, 111.

219 **Williams searched** Conversation with Treve Williams, June 13, 2012.

219 **by war's end** McLynn, *Burma Campaign,* p. 1.

220 **The organization of the defense** Fowler, *We Gave Our Today,* p. 63.

220 **The Royal Air Force** McLynn, *Burma Campaign,* p. 30.

220 **Mandalay was bombed** Fowler, *We Gave Our Today,* p. 77.

220 **Newspapers in India** Goodall, *Exodus Burma.*

221 **only one survived** Ibid.

221 **several survival tricks** Ibid.

222 **"baring the ribs"** "Battle of Asia: Before the Monsoons," *Time* magazine, March 30, 1942.

222 **Stilwell said** "Flight from Burma: Stilwell Leads Way Through Jungle to India," *Life* magazine, August 10, 1942. (Stilwell was in Imphal on May 24, 1942.)

222 **a few defeats** Harper, "Second World War."

222 **Susan gave birth** Susan's passport; *FOEB,* p. 330.

222 **"gnawing ache"** *EB* MS, p. 123.

223 **the largest Commonwealth army** Fowler, *We Gave Our Today,* pp. 5–6.

223 **field of operation** "How Admin Troops Backed-up the Fighting Men," Burma Star Association, http://www.burmastar.org.uk/admin_troops.htm, accessed October 17, 2013.

223 **Fighting with them** James Delingpole, "Our Heroes of Burma," *Mail on Sunday* (London), April 19, 2009.

223 **could be dicey** Ronald Lewin, *Slim the Standardbearer* (Hertfordshire: Wordsworth Editions, 1999), p. 105. Originally published in 1976.

225 **Williams was assigned** Major R. M. Forrester, OC Burma section, "Appendix B, Appreciation for SOE Operations in Burma, 26 August 1943," *Burma Consolidated Reports 1941–1945;* Rev. John Croft, MC, "Gentlemen—'The Elephants,'" *The Army Quarterly and Defence Journal* 13 (April 1983): pp. 192–98; Patrick Howarth, *Undercover: The Men and Women of the SOE* (London: Phoenix Press, 2000), p. 11. Originally published in 1980.

225 **didn't play by the rules** Howarth, *Undercover,* p. 11.

226 **telegraph office** Goodall, *Exodus Burma.*

226 **beneath the weight** *The Calcutta Statesman,* July 14, 1943; Bayly and Harper, *Forgotten Armies,* p. 252.

227 **The first "hire"** Harold Langford Browne's partial war record in the National Archives, London. TNA Ref.: WO374/74943 and WO373/82.

230 **Like the great tusker** Kipling, "Toomai of the Elephants," p. 148.

230 **"Bandoola was presented to me"** Williams, *Bandoola,* p. 240.

CHAPTER 23: THE MAKING OF ELEPHANT BILL

231 **more than three dozen elephants** "Elephants Do Their Bit Against Japs" looks like a wire service story about J. H. Williams written in the early 1940s. From the archives of Treve Williams.

231 **forty miles** *EB* MS, p. 125.

231 **the uzis' wives** Ibid., p. 125. "It was a remarkable get away by night," Williams wrote, "as these riders with their families were taking the gravest of risks in crossing the jungles of the Teelaung Creek as much the Japs' no man's land for patrols as ours."

232 **to escort uzis and elephants** Kahn, "Elephant Bill's Elephants," p. 105.

232 **"That they stayed"** Slim, "Uncommon Adventure."

233 **full of mischief** Email from Treve Williams, November 7, 2012. The nanny, Naw Lah, would sometimes spank him with her hairbrush, the "prickly" side being as painful as the flat side.

234 **"a big-headed Scot"** "British Raid Burma," *Life* magazine, June 28, 1943.

235 **greet visitors naked** Annette Kobak, "The Naked General," *The New York Times,* January 16, 2000.

235 **stabbing himself in the neck** Fowler, *We Gave Our Today,* p. 93.

235 **illuminated map** *EB* MS, p. 133.

236 **On the ground** "Battle of Asia: Before the Monsoons," *Time* magazine, March 30, 1942.

236 **report from the *Daily Mail*** "Elephant Bill Won His War," *Daily Mail,* no date. From the archives of Treve Williams.

236 **plenty of enemy troops** Tillman Durdin, "Patrols Clashes Mark Burma War: . . . Main Defenses of Enemy Are Believed Behind Chindwin and Irrawaddy Rivers," *The New York Times,* December 14, 1943. "The Japanese still hold several points on the west side of the Chindwin," *The New York Times* reported. "They have dug in in the usual fashion with bunkers and machine-gun nests, supported by tree-sitting snipers near trails and open spaces."

236 **no one stepped forward** J. H. Williams, "The Story of a Hard-Boiled Jungle Adventurer: Elephant Bill," *The Sydney Morning Herald,* June 8, 1950. Serialized version of *Elephant Bill* with a number of differences.

237 **constant clashes** Durdin, "Patrols Clashes Mark Burma War." "The uninterrupted harassing warfare going on between Allied and Japanese troops on the India-Burma border is being waged along a jagged, discontinuous 'front' of jungle-covered mountains and valleys stretching 500 miles."

237 **The toll of those killed** Fowler, *We Gave Our Today,* p. 90.

238 **"formidable fighting insect"** Hastings, *Retribution,* p. 49.

238 **traveled as lightly as possible** Associated Press, "British in 3-Month Burma Foray Learn How to Raise Havoc with Foe," *The New York Times,* May 21, 1943.

238 **"an expensive failure"** Kobak, "Naked General."

239 **a letter of gratitude** R. A. Savory, HQ 23 Ind Div., to J. H. Williams, June 12, 1943, from the archives of Treve Williams.

CHAPTER 24: ELEPHANT COMPANY HITS ITS STRIDE

240 **mail from Susan** Conversation with Treve Williams, December 3, 2012.

240 **high jinks** Conversation with Diana Williams Clarke via Skype, May 30, 2013.

241 **supplies of quinine** Joyce Chapman, *The Indian National Army and Japan* (Singapore: Institute of Southeast Asian Studies, 1971), p. 155.

241 **A visiting reporter** T. L. Goodman, "Elephant Bill Commands a Strong Company of Bridge Builders in Burma," *The Sydney Morning Herald,* November 28, 1944.

241 **Imphal, despite its status** McLynn, *Burma Campaign,* p. 294.

241 **Here, the reporters found** Philip Wynter, "Guerilla Tactics in Burma: Traps and Elephants Used Against Japs," *The Argus,* November 25, 1943.

241 **the enemy was so close** *EB,* p. 238. As Williams had put it, "Most of the time there was nothing between us and the Japanese but dripping jungle."

242 **A form of guerilla warfare** Wynter, "Guerilla Tactics in Burma."

242 **After the rains** Fowler, *We Gave Our Today,* p 60.

242 **They suffered from** David W. Tschanz, "Uncommon Misery: The 1944–45 Burma Campaign," Burma Star Association, http://www.burmastar.org.uk /misery.htm, accessed October 21, 2013.

242 **called "yaws"** Mark F. Wiser, "Plasmodium Species Infecting Humans," Tulane University, http://www.tulane.edu/~wiser/protozoology/notes/pl_sp.html, accessed October 21, 2013.

242 **most of all malaria** The Burma Star Association is a collection of information on the war in Burma, including personal memoirs of soldiers. This quote is from Manny Curtis, South Lancashire Regiment, http://www.burmastar.org.uk /mannycurtis.htm, accessed October 21, 2013. One British soldier remembered being hit by the deadly strain of malaria, *p. falciparum,* then known as *malignant tertian.* "Near the banks of the Irrawaddy, I had the great 'pleasure' of developing the next worse strain of malaria—MT. I'd already plodded on through a bout of denghi [sic] fever, but in spite of my daily dose of Mepacrin which was meant to protect us from the dreaded mosquito, I still managed to find a mozzie that hadn't read the label. I'd also had foot rot (who hadn't?), prickly heat, jungle sores, sand fly fever and dysentery. But MT malaria was something apart."

242 **During a particularly bad spell** Tschanz, "Uncommon Misery: The 1944–45 Burma Campaign."

242 **pants cut away** Fowler, *We Gave Our Today,* p. 110.

243 **longest campaign** Ibid., p. xvii.

243 **they owned the skies** Harper, "The Second World War."

243 **they hated the land** Hastings, *Retribution,* p. 67.

243 **American K ration** Fowler, *We Gave Our Today,* p 59.

243 **Among the Japanese generals** Ibid., p. 52.

243 **The engineers had gone** Goodman, "Elephant Bill Commands a Strong Company," p. 2.

244 **He was furious once** Conversation with Diana Williams Clarke and Treve Williams via Skype, June 6, 2013.

244 **The pay scale war** J. H. Williams's army records, National Archives, London. TNA Ref.: W0203-1020, Folio 3B-10A. Provided by Denis Segal.

245 **Then he treated them** *EB,* p. 290; email with Treve Williams: "M&B powder was correctly named M&B 693 and contained a sulphonamide in this case Sulphapyridine. The name M&B presumably came from its maker May & Baker." See also *Wikipedia,* http://en.wikipedia.org/wiki/Sulfapyridine, accessed October 21, 2013.

245 **create a sick camp** *EB,* p. 290. "To my belief," he said, "it was the first field veterinary hospital for elephants ever to be established."

246 *Time* **magazine wrote** "World Battlefronts: Temperamental Transport," *Time* magazine, April 12, 1943.

246 **An Australian newspaper** Goodman, "Elephant Bill Commands a Strong Company of Bridge Builders in Burma," p. 2. Also reported in "A Company of Elephants: A Unique Army Unit in Burma: Bridge Building," from our special correspondent, Kabaw Valley, Burma, November 24 (delayed), no year, no page number. From the archives of Treve Williams.

246 **"The elephant kneels"** Wynter, "*Life's* Reports: Elephants at War / In Burma."

246 **challenged and killed** Document 1, p. 8.

246 **"One forgave Bandoola"** Ibid., p. 9.

247 **looking for bags of salt** Reg Foster, "Elephants Think—But They Forget," *SEAC Souvenir,* April 19, 1945; *EB,* p. 299.

248 **red elephant insignia** Foster, "Elephants Think—But They Forget."

248 **Jim reveled** Conversation with Diana Williams Clarke via Skype, May 30, 2013.

248 **his father's Jeep** Email from Treve Williams, November 7, 2012.

248 **kidney pie** Email from Treve Williams, March 30, 2012.

250 **the winning Allies** Fowler, *We Gave Our Today*, p. 126.

CHAPTER 25: A CRAZY IDEA

252 **Slim had anticipated** David Atkins, *The Forgotten Major: In the Siege of Imphal* (Pulborough, UK: Toat, 1989), p. 78.

252 **the Japanese were risking everything** Hastings, *Retribution*, p. 67.

255 **estimated the value** "World Battlefronts: Temperamental Transport." Five thousand rupees equals about $100 dollars in 1943, according to this website: http://www.likeforex.com/currency-converter/indian-rupee-inr_usd-us-dollar.htm/1943. Then go to the Measuring Worth website (http://www.measuringworth.com) and you can do the conversion to today's value seven different ways, with results from $1,000 to $7,300. Or for all: $330,000. This squares with Foster, "Elephants Think—But They Forget."

255 **High command wanted** "A Company of Elephants."

255 **five mountain ranges** Maps provide by the National Geographic Society map librarian, May 18, 2011.

256 **where Williams had stood** Atkins, *Forgotten Major*, p. 78. There were constant unforeseen appearances by the Japanese all along the route. On March 28, 1944, "Suddenly, without warning at all," one officer, Major David Atkins with the Fourteenth Army, wrote, he found the enemy just behind him at Milestone 105: "How they got there without being seen is quite extraordinary."

257 **Even Slim wondered** Slim, "Uncommon Adventure."

258 **"most forsaken spots"** Chapman, *Indian National Army and Japan*, p. 153.

258 **trench mouth** Conversation with Treve Williams via Skype, February 9, 2013.

259 **He was on musth** Document 1, p. 11.

259 **like the little elephant boy** Kipling, "Toomai of the Elephants," p. 161.

259 **"his musth glands"** Document 1, p. 11.

260 **Balladhun tea plantation** Dave Lamont, "My Memories of a Wonderful Time in India," Koi-Hai.com, http://www.koi-hai.com/Default.aspx?id=490718, accessed October 21, 2013. Details of the plantation filled in by one of the later managers.

261 **a "strong" Japanese patrol** Alan K. Lathrop, "The Employment of Chinese Nationalist Troops in the First Burma Campain," *The Journal of Southeast Asian Studies* 12, no. 2 (September 1981): p. 422; John Parratt, *The Wounded Land* (New Delhi: Mittal Publications, 2005), p. 88; *EB* MS, p. 164.

261 **was captured and, they heard** Atkins, *Forgotten Major*, p. 85; conversation with Treve Williams via Skype, July 29, 2013.

262 **a withering sight** In *EB* MS, p. 167, Williams says 300 to 400 feet high. In at least two other sources, he describes the cliff as 270 feet high: Document fragment 7B, and "Elephant Bill Says: They Are Tops for Intelligence," *Grimsby (UK) Evening Telegraph,* November 4, 1954. In *FOEB,* p. 337, Susan Williams says "about three hundred feet high."

265 **Williams's vertigo** Conversation with Diana Williams Clarke and Treve Williams via Skype, June 6, 2013.

265 **the Japanese had bound** Fowler, *We Gave Our Today,* pp. 24, 42, 48, 49.

266 **"It's strange:"** "A Living Hell in Burma," *Bristol (UK) Evening Post,* June 28, 2005.

266 **"We were not merciful"** Fowler, *We Gave Our Today,* p. 68. Quoting from Second Lieutenant John Randle.

266 **"They'd been slit"** "A Living Hell in Burma."

266 **an astonishing 25 percent** Andrew Roberts, "The Debt Japan Owes These Men," *Daily Mail,* London, September 17, 1993.

CHAPTER 26: THE ELEPHANT STAIRWAY

270 **"All will be well"** *FOEB,* p. 338. Susan's version of what Po Toke says differs from J.H.'s. His own writing changes between the original manuscript for *EB,* p. 169, and the published version, pp. 272–73. I've chosen to use Susan's after consulting with Treve Williams.

272 **Williams wore** Email from Treve Williams, March 31, 2012.

273 **taking a hammering** Associated Press, "Allied Base in India Is Isolated; Foe Is at Last Trail to Imphal," *The New York Times,* April 15, 1944: "Front dispatches said tonight that Japanese troops had reached the Bishenpur–Silchar Trail running southwest and west of the Allied Indian base of Imphal and suffered a dozen casualties in an engagement with Allied troops there."

273 **"Many were my thoughts"** *EB* MS, p. 171.

273 **pain in his stomach** *FOEB,* p. 342.

273 **Bandoola drew** Ibid., pp. 338–39.

273 **Bandoola's great head** *EB* MS, p. 171. Slightly different here from the book.

275 **Here was nothing less** Document 7b, p. 2. A pitch by J. H. Williams either for the book or screenplay: "The final height of the mountain range, when all seems hopeless, is crossed by Bandoola, justifying Williams' life's work."

275–76 **"This is the story"** Slim, "Uncommon Adventure."

278 **On the big elephant's back** *FOEB,* pp. 339–41. And Document 1, p. 11.

278 **It was April 26, 1944** In *Elephant Bill,* p. 283, J. H. Williams says the day after arrival is the twenty-fourth. But in later writing, Document 1, p. 11, he corrected the tally of days on the journey to twenty-one, which would have brought them to the tea estate on April 26, 1944.

278 **The house was built** Lamont, "My Memories of a Wonderful Time in India."

278 **"Faur are ye comin'"** Ibid. Also squares with *EB* MS, p. 176.

280 **After six weeks' recuperation** *FOEB,* p. 342; *EB,* p. 302. Susan and Jim often disagree in their writing over the timing of events. This is one of them. Susan tends to be more reliable on dates, and so I use hers here.

280 **Without that bridge** Croft, "Gentlemen—'The Elephants,'" pp. 192–98; "Bailey Bridge Over Chindwin: Great Engineering Feat in Burma," *The Advertiser* (Adelaide, Australia), December 13, 1944; Brian Bond and Kyoichi Tachikawa, *British and Japanese Military Leadership in the Far Eastern War 1941–1945* (Portland, Ore.: Frank Kass, 2004), p. 49.

281 **For now** Document 1, p.13.

282 **his "religion"** Document fragment 14, p. 4. Handwritten notes on the relationship between man and animals.

EPILOGUE

284 **remote pockets of Burma** Pointon, *Bombay Burmah Trading Corporation Limited,* pp. 92–104.

284 **Treve absolutely hated England** Email from Treve Williams, November 7, 2012.

284 **he did not speak of his distress** *FOEB,* p. 350. Susan wrote, "I could not imagine Jim leaving the jungle and his elephants for good; they had been part of him for so long."

284 **Gone were** Stanford, *Far Ridges,* pp. 18–19.

285 **"in the sawdust ring"** Document fragment 8a, the story of going to the Chipperfield Circus in 1950 or 1951 on a typewritten, single-page. The rest of the document is missing.

285 **a long profile** Williams said within twelve hours, his phone started ringing with calls from publishing houses, and within three days, he was signed on with Rupert Hart-Davis Ltd. Document 25, typewritten speech by J. H. Williams prepared for the London Cornish Association. No date, though clearly the early 1950s. Covers writing and publication of *EB,* elephant intelligence, and movie interest in his story.

285 **a contract** "Tusk of Famous Elephant: Figures at Lecture at Penzance, Col. Williams & his Bandoola," *The Cornishman* (UK), November 16, no year.

285 **In the early fall of 1951** Document fragment 8, p. 1, typewritten story by J. H. Williams about trying to bring elephants to Borneo in the 1950s. See also Document fragment 8a.

285 **Dick Chipperfield** J. H. Williams, *Big Charlie,* p. 15.

285 **"Having said goodbye"** Document fragment 8, p. 1.

285 **"I accepted with alacrity"** J. H. Williams, *Big Charlie,* p. 15.

287 **"Bandoola carried the brunt"** Document 1, pp. 14–16.

288 **Carved on a giant teak tree** Document 7b, p. 2.

288 **an American** Document 21, letter from Richard E. Paulson, dated May 10, 1954. Letterhead: UNITED STATES OF AMERICA, SPECIAL TECHNICAL AND ECONOMIC MISSION TO BURMA, AMERICAN EMBASSY, RANGOON.

288 **He was led to them** J. H. Williams, *Big Charlie,* p. 17.

289 **to rub its lining** Document fragment 8, p. 1.

289 **Williams tried his hand** "Lieut.-Colonel J. H. Williams, 'Elephant Bill,'" *The Times,* July 31, 1958. See also handwritten and typewritten reports on the trip to Ceylon by J. H. Williams, a proposed elephant census for the country, and letters to and from government officials for a proposed trip for 1958 and/or 1959, from the archives of Treve Williams.

290 **purchasing five elephants** Pugh, "Let Animals Teach You to Live."

290 **transporting a huge circus elephant** Noel Whitcomb, "The Elephant Billy Couldn't Forget! To Shift Him Will Cost £1,000-Plus," *Daily Mirror,* June 8, 1952.

290 **As he stood waving** Emails from Treve Williams, August 1 and 2, 2012.

INDEX

Page numbers of photographs and illustrations appear in *italics*.

ABOUT THE AUTHOR

VICKI CONSTANTINE CROKE has been exploring animal life for more than two decades—tracking the fossa in Madagascar, polar bears in the Arctic Circle, and Tasmanian devils in, of course, Tasmania. She now covers animal issues for WBUR-FM, Boston's NPR news station, on air (*Here and Now*) and on WBUR's The Wild Life online at thewildlife.wbur.org. Her work there earned a 2013 regional Edward R. Murrow Award. She is the author of *The Lady and the Panda: The True Adventures of the First American Explorer to Bring Back China's Most Exotic Animal, The Modern Ark: The Story of Zoos—Past, Present and Future,* and *Elephant Company: The Inspiring Story of an Unlikely Hero and the Animals Who Helped Him Save Lives in World War II.* Croke has worked on nature documentaries for Disney and for the A&E channel and anchored *The Secret Life of Animals* on NECN-TV. She also wrote *The Boston Globe*'s "Animal Beat" column for 13 years, and has contributed to *The New York Times, The Washington Post, The London Sunday Telegraph, Time, Popular Science, O: The Oprah Magazine, Gourmet, National Wildlife,* and *Discover* magazine, among others. She lives in the Boston area.

www.vickicroke.com
Facebook.com/vicki.c.croke
@VickiCroke

A B O U T   T H E   T Y P E

This book was set in Bembo, a typeface based on an old-style Roman face that was used for Cardinal Pietro Bembo's tract *De Aetna* in 1495. Bembo was cut by Francesco Griffo (1450–1518) in the early sixteenth century for Italian Renaissance printer and publisher Aldus Manutius (1449–1515). The Lanston Monotype Company of Philadelphia brought the well-proportioned letterforms of Bembo to the United States in the 1930s.